# PRENTICE-HALL FOUNDATIONS OF PHILOSOPHY SERIES

| | |
|---|---|
| *Virgil Aldrich* | Philosophy of Art |
| *William Alston* | Philosophy of Language |
| *Roderick M. Chisholm* | Theory of Knowledge   2E |
| *Lawrence H. Davis* | Theory of Action |
| *William Dray* | Philosophy of History |
| *C. Dyke* | Philosophy of Economics |
| *Joel Feinberg* | Social Philosophy |
| *William K. Frankena* | Ethics   2E |
| *Martin P. Golding* | Philosophy of Law |
| *Carl Hempel* | Philosophy of Natural Science |
| *John Hick* | Philosophy of Religion   3E |
| *David L. Hull* | Philosophy of Biological Science |
| *James C. McClellan* | Philosophy of Education |
| *Joseph Margolis* | Philosophy of Psychology |
| *Willard Van Orman Quine* | Philosophy of Logic |
| *Richard Rudner* | Philosophy of Social Science |
| *Wesley C. Salmon* | Logic   3E |
| *Jerome Shaffer* | Philosophy of Mind |
| *Richard Taylor* | Metaphysics   3E |

*Elizabeth Beardsley, Monroe Beardsley,*
*and Tom L. Beauchamp, editors*

Third Edition
# LOGIC

**Wesley C. Salmon**
University of Pittsburgh

*PRENTICE-HALL, INC., Englewood Cliffs, New Jersey 07632*

*Library of Congress Cataloging in Publication Data*

SALMON, WESLEY C.
  Logic.

  (Prentice-Hall foundations of philosophy series)
  Bibliography: p.
  Includes index.
  1. Logic.  I. Title  II. Series.
BC108.S2 1984        160        83-13924
ISBN  0-13-540021-X

Editorial/production supervision:
  Chrystena Chrzanowski
Manufacturing buyer: Harry P. Baisley

Printed in the United States of America

10  9  8  7  6  5  4  3  2

ISBN  0-13-540021-X

PRENTICE-HALL INTERNATIONAL, INC., *London*
PRENTICE-HALL OF AUSTRALIA PTY. LIMITED, *Sydney*
EDITORA PRENTICE-HALL DO BRASIL, LTDA., *Rio de Janeiro*
PRENTICE-HALL CANADA INC., *Toronto*
PRENTICE-HALL OF INDIA PRIVATE LIMITED, *New Delhi*
PRENTICE-HALL OF JAPAN, INC., *Tokyo*
PRENTICE-HALL OF SOUTHEAST ASIA PTE. LTD., *Singapore*
WHITEHALL BOOKS LIMITED, *Wellington, New Zealand*

In Memory of
My Mother,
*Ruth Elizabeth Salmon*

# Contents

## THREE
# Induction
**87**

## FOUR
# Logic and Language
**140**

# Foundations
# of Philosophy

Many of the problems of philosophy are of such broad relevance to human concerns, and so complex in their ramifications, that they are, in one form or another, perennially present. Though in the course of time they yield in part to philosophical inquiry, they may need to be rethought by each age in the light of its broader scientific knowledge and deepened ethical and religious experience. Better solutions are found by more refined and rigorous methods. Thus, one who approaches the study of philosophy in the hope of understanding the best of what it affords will look for both fundamental issues and contemporary achievements.

Written by a group of distinguished philosophers, the Foundations of Philosophy Series aims to exhibit some of the main problems in the various fields of philosophy as they stand at the present stage of philosophical history.

While certain fields are likely to be represented in most introductory courses in philosophy, college classes differ widely in emphasis, in method of instruction, and in rate of progress. Every instructor needs freedom to change his course as his own philosophical interests, the size and makeup of his class, and the needs of his students vary from year to year. The nineteen volumes in the Foundations of Philosophy Series—each complete in itself, but complementing the others—offer a new flexibility to the instructor, who can create his own textbook by combining several volumes as he wishes, and choose different combinations at different times. Those volumes that are not used in an introductory course will be found valuable, along with other texts or collections of readings, for the more specialized upper-level courses.

*Elizabeth Beardsley*  /  *Monroe Beardsley*  /  *Tom L. Beauchamp*
Temple University       Temple University       Georgetown University

# Preface

Although logic is generally regarded as a branch of philosophy, its applications extend far beyond the limits of any single discipline. The critical standards of logic have application in any subject that employs inference and argument—in any field in which conclusions are supposed to be supported by evidence. This includes every domain of serious intellectual endeavor, as well as the practical affairs of everyday life.

There are many logic textbooks—that is, books intended mainly for use as texts in logic courses. This book has a different purpose. It is designed primarily for readers who, for various reasons, would find a basic knowledge of logic helpful. They might be taking courses in other branches of philosophy. They might be students of mathematics, science, language, history, or law. They might be interested in the presentation and criticism of reasoned arguments as they occur in exposition and debate. Or they might want to learn a little logic to help them evaluate their own thinking, as well as the enormous barrage of words—directed at all of us in our everyday lives by television, radio, newspapers, magazines, colleagues, and friends—that are intended to persuade us to purchase a certain product or to take a particular stand on some issue of public policy, politics, or religion. I am offering them a concise treatment of a wide range of topics in logic in the hope that it will be a practical supplement to the materials in their various areas of interest. If they are stimulated to pursue the study of logic a little bit farther, I would be most gratified. Looking to that end, a brief list of additional readings is given at the conclusion of the book.

Like many serious disciplines, logic may be studied for its intrinsic interest or for the purpose of application. These two aims are not mutually exclusive. I have tried to satisfy each purpose to some extent. On the one hand, I have said quite a bit throughout the book concerning the scope, nature, and function of logic. I have tried to show the kinds of questions logic deals with and the kinds that are outside of its domain, hoping that readers will get a good basic idea of what logic is all about. On the other hand, I have tried to present topics that have important applications. In particular, every effort has been made to apply logical considerations to significant examples.

This book had its modest beginnings over twenty years ago as a sixteen-page mimeographed pamphlet, which was distributed to students in introductory philosophy courses at Brown University. It was designed as a small handbook containing just a few basic logical concepts and argument forms to supplement the textbooks in these courses. Its basic purpose has not changed, but I believe that later versions provide a far more useful supplement in a broader range of contexts. It has subsequently gone through two previous editions in the Prentice-Hall Foundations of Philosophy Series. In each case the content of the book was substantially expanded to cover additional topics that had been omitted from earlier versions.

The third edition continues the trend. The main shortcoming of the second edition, I felt, was its rather cursory treatment of causal reasoning. It has become increasingly clear to me in recent years that arguments involving causal relationships occur with astonishing frequency in a wide variety of contexts. It is of vital importance for us to learn about how smoking, diet, and exposure to radiation bear upon the occurrence of cancer. News on such issues, and reports of studies that purport to furnish answers, appear regularly in newspapers and magazines. We are often informed about investigations into the causes of airplane crashes, fires, nuclear accidents, and a variety of other large or small catastrophes. We need to know much more about the causes of inflation, traffic fatalities, birth defects, and various diseases. We need to know more about the effects of the increased levels of carbon dioxide in the atmosphere that result from the use of coal as a fuel, as well as the effects of innumerable other chemicals that we introduce into the environment. Scientists are constantly trying to find out more about the effects of all sorts of drugs—marijuana, alcohol, diet drugs, oral contraceptives, and new therapeutic agents. We all want to know why our tomato plants are not doing well this year, why our college-aged children have such strange taste in popular music, why last winter was especially cold, and why our cars would not start this morning. The list seems virtually endless, and each item in some fashion involves causal reasoning.

In an effort to do some justice to this important domain of logic, I have incorporated into the present edition three sections, 27–29, that deal with causal reasoning. Mill's methods (with the exception of the method of residues) are presented as basic tools for dealing with causal relations, and they are used to lead into more modern approaches that employ controlled experiments and statistical considerations. The treatment of the causal fallacies is, I believe, much improved in this edition. I hope that these three sections, which constitute the most important change, provide a more satisfactory introduction to causal reasoning.

Another significant change in this edition is the inclusion of a treatment of operational definitions in section 32. Given the widespread reference to operational definitions in virtually every scientific discipline, it seems essential to include them in a general discussion of definitions.

In addition, many small but important changes that correct and update the text have been incorporated. Especially significant, in my opinion, is the sincere attempt to remove any traces of sexual bias that were present in earlier editions. Events of the past decade have thoroughly convinced me of the harm that can result even from unintentional inequalities. I hope no infractions remain.

There is one revision that I seriously considered making, but in the end decided against. Robert McLaughlin has argued quite cogently that the traditional discovery/justification distinction (section 3) is better described as a distinction between invention and appraisal. In spite of the advantages of his new terminology, I decided—since the traditional terms were used in the previous editions—to stick with them in order to avoid terminological confusion. More importantly, however, he has shown that there can be helpful rational guidelines in the process of invention; thus there is, in some sense, a logic of discovery. Nevertheless it is not the sort of logic of discovery that I reject in this book, so I decided to confine mention of it to this Preface, instead of revising the discussion in section 3. An elementary handbook is not an appropriate place to report on the results of recent research.[1]

I am grateful to Prentice-Hall for the opportunity to bring out this third edition; I hope the new material will make the book more adequate for contemporary readers. I should like to express my warm thanks to Elizabeth and Monroe Beardsley, editors of this series, for their help and encouragement ever since I began work on the first edition, and to Tom Beauchamp, who has recently joined the group of editors, for valuable help on this edition. I am grateful to Chrystena Chrzanowski of Prentice-Hall for her skill and sensitivity in bringing the production of this book to a successful and timely conclusion. Finally, I should like to express my deepest gratitude to my wife, Merrilee Salmon, for her extremely useful suggestions and criticisms based upon many years' experience as a successful teacher of logic. Her help has been invaluable.

**Wesley C. Salmon**

[1]See his essay, "Invention and Appraisal" in Robert McLaughlin, ed., *What? Where? When? Why?* (Dordrecht: D. Reidel Publishing Co., 1982).

# CHAPTER ONE

# The Scope of Logic

When people make statements, they may offer evidence to support them or they may not. A statement that is supported by evidence is the conclusion of an argument, and logic provides tools for the analysis of arguments. Logical analysis is concerned with the relationship between a conclusion and the evidence given to support it.

When people reason, they make inferences. These inferences can be transformed into arguments, and the tools of logic can then be applied to the resulting arguments. In this way, the inferences from which they originate can be evaluated.

Logic deals with arguments and inferences. One of its main purposes is to provide methods for distinguishing those that are logically correct from those that are not.

## 1. ARGUMENT

In one of his celebrated adventures, Sherlock Holmes comes into possession of an old felt hat. Although Holmes is not acquainted with the owner of the hat, he tells Dr. Watson many things about the man—among them, that he is highly intellectual. This assertion, as it stands, is unsupported. Holmes may have evidence for his statement, but so far he has not given it.

Dr. Watson, as usual, fails to see any basis for Holmes's statement, so he asks for substantiation. "For answer Holmes clapped the hat upon his head. It came right over the forehead and settled upon the bridge of his nose. 'It is a question of cubic capacity,' said he; 'a man with so large a brain must have something in it.' "[1] Now, the statement that the owner of the hat is highly intellectual is no longer an unsupported assertion. Holmes has given the evidence, so his statement is supported. It is the conclusion of an argument.

We shall regard assertions as unsupported unless evidence is actually *given* to support them, whether or not anyone *has* evidence for them. There is a straightforward reason for making the distinction in this way. Logic is concerned with arguments. An argument consists of more than just a statement; it consists of a conclusion along with supporting evidence. Until the evidence is given, we do not have an argument to examine. It does not matter who gives the evidence. If Watson had cited the size of the hat as evidence for Holmes's conclusion, we would have had an argument to examine. If we, as readers of the story, had been able to cite this evidence, again, there would have been an argument to examine. But, by itself, the statement that the owner is highly intellectual is an unsupported assertion. We cannot evaluate an argument unless the evidence, which is an indispensable part of the argument, is given.

To distinguish assertions for which no evidence is given from conclusions of arguments is not to condemn those of the former kind. The purpose is only to make clear the circumstances in which logic is applicable and those in which it is not. If a statement is made, we may be willing to accept it as it stands. If so, the question of evidence does not arise. If, however, the statement is one we are not ready to accept, the question of evidence does arise. When evidence has been supplied, the unsupported assertion is transformed into a supported conclusion. An argument is then available, to which logic may be applied.

The term "argument" is a basic one in logic. We must explain its meaning. In ordinary usage, the term "argument" often signifies a dispute. In logic, it does not have this connotation. As we use the term, an argument can be given to justify a conclusion, whether or not anyone openly disagrees. Nevertheless, intelligent disputation—as opposed to the sort of thing that consists of loud shouting and name-calling—does involve argument in the logical sense. Disagreement is an occasion for summoning evidence if an intelligent resolution is sought.

Arguments are often designed to convince, and this is one of their important and legitimate functions; however, logic is not concerned with the persuasive power of arguments. Arguments that are logically incorrect often do convince, whereas logically impeccable arguments often fail to persuade. Logic is concerned with an objective relation between evidence

---

[1]A. Conan Doyle, "The Adventure of the Blue Carbuncle," *Adventures of Sherlock Holmes* (New York and London: Harper & Row, Publishers, Inc., n.d.), p. 158. Direct quotation and use of literary material from this story by permission of the Estate of Sir Arthur Conan Doyle.

and conclusion. An argument may be logically correct even if nobody recognizes it as such; or it may be logically incorrect even if everyone accepts it.

Roughly speaking, an argument is a conclusion standing in relation to its supporting evidence. More precisely, *an argument is a group of statements standing in relation to each other.*[2] An argument consists of one statement that is the conclusion and one or more statements of supporting evidence. The statements of evidence are called *premises*. There is no set number of premises that every argument must have, but there must be at least one.

When Watson requested a justification for the statement about the owner of the hat, Holmes gave an indication of an argument. Although he did not spell out his argument in complete detail, he did say enough to show what it would be. We can reconstruct it as follows:

a]    1. This is a large hat.
      2. Someone is the owner of this hat.
      3. The owners of large hats are people with large heads.
      4. People with large heads have large brains.
      5. People with large brains are highly intellectual.
      6. The owner of this hat is highly intellectual.

This is an argument; it consists of six statements. The first five statements are the premises; the sixth statement is the conclusion.

The premises of an argument are supposed to present evidence for the conclusion. Presenting evidence in premises involves two aspects. First, the premises are statements of fact. Second, these facts are offered as *evidence for* the conclusion. There are, consequently, two ways in which the premises may fail to present evidence for the conclusion. First, one or more of the premises may be false. In this case, the *alleged* facts are not facts at all; the *alleged* evidence does not exist. Under these circumstances, we can hardly be said to have good grounds for accepting the conclusion. Second, even if the premises are all true—that is, even if the premises do accurately state the facts—they may not have an appropriate relation to the conclusion. In this case, the facts are as stated in the premises, but these facts are not *evidence for* the conclusion. In order for facts to be evidence for a conclusion they must be properly relevant to that conclusion. Obviously, it will not do merely to give any true statements to support a conclusion. The statements must have some bearing upon that conclusion.

If an argument is offered as a justification of its conclusion, two questions arise. First, are the premises true? Second, are the premises properly

---

[2]The term "statement" is used to refer to components of arguments because it is philosophically more neutral than alternatives such as "sentence" or "proposition." No technical definition of "statement" is offered here because any definition would raise controversies in the philosophy of language that need not trouble the beginner. More sophisticated readers may supply whatever technical definition seems most appropriate to them.

related to the conclusion? If either question has a negative answer, the justification is unsatisfactory. It is absolutely essential, however, to avoid confusing these two questions. In logic we are concerned with the second question only.[3] When an argument is subjected to logical analysis, the question of relevance is at issue. *Logic deals with the relation between premises and conclusion, not with the truth of the premises.*

One of our basic purposes is to provide methods of distinguishing between logically correct and incorrect arguments. *The logical correctness or incorrectness of an argument depends solely upon the relation between premises and conclusion.* In a logically correct argument the premises, whether they are actually true or actually false, have the following relation to the conclusion: *If the premises were true, this fact would constitute good grounds for accepting the conclusion as true.* If the facts alleged by the premises are, indeed, facts, then they *do* constitute good evidence for the conclusion. But even if one or more premises are false, the facts alleged by the premises would constitute good evidence for the conclusion if the facts were what the premises claim them to be. That is what we shall mean by saying that the premises of a logically correct argument *support* the conclusion. The premises of an argument support the conclusion if the truth of the premises would constitute good reason for asserting that the conclusion is true. When we say that the premises of an argument support the conclusion, we are *not* saying that the premises are true; we are saying that there would be good evidence for the conclusion *if* the premises were true.

The premises of a logically incorrect argument may *seem* to support the conclusion but actually they do not. Logically incorrect arguments are called *fallacious*. Even if the premises of a logically incorrect argument were true, this would not consistute good grounds for accepting the conclusion. The premises of a logically incorrect argument do not have the proper relevance to the conclusion.

Since the logical correctness or incorrectness of an argument depends solely upon the relation between premises and conclusion, *logical correctness or incorrectness is completely independent of the truth of the premises.* In particular, it is wrong to classify an argument as fallacious just because it has one or more false premises. Consider the argument concerning the hat in example *a*. You may already have recognized that there is something wrong with the argument from the size of the hat to the intellectuality of the owner; you might have been inclined to reject it on grounds of faulty logic. It would have been a mistake to do so. The argument is logically correct—it is not fallacious—but it does have at least one false premise. As a matter of fact, not everyone who has a large brain is highly intellectual. However, you

---

[3]There are important exceptions to this statement. They will be discussed in sections 12 and 33, but they can safely be ignored until then.

should be able to see that the conclusion of this argument would have to be true if all of the premises were true. It is not the business of logic to find out whether people with large brains are intellectual; this matter can be decided only by scientific investigation. Logic *can* determine whether these premises support their conclusion.

As we have just seen, a logically correct argument may have one or more false premises. A logically incorrect or fallacious argument may have true premises; indeed, it may have a true conclusion as well.

*b*]   *Premises:*   All mammals are mortal.
                  All dogs are mortal.
   *Conclusion:*   All dogs are mammals.

This argument is obviously fallacious. The fact that the premises and the conclusion are all true statements does not mean that the premises support the conclusion. They do not. In section 5 we shall prove this argument fallacious by using a general method for treating fallacies. The techniques of section 14 also apply to arguments of this type. For the present, we can indicate the fallacious character of *b* by pointing out that the premises would still be true even if dogs were reptiles (not mammals). The conclusion would then be false. It happens that the conclusion, "All dogs are mammals," is true, but there is nothing in the premises that provides any basis for it.

Since the logical correctness or incorrectness of an argument depends solely upon the relation between the premises and the conclusion and is completely independent of the truth of the premises, we can analyze arguments without knowing whether the premises are true—indeed, we can do so even when they are known to be false. This is a desirable feature of the situation. It is often useful to know what conclusions can be drawn from false or doubtful premises. For example, intelligent deliberation involves the consideration of the consequences of various alternatives. We may construct arguments with various premises in order to see what the consequences are.

*c*]   Perhaps you are thinking of buying an expensive foreign sports car. You might suppose to yourself (as a hypothetical premise) that you purchase it. In addition to the cost of the car, there would be other expenses, such as maintenance, license, and insurance. When you add up all of these items, you see that it would create a severe strain on your budget. You recognize, moreover, that one of the main attractions of such a car involves driving at high speeds; in view of the 55-mile-per-hour speed limit, you realize that having it would create a strong temptation to violate the law, thus posing a serious risk of expensive speeding citations and a possible suspension of your driver's license. These considerations might convince you not to purchase such a car at this time.

In constructing such arguments, we do not pretend that the premises are true; rather, we can examine the arguments without even raising the question of the truth of the premises. Up to this point we have proceeded as if the only function of arguments is to provide justifications for conclusions. We see now that this is only one among several uses for arguments. In general, arguments serve to show the conclusions that can be drawn from given premises, whether these premises are known to be true, known to be false, or are merely doubtful.

For purposes of logical analysis it is convenient to present arguments in standard form. We shall adopt the practice of writing the premises first and identifying the conclusion by a triplet of dots.

d]      Everyone who served on the jury was a registered voter.
        Jones served on the jury.
        ∴ Jones was a registered voter.

This argument is logically correct. Outside of logic books, we should not expect to find arguments expressed in this neat form. We must learn to recognize arguments when they occur in ordinary prose, for they are not usually set off in the middle of the page and labeled. Furthermore, we have to identify the premises and the conclusion, for they are not usually explicitly labeled. It is not necessary for the premises to precede the conclusion. Sometimes the conclusion comes last, sometimes first, and sometimes in the middle of the argument. For stylistic reasons arguments may be given in a variety of ways; for example, any of the following variations of d would be quite proper:

e]      Everyone who served on the jury was a registered voter and Jones served on the jury; *therefore,* Jones was a registered voter.

f]      Jones was a registered voter *because* Jones served on the jury, and everyone who served on the jury was a registered voter.

g]      *Since* everyone who served on the jury was a registered voter, Jones *must have been a* registered voter, *for* Jones served on the jury.

The fact that an argument is being given is usually conveyed by certain words or phrases which indicate that a statement is functioning as a premise or as a conclusion. Terms like "therefore," "hence," "consequently," "so," and "it follows that" indicate that what comes immediately after is a conclusion. The premises from which it follows should be stated nearby. Also, certain verb forms that suggest necessity, such as "must have been," indicate that the statement in which they occur is a conclusion. They indicate that this statement follows necessarily (i.e., deductively) from stated premises. Other terms indicate that a statement is a premise: "since," "for," and "because" are examples. The statement that follows such a word is a premise. The conclusions based upon this premise should be found nearby. Terms that indicate parts of arguments should be used if, and only if, arguments are being presented. If no argument occurs, it is misleading to use these terms. For instance, if a statement is prefaced by the word "therefore," the reader has every right to expect that it follows from something that has already been said. When arguments are given, it is important to indicate that fact, and to indicate exactly which statements are intended as premises and which as conclusions. It is up to the readers to be sure they understand which statements are premises and which are conclusions before they proceed to subject arguments to analysis.

There is another respect in which arguments encountered in most contexts fail to have the standard logical form. When we subject arguments to logical analysis, all the premises must be given explicitly. Many arguments, however, involve premises so obvious that it would be sheer pedantry to state them in ordinary speech and writing. We have already seen an example of an argument with missing premises. Holmes's argument about the hat was incomplete; we attempted to complete it in example *a*. Outside of a logic book, example *d* might appear in either of the following forms, depending upon which premise is considered more obvious:

*h*]   Jones must have been a registered voter, for she served on the jury.

*i*]   Jones was a registered voter, because everyone who served on the jury was a registered voter.

In neither case would there be any difficulty in finding the missing premise.[4]

It would be unreasonable to insist that arguments always be presented in complete form without missing premises. The person who puts forth an argument has every right to expect us to try to make the argument as strong as possible. In reconstructing arguments, we should do our best to find *plausible premises* which will make the argument *logically correct*. As we shall see, however, in some cases there appears to be no way to make the argument into a strong one. The premises needed to make the argument logically correct do not seem to be true, and those that we are prepared to believe true do not make the argument logically correct (see example *z* of section 7 and example *v* of section 14).

Although the missing premise is often a statement too obvious to bother

---

[4]Arguments with missing premises have traditionally been called *enthymemes*—literally translated, "in the mind"—but there is no need to memorize that fancy word. It is entirely proper to call them simply *incomplete arguments*. Moreover, in some arguments the conclusion is unstated; the premises are given and we are left to draw our own conclusion. Such arguments have also been called *enthymemes*, but we shall call them *incomplete arguments* as well.

making, it can also be a great pitfall. A missing premise can sometimes constitute a crucial hidden assumption. When we attempt to complete the arguments we encounter—including those we ourselves put forth—we bring to light the assumptions that would be required to make them logically correct. This step is often the most illuminating aspect of logical analysis. It sometimes turns out that the required premises are extremely dubious or obviously false.

Logical analysis of discourse involves three preliminary steps that we have discussed.

1. Arguments must be recognized; in particular, unsupported statements must be distinguished from conclusions of arguments.
2. When an argument has been found, the premises and conclusions must be identified.
3. If the argument is incomplete, the missing premises must be supplied.

When an argument has been set out in complete and explicit form, logical standards can be applied to determine whether it is logically correct or fallacious.

## 2. INFERENCE

In the preceding section we discussed arguments and said that logic can be used to analyze and evaluate them. This is one important function of logic. In the minds of most people, however, logic has another function: it has something to do with thinking and reasoning. Thinking and reasoning consist, in part at least, of making inferences. In this section we shall discuss the application of logic to inferences.

Many of our beliefs and opinions—indeed, much of our knowledge—are results of inference. The Sherlock Holmes example provides a simple illustration of this point. Holmes did not *see* that the owner of the hat was highly intellectual; he saw that the hat was large, and he *inferred* that the owner was highly intellectual. In the preceding section we discussed Holmes's argument; now let us consider his inference. Holmes had come to the conclusion that the owner of the hat was highly intellectual. This conclusion was a belief or opinion that he held. When Dr. Watson paid him a visit, he *stated* this conclusion. Holmes had arrived at his conclusion on the basis of evidence that he had. When called upon to do so, he *stated* his evidence for his conclusion. By stating his evidence and his conclusion, he presented an *argument*. Before he presented his argument, he had made an *inference* from his evidence to his conclusion.

There are close parallels between arguments and inferences. Both arguments and inferences involve evidence and conclusions standing in relation to each other. The main difference lies in the fact that an argument is a linguistic entity, a group of statements; an inference is not.

In the first place, the conclusion of an argument is a statement. The conclusion of an inference is an opinion, belief, or some such thing. We began our discussion of logic by dealing with statements, distinguishing between those that are supported and those that are not. A supported statement is the conclusion of an argument. It may have occurred to you that a similar distinction could have been made between beliefs and opinions that are supported and those that are not. We have evidence for some of our beliefs and opinions, whereas for others we do not. A supported belief or opinion would then be the conclusion of an inference.

If we wish to consider the justification of a belief or opinion, we must examine the evidence for it. In an argument, the evidence is given in statements: the premises. In an inference, the person who makes the inference must *have* the evidence. To say that a person has evidence is to say that he or she has knowledge, beliefs, or opinions of a certain kind. For instance, Holmes knew that the hat was large. In addition, he believed that there is a relation between hat size and intellectual ability. This was part of his evidence.

Making an inference is a psychological activity; it consists of drawing a conclusion from evidence, of arriving at certain opinions or beliefs on the basis of others. But logic is not psychology; it does not attempt to describe or explain the mental processes that occur when people infer, think, or reason. Some inferences are, nevertheless, logically correct; others are logically incorrect. Logical standards can be applied to inferences in order to subject them to critical analysis.

In order to evaluate an inference, we must consider the relation between a conclusion and the evidence from which the conclusion is drawn. The conclusion must be stated, and so must the evidence. When the evidence is stated, we have the *premises of an argument*. When the conclusion is stated, it becomes the *conclusion of that argument*. The statement of the inference is thus an argument, and it can be subjected to logical analysis and evaluation, as we indicated in the preceding section. In the logical analysis of an inference we are not concerned with how the person who made the inference reached the conclusion. We are concerned only with the question of whether the conclusion is supported by the evidence upon which it is based. In order to answer this question, the inference must be stated; if it is stated, it becomes an argument. This is true even if the people who make the inferences state them only to themselves.

As we explained in the preceding section, the logical correctness of an argument does not depend upon the truth of its premises. In precisely the same manner, the logical correctness of an inference is independent of the truth of the beliefs or opinions that constitute its evidence. The beliefs or opinions upon which the conclusion of an inference is based may support that conclusion even if these beliefs or opinions are false. Just as we sometimes construct arguments with premises that are dubious or known to be false, so also we often make inferences from suppositions that are dubious or believed to be false. For example, we might make an inference from the suppositions that we will go camping for the next two weeks and that the weather will be rainy during that period. This inference might be an important part of the deliberation that helps us decide how to spend a vacation. In making an inference of this kind we need not believe our suppositions; rather, we want to see what the consequences would be if the suppositions were true.

You may still feel uneasy about limiting the application of logic to arguments. Is it true, you might ask, that all inferences can be rendered in language? Are there not, perhaps, some beliefs that cannot be expressed in statements? Is there not, perhaps, some evidence that cannot be stated in words? Is it impossible for someone to have a belief supported by evidence, and yet either the belief itself or the evidence for it defies formulation in language? This possibility cannot be denied, but caution is required. Suppose the following incident had occurred:

a]    Holmes handed the hat to Watson and asked him what he could infer concerning its owner. Watson examined it carefully, and at last he said, "Something about the character of the man is clearly indicated, but it is one of those facets of his spirit which cannot be expressed in words." Hiding his impatience, Holmes asked Watson what evidence he had for this conclusion. Watson replied, "It is an ineffable quality about the hat—something I couldn't possibly describe."

Such a performance (which never occurred and is completely out of character for Dr. Watson) would surely arouse a reasonable suspicion that no inference had been made, no conclusion drawn, and no evidence found. Whether this suspicion is correct or not, it would be impossible for anyone, including Watson, to subject the alleged inference to logical analysis. Thus, we shall regard the analysis of arguments as the primary function of logic, recognizing that inferences may be dealt with by transforming them into arguments. This means that there is an extremely close relationship between logic and language. We shall see this intimate connection repeatedly as our discussion proceeds.

## 3. DISCOVERY AND JUSTIFICATION

When a statement has been made, two important questions may be raised: How did it come to be thought of? and What reasons do we have for accepting it as true? These are different questions. It would be a serious error to confuse the questions, and it would be at least as serious to confuse the answers. The first question is one of *discovery;* circumstances pertaining to this question are within the *context of discovery*. The second question is one of *justification;* matters relevant to this question belong to the *context of justification.*

Whenever the support of a statement is at issue, it is essential to keep clear the distinction between the context of discovery and the context of justification. *The justification of a statement consists of an argument.* The statement to be justified is the conclusion of the argument. The argument consists of that conclusion and its supporting evidence standing in relation to each other. The discovery of the statement, by contrast, is a psychological process whereby the statement is thought of, entertained, or even accepted.

The distinction between discovery and justification is clearly illustrated by the following example:

*a]*   The Indian mathematical genius Ramanujan (1887–1920) claimed that the goddess of Namakkal visited him in his dreams and gave him mathematical formulas. Upon awaking, he would write them down and verify them.[5]

There is no reason to doubt that Ramanujan received inspiration in his sleep, whether from the goddess of Namakkal or from more natural sources. These circumstances have nothing to do with the truth of the formulas. The justification relates to their proofs—mathematical arguments—which in some cases he supplied after he awakened.

The following example illustrates the same point:

*b]*   There is a famous story about Sir Isaac Newton's discovery of the law of gravitation. According to this (probably apocryphal) tale, Newton was sitting in the garden one day and saw an apple fall to the ground. Suddenly he had a brilliant insight: the planets in their courses, objects falling to earth, the tides—all are governed by the law of universal gravitation.

This is a charming anecdote about the discovery of the theory, but it has no bearing upon its justification. The question of justification can be answered only in terms of observations, experiments, and arguments—in short, the justification depends upon evidence for the theory and not upon the psychological factors that made the theory occur to Newton in the first place.

Questions of justification are questions about the acceptability of statements. Since a justification of a statement is an argument, justification involves two aspects: the truth of the premises and the logical correctness of the argument. As we have previously emphasized, these two aspects are independent of each other. A justification can fail because of either one. If we show that the premises are false or dubious, we have shown that the justification is inadequate. Similarly, if we show that the argument is log-

---

[5]G. H. Hardy, P. V. Seshu Aiyar, and B. M. Wilson, eds., *Collected Papers of Srinivasa Ramanujan* (Cambridge, Eng.: University Press, 1927), p. xii.

ically incorrect, we have shown that the justification is unsatisfactory. *Showing that a justification is inadequate, on either of these grounds, does not show that the conclusion is false.* There may be another, adequate justification for the same conclusion. If we have shown that a justification is inadequate, we have merely shown that it does not provide good reason for believing the conclusion to be true. Under these circumstances, we have neither reason to accept the conclusion as true nor reason to reject it as false; there is simply no justification. It will be important to remember this fact as you read the remaining sections of this book. We shall consider many arguments that either have false premises or are logically incorrect. It does not follow that these arguments have false conclusions.

There is, however, such a thing as *negative justification.* It is sometimes possible to show that a statement is false. As we shall see, the *reductio ad absurdum* (section 8) and the argument against the person (section 25) are often used in this way. Negative justifications are as much within the context of justification as are positive justifications. Questions concerning the adequacy of a justification are also within the context of justification.

The error of treating items in the context of discovery as if they belonged to the context of justification is called the *genetic fallacy.* It is the fallacy of considering factors in the discovery, or genesis, of a statement relevant, *ipso facto,* to the truth or falsity of it. For example,

c]     The Nazis condemned the theory of relativity because Einstein, its originator, was a Jew.

This is a flagrant case of the genetic fallacy. The national or religious background of the discoverer of a theory is certainly relevant only to the context of discovery. The Nazis used such a fact as if it belonged to the context of justification.

The genetic fallacy must, however, be treated with care. As we shall see (sections 24 and 25), both the argument from authority and the argument against the person have fallacious forms, often cases of the genetic fallacy. Both arguments, however, also have correct forms, which must not be confused with the genetic fallacy. The difference is this. Items within the context of discovery can sometimes be correctly incorporated into the context of justification by showing that there is an objective connection between that aspect of the discovery and the truth or falsity of the conclusion. The argument then requires a premise stating this objective connection. The genetic fallacy, in contrast, consists of citing a feature of the discovery without providing any such connection with justification.

The distinction between discovery and justification is closely related to the distinction between inference and argument. The psychological activity of making an inference is a process of discovery. People who make inferences must think of the conclusions, but this is not the entire problem of discovery. They must discover the evidence, and they must discover the relationship between the evidence and the conclusions. The inference is sometimes described as the transition from the evidence to the conclusion. If this statement is taken to mean that thinking, reasoning, and inferring consist in starting from evidence that is somehow given and proceeding by neat logical steps to a conclusion, then it is certainly inaccurate. In the first place, the evidence is not always given before the conclusion. Sometimes a conclusion occurs to us first; then we have to try to find evidence to support it or show it to be false. Sometimes we have a little evidence, then we think of a conclusion, and finally we have to discover more evidence before we have a completed inference. Even if we start with some evidence and simply proceed from it to a conclusion, in most cases thinking does not proceed in logical steps. Our minds wander, we daydream, reveries intrude, irrelevant free associations occur, and blind alleys are followed. No matter how it happens, however, the inference is sometimes completed, and we end up with evidence and conclusion standing in relation to each other. All of this pertains to discovery. When the process of discovery is finished, the inference can be transformed into an argument, as we explained in the preceding section, and the argument can be examined for logical correctness. The resulting argument is not by any means a description of the thought processes that led to the conclusion.

It should be evident that logic does not attempt to describe the ways in which people actually think. You may wonder, however, whether it is the business of logic to lay down rules to determine how we *ought* to think. Does logic provide a set of rules to guide us in reasoning, in problem solving, in drawing conclusions? Does logic prescribe the steps we should follow in making inferences? This conception is a common one. People who reason effectively are often said to have "logical minds," and they are said to reason "logically."

Sherlock Holmes is a prime example of a man with superb reasoning powers. He is extremely skillful at making inferences and drawing conclusions. When we examine this ability we see, however, that it does not lie in utilizing a set of rules to guide his thinking. For one thing, Holmes is vastly superior to his friend Watson in making inferences. Holmes is willing to teach Watson his methods, and Watson is an intelligent man. Unfortunately, there are no rules Holmes can communicate to Watson that will make Watson capable of Holmes's feats of reasoning. Holmes's abilities consist of such factors as his keen curiosity, his high native intelligence, his fertile imagination, his acute powers of perception, his wealth of general information, and his extreme ingenuity. No set of rules can provide a substitute for such abilities.

If there were a set of rules for making inferences, these rules would constitute rules for discovery. Actually, effective thinking requires free play of thought and imagination. To be bound by rigid methods or rules would tend only to hamper thought. The most fruitful ideas are often precisely those that rules could not produce. Of course, people can improve their reasoning abilities by education, practice, and training, but all this is a far cry from learning and adopting a set of rules of thought. In any case, when we discuss the specific rules of logic we shall see that they could not begin to be adequate as methods of thinking. The rules of logic, if imposed as limitations on ways of thinking, would become a straitjacket.

What we have said about logic may be disappointing. We have placed a good deal of emphasis on the negative side by saying what logic cannot do. Logic cannot provide a description of actual thought processes—such problems are in the domain of psychology. Logic cannot provide rules for making inferences—such matters pertain to discovery. What, then, is logic good for? Logic provides critical tools with which we can make sound evaluations of inferences. This is the sense in which logic does tell us how we ought to think. Once an inference has been made, it can be transformed into an argument, and logic can be applied to determine whether or not it is correct. Logic does not tell us how to *make* inferences, but it does tell us which ones we ought to *accept*. A person who accepts incorrect inferences is being illogical.

To appreciate the value of logical tools, it is important to have realistic expectations about their use. If you expect a hammer to do the job of a screwdriver you are bound to be disappointed, but if you understand its function you can see what it is good for. Logic deals with justification, not with discovery. Logic provides tools for the analysis of discourse; such analysis is indispensable to the intelligent expression of our own views and the clear understanding of the claims of others.

## 4. DEDUCTIVE AND INDUCTIVE ARGUMENTS

What we have said so far applies to all types of arguments. The time has come to distinguish two major types: *deductive* and *inductive*. There are logically correct forms of each, and we can roughly distinguish incorrect forms (fallacies) of each type. Here are correct examples:

*a]*  *Deductive:*  Every mammal has a heart.
                          All horses are mammals.
                          ∴Every horse has a heart.

*b]*  *Inductive:*  Every horse that has ever been observed has had a heart.
                          ∴Every horse has a heart.

There are certain fundamental characteristics that distinguish between correct deductive and correct inductive arguments. We will mention two primary ones.

|                DEDUCTIVE                |                INDUCTIVE                |
|-----------------------------------------|----------------------------------------|
| I. If all of the premises are true, the conclusion *must be true*. | I. If all of the premises are true, the conclusion is probably true but not necessarily true. |
| II. All of the information or factual content in the conclusion was already contained, at least implicitly, in the premises. | II. The conclusion contains information not present, even implicitly, in the premises. |

It is not difficult to see that the two examples satisfy these conditions.

*Characteristic I.* The only way in which the conclusion of *a* could be false—that is, the only possible circumstance under which it could fail to be true that every horse has a heart—is that either not all horses are mammals or not all mammals have hearts. In other words, for the conclusion of *a* to be false, one or both of the premises must be false. If both premises are true, the conclusion must be true. On the other hand, in *b*, it is quite possible for the premise to be true and the conclusion false. This would happen if at some future time a horse is observed that does not have a heart. The fact that no horse without a heart has yet been observed is some evidence that none ever will be. In this argument, the premise does not necessitate the conclusion, but it does lend some weight to it.

*Characteristic II.* When the conclusion of *a* says that all horses have hearts, it says something that has already been said, in effect, by the premises. The first premise says that all mammals have hearts, and that includes all horses according to the second premise. In this argument, as in all other correct deductive arguments, the conclusion states explicitly or reformulates information already given in the premises. It is for this reason that deductive arguments also have characteristic I. The conclusion must be true if the premises are true, *because* the conclusion says nothing that was not already stated by the premises. However, the premise of our inductive argument *b* refers only to horses that have been observed up to the present, whereas the conclusion refers to horses that have not yet been observed. Thus, the conclusion makes a statement that goes beyond the information given in the premise. It is because the conclusion says something not given in the premise that the conclusion might be false even though the premise is true. The additional content of the conclusion might be false, rendering the conclusion as a whole false. Deductive and inductive arguments fulfill different functions. The deductive argument is designed to make explicit the content of the premises; the inductive argument is designed to extend the range of our knowledge.

We may summarize by saying that the inductive argument expands the content of premises by sacrificing necessity, whereas the deductive argument achieves necessity by sacrificing any expansion of content.

It follows immediately from these characteristics that deductive correctness (known as *validity*—see section 5) is an all-or-nothing affair. An argument either qualifies fully as a correct deduction or fails completely; there are no degrees of deductive validity. The premises either completely necessitate the conclusion or fail entirely to do so. Correct inductive arguments, in contrast, admit of degrees of strength, depending upon the amount of support the premises furnish for the conclusion. There are degrees of probability that the premises of an inductive argument can supply to a conclusion, but the logical necessity that relates premises to conclusion in a deductive argument is never a matter of degree.

Examples *a* and *b* illustrate clearly the basic properties of inductive and deductive arguments and the important differences between them. These same characteristics can be used to classify far less trivial arguments.

*c*]    The relation between a scientific generalization and its supporting observational evidence is *inductive*. For example, according to Kepler's first law, the orbit of Mars is an ellipse. The observational evidence for this law consists of a number of isolated observations of the position of Mars. The law itself refers to the position of the planet, whether it is observed or not. In particular, the law states that the future motion of the planet will be elliptical, that its motion was elliptical before any person observed it, and that its motion is elliptical when clouds obscure the sky. Clearly, this law (the conclusion) has far more content than the statements describing the observed positions of Mars (the premises).[6]

*d*]    Mathematical argument is *deductive*. The most familiar example is Euclidean plane geometry, which almost everyone studies in high school. In geometry, theorems are proved on the basis of axioms and postulates. The method of proof is to deduce the theorems (conclusions) from the axioms and postulates (premises). The method of deduction assures us that the theorems *must* be true if the axioms and postulates are true. This example shows, incidentally, that deductive arguments are not always trivial. Although the content of the theorem is given in the axioms and postulates, this content is by no means completely obvious. Making the implicit content of the axioms and postulates explicit is genuinely illuminating.

One of the main reasons for emphasizing the basic characteristics of inductive and deductive arguments is to make clear what can be expected of them. In particular, deduction has a severe limitation. The content of the conclusion of a correct deductive argument is present in the premises. An

---

[6]The fact that Kepler's first law is a consequence of Newton's laws does not affect the example, for Newton's laws, themselves, have content that goes far beyond the observational evidence on which they rest. In either case, there is an inductive relation between the observational evidence and the laws.

argument, therefore, cannot be a logically correct deduction if it has a conclusion whose content exceeds that of its premises. Let us apply this consideration to two extremely important examples.

*e*]     René Descartes (1596–1650), often considered the founder of modern philosophy, was deeply disturbed by the error and uncertainty of what passed for knowledge. To remedy the situation, he attempted to found his philosophical system upon indubitable truths and derive a variety of far-reaching consequences from them. In his *Meditations* he takes great pains to show that the proposition "I think, therefore, I exist" cannot be doubted. He then proceeds to elaborate a comprehensive philosophical system in which, eventually, he arrives at conclusions concerning the existence of God, the nature and existence of material objects, and the basic dualism of the physical and the mental. It is easy to form the impression that Descartes is attempting to deduce these consequences from the preceding premise alone, but no such deduction could be logically correct, for the content of the conclusions far exceeds that of the premise. Unless Descartes was guilty of gross logical blunders, he must have used additional premises, nondeductive arguments, or both. These simple considerations should serve as a warning that the initial interpretation of Descartes's argument is probably mistaken and that a closer examination is required.

*f*]     One of the most profound and vexing problems in moral philosophy is that of providing a justification for value judgments. The British philosopher David Hume (1711–1776) saw clearly that value judgments cannot be justified by deducing them from statements of fact alone. He writes, "In every system of morality which I have hitherto met with, I have always remarked that the author proceeds for some time in the ordinary way of reasoning, and establishes the being of a god, or makes observations concerning human affairs; when of a sudden I am surprised to find that instead of the usual copulations of proposition *is* and *is not*, I meet with no proposition that is not connected with an *ought* or an *ought not*. This change is imperceptible, but is, however, of the last consequence. For as this *ought* or *ought not* expresses some new relation or affirmation, it is necessary that it should be observed and explained; and at the same time that a reason should be given for what seems altogether inconceivable, how this new relation can be a deduction from others which are entirely different from it."[7]

The characteristics just described serve to distinguish *correct* deductive from *correct* inductive arguments. At this point you might be wondering how to identify incorrect deductions and inductions. We shall, after all, encounter some well-known invalid forms of deductive argument (e.g., in sections 7 and 14), as well as some inductive fallacies (e.g., in sections 21 and 22). Nevertheless, strictly speaking there are no incorrect deductive or inductive arguments; there are valid deductions, correct inductions, and assorted fallacious arguments. There are, of course, invalid arguments that look something like valid deductions; these are loosely called "invalid de-

[7]David Hume, *A Treatise of Human Nature*, Book III, Part I, Sec. I.

ductions" or "deductive fallacies." They are identified as deductive fallacies because they can easily be confused with correct deductions. Similar remarks could be made about the mistakes that plague inductive reasoning. There are no precise logical characteristics that delineate incorrect deductions and incorrect inductions; basically it is a psychological matter. An incorrect argument that might be offered as a valid deduction, either because the author of the argument is making a logical error or because he or she hopes to fool someone else, would normally be considered a deductive fallacy. Incorrect induction could be described analogously.

You may have noticed, quite correctly, that any inductive argument can be transformed into a deductive argument by the addition of one or more premises. It might, therefore, be tempting to regard inductive arguments as incomplete deductive arguments rather than as an important and distinct type. This would be a mistake. Even though every inductive argument can be made into a deductive argument by the addition of premises, the required premises are often statements whose truth is very doubtful. If we are trying to justify conclusions, it will not do to introduce highly dubious premises. Actually, the kind of argument which extends our knowledge is indispensable. For instance, if no such mode of argument were available, it would be impossible to establish any conclusions about the future on the basis of our experience of the past and present. Without some type of inductive reasoning, we would have no grounds for predicting that night will continue to follow day, that the seasons will continue to occur in their customary sequence, or that sugar will continue to taste sweet. All such knowledge of the future, and much else as well, depends upon the power of inductive arguments to support conclusions that go beyond the data presented in their premises.

# CHAPTER TWO

# Deduction

The validity of deductive arguments is determined by their logical form, not by the content of the statements comprising them. After analyzing the relation between form and validity, we shall examine some of the most important valid forms of deductive argument and some common deductive fallacies. We shall also discuss some basic methods for ascertaining the validity or invalidity of deductive argument forms.

## 5. VALIDITY

As we have seen, logic is concerned with the correctness of arguments, not with the truth or falsity of premises or conclusions. Correct deductive arguments are called *valid*. The validity of a deductive argument depends solely upon the relation between the premises and the conclusion. To say that a deductive argument is "valid" means that the premises are related to the conclusion in such a way that *the conclusion must be true if the premises are true*. *Validity* is a property of arguments, which are groups of statements, not of individual statements. *Truth,* on the other hand, is a property of individual statements, not of arguments. It is meaningless to call an argument "true," and it is meaningless to call a single statement "valid." Arguments that purport to be valid deductions but are logically incorrect or fallacious are also called *invalid*. An alleged deductive argument is invalid if there is any possibility that the premises could be true and the conclusion false.

An argument is not proved valid by showing that it has a true conclusion. An argument is not proved invalid by showing that it has a false conclusion. Each of the following three combinations is possible for valid deductive arguments:

1. True premises and a true conclusion.
2. Some or all premises false and a true conclusion.
3. Some or all premises false and a false conclusion.

The following arguments, which exemplify the foregoing combinations, are valid (see section 14):

*a*]     All diamonds are hard.                      *True*
       Some diamonds are gems.                 *True*
      ∴Some gems are hard.                    *True*

*b*]     All cats have wings.                        *False*
       All birds are cats.                       *False*
      ∴All birds have wings.                  *True*

*c*]     All cats have wings.                        *False*
       All dogs are cats.                        *False*
      ∴All dogs have wings.                  *False*

In each of these arguments, if the premises were true, the conclusion would have to be true. It is impossible for a valid deductive argument to have true premises and a false conclusion.

Invalid arguments may have any combination of truth and falsity for premises and conclusion. We shall not give examples of all possible combinations, but we must re-emphasize the fact that an invalid argument may have true premises and a true conclusion. This point was illustrated by example *b* of section 1.

In order to study validity and invalidity, we classify arguments in terms of their *forms*. From the standpoint of deductive logic, the subject matter of an argument is unimportant; the form or structure is what counts. Validity or invalidity is determined by the form, not by what the premises and conclusion talk about. By examining the form of an argument, in abstraction from the content of the premises and conclusion, we can investigate the relation between the premises and conclusion without considering their truth or falsity.

Different arguments may share the same form; and since form determines validity, we may speak of the validity of a form as well as the validity of an argument. If we say that a form is valid, we mean that it is impossible for any argument that has that form to have true premises and a false conclusion. Any argument that has a valid form is a valid argument. We test an argument for validity by seeing whether it has a valid form.

Consider example *b*. This argument contains terms referring to three classes of things: birds, cats, and things that have wings. If we are dealing with the form of this argument, we do not care about the particular characteristics of these things, so we may deliberately refuse to mention them. We may substitute letters for each of these terms, using the same letter to replace the same term each time it occurs and different letters to replace different terms.

Using the letters "*F*," "*G*," and "*H*," respectively, we get

*d*]     All *G* are *H*.
         All *F* are *G*.
         ∴All *F* are *H*.

We may do the same thing with example *c*. This time, let "*F*," "*G*," and "*H*" stand for dogs, cats, and things that have wings, respectively. Again, the result is *d*. Examples *b* and *c* have the same form; this form is given by *d*. Schema *d* is not, itself, an argument; it is a form that becomes an argument if particular terms are substituted for the three letters. It is a valid form. Regardless of what terms are substituted for "*F*," "*G*," and "*H*," provided the same term is substituted for a given letter each time it occurs, the result will be a valid argument. It does not matter to what kinds of things "*F*," "*G*," and "*H*" refer. If it is true that all *G* are *H*, and it is true that all *F* are *G*, then it must be true that all *F* are *H*.

We can easily illustrate the fact that the validity of an argument depends only upon its form, not upon its content or the truth or falsity of the statements occurring in it.

*e*]     All flageolets are fipple-flutes.
         All monauli are flageolets.
         ∴All monauli are fipple-flutes.

Argument *e* has the form *d*. You may not have any idea which statements, if any, in this argument are true; however, it is obvious that the argument is valid: If the premises are true the conclusion cannot fail to be true. We can see this by examining the form. It is not necessary to find out what the statements mean, let alone whether they are true or false. The form is valid.

An invalid form of argument is called a deductive *fallacy*. A common way of exposing a fallacious argument is to compare it with another argument of the same form in which the premises are true but the conclusion is false. We shall call this method of proving invalidity the *method of counterexample*. To say that an argument is valid means that it has a valid form. To say that a form is valid means that *no argument with that form can have true premises and a false conclusion*. Thus, when we say that an argument is valid, we are making a universal statement about all arguments of that form.

A universal statement can be refuted by one negative instance—one counterexample. In order to prove that a form is fallacious, it is sufficient to find a counterexample, an argument having that form but having true premises and a false conclusion. At this point we must insert a word of caution about the method of counterexample. It is important to note that this method conclusively proves the invalidity of a *form* but not necessarily that of a particular *argument*. To say that an argument is fallacious means that there is *no* valid form that it exemplifies. Hence, if we merely show that an argument has a certain form, and that this form is invalid, we have not thereby proved that the argument is invalid. In order to establish conclusively the invalidity of an argument, it is necessary to show that there is no other form it possesses by virtue of which it is valid.

Any particular argument exemplifies more than one logical form as the following consideration makes obvious. As we shall see in section 10, certain kinds of arguments depend for their validity only upon the relationships among simple statements viewed as wholes; the internal structures of these statements do not matter. Arguments of this sort—so-called *truth-functional arguments*—can best be symbolized by using a single letter to stand for a given statement. If we analyze argument *e*, for example, by the method of section 10, its form would be given by

$f]$    $p$
     $q$
    $\therefore r$

where the letters "*p*," "*q*," "*r*" can stand for any statements whatever. Obviously, *f* is not a valid form. If, however, we analyze argument *e* by the *syllogistic method* of section 14, its form would be *d*. Thus, *e* may be said to have a truth-functional form *f* and a syllogistic form *d*. You might be tempted to say that *d* rather than *f* is *the* form of argument *e*, but that would not be quite correct. Both *d* and *f* are forms of argument *e*; however, *d* is a valid form whereas *f* is a fallacious form. By showing that argument *e* has form *d* we show that argument *e* is valid. By showing that argument *e* exemplifies form *f* as well, we certainly do not show that it is an invalid argument. We may say that *d* is the form by virtue of which *e* is a valid argument, whereas form *f* has no such unique or important role. The point is this: If we had started by analyzing argument *e* truth-functionally (see section 10) and attributed form *f*, we would not have shown that argument *e* is invalid. We could only have concluded that it is not valid by virtue of form *f* and that we shall have to find another form it possesses if we are to show it to be a valid argument.

In practice, we can often tell which form reveals the essential logical structure of a given argument. If that form happens to be valid, our job is done, for an argument is valid if it possesses any valid form, regardless of which other forms it might exemplify. If the form we choose to represent the given argument is fallacious, we can usually conclude at least tentatively that the argument is invalid. Anyone who wishes to convince us otherwise must show us a valid form the argument possesses.

We shall use the method of counterexample to show that the various fallacies we discuss are, indeed, invalid. As a preliminary illustration of the method, let us consider example *b* of section 1.

g]     All mammals are mortal.
        All dogs are mortal.
        ∴All dogs are mammals.

This argument has true premises and a true conclusion; nevertheless, it has an invalid form.

h]     All *F* are *H*.
        All *G* are *H*.
        ∴All *G* are *F*.

For "*F*" substitute "mammals," for "*G*" substitute "reptiles," and for "*H*" substitute "mortal." This yields

i]     All mammals are mortal.                                    *True*
        All reptiles are mortal.                                    *True*
        ∴All reptiles are mammals.                              *False*

The resulting argument *i* has the same form as *g*, but its premises are obviously true, whereas its conclusion is patently false. Hence, *i* is a counterexample, proving that *h* is an invalid form. Since *h* seems to exhibit the basic logical structure of argument *g*, we conclude that it is an invalid argument.

## 6. CONDITIONAL STATEMENTS

The first few valid and invalid forms of argument we shall examine contain a very important type of statement used as a premise: the *conditional* (or *hypothetical*) statement. It is a complex statement composed of two component statements joined by the connective "if . . . then . . ." For example,

a]     If today is Wednesday, then tomorrow is Thursday.

b]     If Newton was a physicist, then he was a scientist.

Both statements are conditional or hypothetical. In a conditional statement, the part that is introduced by "if" is called the *antecedent;* the part that comes immediately after "then" is called the *consequent.* "Today is Wednesday" is the antecedent of *a;* "Newton was a physicist" is the antecedent of *b.*

"Tomorrow is Thursday" is the consequent of $a$; "he [Newton] was a scientist" is the consequent of $b$. The antecedents and consequents of conditional statements are, themselves, statements. A conditional statement has a definite *form*, which may be expressed

$c$]     If $p$, then $q$

where it is understood that statements are to replace "$p$" and "$q$." The *content* of a conditional statement depends upon the particular statements that occur as antecedent and consequent. The *form* is determined by the fact that the connective "if . . . then . . ." places these two statements, whatever their content, in definite relation to each other.

In logic, it is useful to have standard forms, and we shall take $c$ as our standard form for a conditional statement. Nevertheless, it is important to realize that a conditional statement can be equivalently reformulated in a variety of ways. We must expect to encounter the alternatives when we are dealing with arguments that we find in ordinary contexts. Examination of some of these different formulations will help us to recognize them when they occur, and it will deepen our understanding of the extremely important conditional form.

1.   "If $p$, then $q$" is equivalent to "If not-$q$, then not-$p$." This relation is so fundamental that it has a special name: "contraposition." "If not-$q$, then not-$p$" is the contrapositive of "If $p$, then $q$."

Application of contraposition to $b$ gives

$d$]     If Newton was not a scientist, then he was not a physicist.

You should satisfy yourself that $b$ and $d$ are equivalent to each other (see p. 49).

2.   "Unless" means the same as "if not . . . ."

Thus, $d$ can be translated directly into

$e$]     Unless Newton was a scientist, he was not a physicist.

Again, you should satisfy yourself that $e$ is equivalent to $d$ and also to $b$.

3.   "Only if" is the exact converse of "if"; that is, "If $p$, then $q$" is equivalent to "Only if $q$, $p$."

Applying this equivalence to $b$ we get

$f$]     Only if Newton was a scientist was he a physicist.

You should satisfy yourself that *f* is equivalent to *b*. Furthermore, you should be perfectly clear that *b* differs in meaning from

g]    Only if Newton was a physicist was he a scientist.

This statement says that Newton would not have been a scientist if, instead of being a physicist, he had been a chemist or a biologist. Statement *b* is certainly true, but *g* is surely false; *g* means the same as

h]    If Newton was a scientist, then he was a physicist

which is clearly different from *b* in content.

4.   The word order of conditional statements can be inverted without changing the meaning, provided that the same clause is still governed by "if." The antecedent of the conditional statement need not come first; it may come after the consequent. The antecedent is the statement introduced by "if," wherever "if" happens to occur. The same thing may be said of conditional statements expressed in terms of "only if" and "unless." The statement may be inverted, provided the same clause is still governed by "only if" or "unless."

Using this equivalence, *b, d, e,* and *f,* respectively, may be expressed as follows without changing their meaning:

i]    Newton was a scientist if he was a physicist.

j]    Newton was not a physicist if he was not a scientist.

k]    Newton was not a physicist unless he was a scientist.

l]    Newton was a physicist only if he was a scientist.

This list by no means exhausts the possible ways of expressing conditional statements, but it gives a fair idea of the kinds of alternatives that exist. In the arguments we examine subsequently we shall encounter some of these alternatives.

## 7. CONDITIONAL ARGUMENTS

Our examination of specific argument forms will begin with the consideration of four very simple and basic ones. Two of them are valid, and the other two are invalid. In each case there are two premises, the first premise being a conditional statement.

The first valid argument form is called *affirming the antecedent* (or sometimes *modus ponens*). Consider the following example:

*a*]　If Smith fails her English examination, then she will be disqualified for the swimming meet.
Smith fails her English examination.
∴Smith will be disqualified for the swimming meet.

This argument is obviously valid; its form is described by the following schema:

*b*]　If *p*, then *q*.
*p*.
∴*q*.

Here is another example of the transition from an argument to its form or structure: *b* is not an argument but the schema of an argument. The letters "*p*" and "*q*" are not statements—they are merely letters—but if statements are substituted for these letters, an argument results. Of course, it is essential that the same statement be substituted for "*p*" in each place it occurs and that the same statement be substituted for "*q*" in each place it occurs. If the substitution is made in this way, the resulting argument will be valid, regardless of what statements are substituted for "*p*" and "*q*." Indeed, we may substitute statements for "*p*" and "*q*" in such a way that the premises are either doubtful or known to be false, and still we may be assured that *the conclusion would be true if the premises were true*. This again illustrates the fact that the validity of an argument depends only upon its form and not upon its content.

It is easy to see why form *b* is called *affirming the antecedent*. The first premise is a conditional statement, and the second premise affirms (asserts) the antecedent of this conditional. The conclusion of the argument is the consequent of the first premise. Here is another example of affirming the antecedent:

*c*]　Is 288 divisible by 9? It is if its digits add up to a number that is divisible by 9. Since $2 + 8 + 8 = 18$, which is divisible by 9, the answer is "yes."

Like most arguments we encounter, *c* is not given in standard logical form. We rewrite it:

*d*]　If the sum of the digits of 288 is evenly divisible by 9, then 288 is evenly divisible by 9.
The sum of the digits of 288 is evenly divisible by 9.
∴288 is evenly divisible by 9.

This argument has form *b*.

Another valid form of deductive argument is *denying the consequent* (sometimes called *modus tollens*).

*e]*    If there is going to be a storm tonight, then the barometer is falling. The
       barometer is not falling.
       ∴There is not going to be a storm tonight.

This argument has the form

*f]*    If *p*, then *q*.
       Not-*q*.
       ∴Not-*p*.

It is easy to see why this form is called *denying the consequent*. The first
premise is a conditional statement, and the second premise is the denial or
negation of the consequent of that conditional. Here is another example:

*g]*    He would not take the crown;
       Therefore, 'tis certain he was not ambitious.[1]

Again, we have an argument that must be translated into standard form.
This time a premise is missing, but we can easily supply it.

*h]*    If Caesar had been ambitious, then he would have taken the crown.
       He did not take the crown.
       ∴Caesar was not ambitious.

The term "therefore" indicates the conclusion; the phrase " 'tis certain"
indicates the necessity of a deductive argument. Clearly, *h* has the form *f*.
   Denying the consequent often takes a slightly different form. For
example,

*i]*    BRUTUS:    Ay, Casca; tell us what hath chanced today, That Caesar looks so
                  sad.
       CASCA:     Why, you were with him, were you not?
       BRUTUS:    I should not then ask Casca what had chanced.[2]

This argument can be reconstructed as follows:

*j]*    If I had been with Caesar, then I would not have asked what happened.
       I have asked what happened.
       ∴I was not with Caesar.

The consequent of the first premise is a negative statement, so the second
premise, which is its denial, is affirmative. This gives rise to a slight variant
of *f*, namely,

[1]William Shakespeare, *Julius Caesar*, Act III, Scene II.
[2]*Ibid.*, Act I, Scene III.

k]   If *p,* then not-*q.*
     *q.*
     ∴Not-*p.*

This form is also called *denying the consequent.*

Further examples of these two forms of argument lie at the heart of the philosophical problem of free will. We cite a classical source:

l]   Lucretius, a Roman poet of the first century B.C., in his famous work, *De Rerum Natura,* argued that everything consists of atoms. Furthermore, he held that these atoms are subject to spontaneous and indeterminate swervings; for if each atomic motion were rigidly determined by prior motions, where could we find a source for free will? To Lucretius, it was clear that living things do have free will, so he concluded that determinism cannot hold.

The central core of the argument may be put as follows:

m]   If determinism holds, then people do not have free will.
     People have free will.
     ∴Determinism does not hold.

This argument is valid; it is an instance of denying the consequent. The only grounds upon which it can be attacked are by attacking the truth of the premises. Some people, however, taking it as more obvious that determinism holds than that man has free will, have constructed a different argument.

n]   If determinism holds, then people do not have free will.
     Determinism holds.
     ∴People do not have free will.

This argument is also valid; it is an instance of affirming the antecedent (schema *b*). In order to accept the conclusion of this argument, however, one must deny the truth of the second premise of *m.* The controversy between those who accept *m* and those who accept *n* does not lie in the validity of the arguments; they are both valid. It lies in the question of the truth of the premises. Between the two arguments we have three premises; they cannot all be true, for they are mutually incompatible. The philosophical controversy hinges upon the question of which premises are false.

There are two invalid forms of argument that are deceptively similar to the two valid forms we have just discussed. The first of these is called *the fallacy of affirming the consequent.* For example,

o]   Men, we will win this game unless we go soft in the second half. But I know we're going to win, so we won't go soft in the second half.

In standard form this argument becomes

*p*]    If we do not go soft in the second half, then we will win this game.
       We will win this game.
       ∴We will not go soft in the second half.

This argument has the form

*q*]    If *p*, then *q*.
       *q*.
       ∴*p*.

This form bears some resemblance to the valid form of affirming the
antecedent (schema *b*), but there are crucial differences. In affirming the
antecedent, the second premise asserts the *antecedent* of the first premise,
and the conclusion is the consequent of the first premise. In the fallacy of
affirming the consequent, the second premise asserts the *consequent* of the
first premise and the conclusion is the antecedent of the first premise.

The invalidity of affirming the consequent can easily be shown by the
method of counterexample (section 5). We construct an argument of this
form that has true premises and a false conclusion.

*r*]    If Harvard University is in Vermont, then it is in New England.
       Harvard University is in New England.
       ∴Harvard University is in Vermont.

The second invalid form of argument is called *the fallacy of denying the
antecedent*. This one bears some resemblance to the valid form of denying
the consequent. Consider the following argument:

*s*]    If Richard Roe is willing to testify, then he is innocent.
       Richard Roe is not willing to testify.
       ∴Richard Roe is not innocent.

This argument has the form

*t*]    If *p*, then *q*.
       Not-*p*.
       ∴Not-*q*.

The following fictitious bit of campaign oratory provides another instance
of this fallacy:

*u*]    So I say to you, ladies and gentlemen, that you should vote for my opponent *if*
       you want to pay higher taxes and get less for your money—*if* you feel that

clean and honest government is not worth having. But I know that you are
decent and intelligent people, so I ask for your support on election day.

This argument may be analyzed as follows:

*v]*   If you want to pay higher taxes and get less for your money, and you feel that
clean and honest government is not worth having, then you should vote for
my opponent.
It is not true that you want to pay higher taxes and get less for your money or
that you feel that clean and honest government is not worth having.
∴You should not vote for my opponent.

Actually, people often say "if" when they mean "if and only if"; if the first
premise is construed in that way, the argument, of course, becomes valid,
though it loses some of its rhetorical force.

It is easy to show that denying the antecedent is invalid by the method of
counterexample.

*w]*   If Columbia University is in California, then it is in the United States.
Columbia University is not in California.
∴Columbia University is not in the United States.

Both the fallacy of affirming the consequent and the fallacy of denying the
antecedent have special instances that deserve explicit mention. As we have
explained, in a valid deductive argument, if the premises are true the
conclusion must be true. Suppose we have an argument that is known to be
valid and that is known to have a true conclusion. What can we say about
the premises? It might be tempting to say that the premises of this argument are true. To do so would be to commit the fallacy of affirming the
consequent.

*x]*   If the premises of this argument are true, then the conclusion of this argu-
ment is true (i.e., the argument is valid).
The conclusion of this argument is true.
∴The premises of this argument are true.

It is a logical error to infer the truth of the premises from the truth of the
conclusion. Similarly, if we have a valid argument with false premises it
might be tempting to say that the conclusion is false. This would be the
fallacy of denying the antecedent.

*y]*   If the premises of this argument are true, then the conclusion of this argu-
ment is true (i.e., the argument is valid).
The premises of this argument are not true.
∴The conclusion of this argument is not true.

When an argument is given with missing premises, it is sometimes impossible to tell what premises the person had in mind. It is up to us to choose, and more than one choice may be available. Consider the following imaginary conversation:

z] It was Monday morning. Neither John nor Harvey felt much like working, so they killed a bit of time at the water cooler, gossiping about their fellow workers.

"Have you noticed," John asked, "that Henry never seems to take a drink? After work last Friday, we all stopped at that little lounge over on Elm Street—sorry you couldn't make it, Harv—and Henry had nothing but coffee. And at the company picnic last spring—man, the beer was really flowing that time, wasn't it?—he was drinking iced tea. What is it with him?"

"Well, as you know," Harvey answered, "I've known old Hank for many years, and I've never seen him touch a drop."

"You mean he really is a teetotaler?" John asked in some amazement. "That's funny, he never struck me as the puritanical sort."

This conversation involves arguments, but as usual they need to be sorted out. In the first place, an inductive argument is given to support the conclusion that Henry is a total abstainer from alcoholic beverages. Using that conclusion as a premise, John goes on to infer that Henry is puritanical, that is, that he has moral principles which prevent him from drinking. Clearly, a premise is missing from the argument, so we must supply it. We might reconstruct it as follows:

aa] If Henry never drinks, then he has moral scruples against drinking.
Henry never drinks.
∴Henry has moral scruples against drinking.

This argument is an instance of affirming the antecedent and is, therefore, valid. The trouble is that there is not much reason to believe that the premise we have supplied is true. Henry might, for all we know, abstain for reasons of health or because he doesn't like the taste of alcoholic beverages. We might try a different premise.

ab] If Henry has moral scruples against drinking, then Henry never drinks.
Henry never drinks.
∴Henry has moral scruples against drinking.

The premise we have introduced this time is far more plausible than the one we used previously, but now the argument is invalid, for it is an instance of the fallacy of affirming the consequent, and it is hard to see any alternative form it could have that would make it valid. Following the advice offered in section 1, we have done our best to reconstruct the argument as one that has a valid form and true—or, at least, plausible—premises. In this case, there seems to be no way in which this can be done.

## 8. REDUCTIO AD ABSURDUM

The *reductio ad absurdum* is a valid argument form that is widely used and highly effective. Sometimes it is used to establish a positive conclusion; often it is used to refute the thesis of an opponent. The idea of this form of argument is quite simple. Suppose we wish to prove that a statement *p* is true. We begin by assuming that *p* is false; that is, we assume *not-p*. On the basis of this assumption, we deduce a conclusion that is known to be false. Since a false conclusion follows from our assumption of *not-p* by a valid deductive argument, the assumption must have been false. If *not-p* is false, *p* must be true, and *p* was the statement we set out to prove in the first place.

Let us call the argument by which we deduce a false statement from the assumption *not-p* the *sub-deduction*. It may have any form whatever, as long as it is valid. The validity of any particular *reductio ad absurdum* depends upon the validity of its sub-deduction. A particular *reductio ad absurdum* may be attacked by showing that the sub-deduction is invalid, but the general form of *reductio ad absurdum* (which requires that the sub-deduction be valid) is not open to attack, for it is a valid form. Furthermore, the conclusiveness of the proof of *p* by *reductio ad absurdum* depends upon the falsity of the conclusion of the sub-deduction. The conclusion of the sub-deduction may be either some statement we are simply willing to accept as false or it may be an actual self-contradiction (see section 33). Often, the conclusion of the sub-deduction is *p* itself. This is a special case of a self-contradiction. If, on the assumption of *not-p*, we can deduce *p*, then, on the assumption of *not-p*, we have both *p* and *not-p*, which is a self-contradiction.

The *reductio ad absurdum* may be schematized as follows:

*a*]     *To prove:*   *p*.
         *Assume:*    Not-*p*.
         *Deduce:*    A false statement; either
                      *p* (which contradicts the assumption not-*p*), or
                      *q* and not-*q* (a self-contradiction), or
                      some other statement *r*, which is known to be false.
         *Conclude:* ∴ Not-*p* is false; therefore, *p*.

*Reductio ad absurdum* is closely related to denying the consequent. This relation is shown by the following argument:

*b*]     If the premise (assumption) of the sub-deduction is true, then the conclusion of the sub-deduction is true (i.e., the sub-deduction is valid).
         The conclusion of the sub-deduction is not true.
         ∴ The premise of the sub-deduction is not true.

*Reductio ad absurdum* is frequently used in mathematics, where it is often called *indirect proof*. Here is a classical mathematical example that is famous for its simplicity and elegance:

c]    A rational number is one that can be expressed as a simple fraction, that is, as the ratio of two integers (whole numbers). The Greek philosopher and mathematician Pythagoras (sixth century B.C.) is credited with the discovery that there is no rational number whose square equals two—in other words, that the square root of two is an irrational number. This conclusion is easily proved by *reductio ad absurdum.*

Assume that there is some rational number whose square is equal to two. Let this number be expressed in lowest terms; that is, if the numerator and denominator have a common factor greater than one, remove it. Thus we have

$$2 = (a/b)^2 \text{ or } a^2 = 2b^2$$

where $a$ and $b$ have no common factor greater than one. $a^2$ is an even number because it is twice $b^2$; hence, $a$ is an even number because the square of any odd number is odd. Since $a$ is even, it can be written as $2c$; $a^2$ equals $4c^2$. Then

$$4c^2 = 2b^2 \text{ and } 2c^2 = b^2.$$

It follows that $b^2$ is even, and so is $b$. We have shown that $a$ and $b$ are both even. This contradicts the assumption that $a/b$ is a rational number written in lowest terms. Therefore, there is no rational number whose square equals two.

Another excellent source of *reductio ad absurdum* arguments is the dialogues of Plato. Typically, in these dialogues, Socrates asks a question and proceeds to refute the answers given by showing that they lead to unacceptable consequences. Here is a brief and simple example:

d]    Well said, Cephalus, I replied; but as concerning justice, what is it?—to speak the truth and pay your debts—no more than this? And even to this are there not exceptions? Suppose that a friend when in his right mind has deposited arms with me and he asks for them when he is not in his right mind, ought I to give them back to him? No one would say that I ought or that I should be right in doing so, any more than they would say that I ought always to speak the truth to one who is in his condition.

You are quite right, he replied.

But then, I said, speaking the truth and paying your debts is not a correct definition of justice.[3]

The structure of the argument is quite clear.

e]    *To prove:*   Speaking the truth and paying debts is not a correct definition of justice.

    *Assume:*   Speaking the truth and paying debts is a correct definition of justice.

    *Deduce:*   It is just to give weapons to a madman. But this is absurd.

    *Conclude:* ∴ Speaking the truth and paying debts is not a correct definition of justice.

[3]Plato, *The Republic*, Book I. From *The Dialogues of Plato*, trans. B. Jowett (New York: Macmillan, Inc., 1892), III, 6.

For a final example of *reductio ad absurdum* we go to Kant's antinomies. Each of the four antinomies involves the proof of a thesis and the proof of an antithesis. Each of these eight proofs is by *reductio ad absurdum*. We illustrate with the proof of part of the thesis of the first antinomy.

*f]*    *Thesis:*    The world has a beginning in time. . . .
       *Proof:*    Granted, that the world has no beginning in time; up to every given moment of time, an eternity must have elapsed, and therewith passed away an infinite series of successive conditions or states of the things in the world. Now the infinity of a series consists in the fact that it never can be completed by means of a successive synthesis. It follows that an infinite series already elapsed is impossible, and that consequently a beginning of the world is a necessary condition of its existence. And this was the first thing to be proved.[4]

In the examples we have cited, we are not particularly concerned with the validity of the sub-deduction; rather, we wish to show the form of the *reductio ad absurdum*. We might remark, however, that the sub-deduction in example *c* is correct, the sub-deduction in example *f* is almost certainly incorrect, and the sub-deduction in *d* is at best somewhat dubious.


## 9. THE DILEMMA

In everyday language, we say that one faces a dilemma if one is forced to make a choice between two undesirable alternatives. For example,

*a]*    Brown has been compelled to appear in court because she has been charged with a minor traffic violation of which she is innocent. The judge asks whether she pleads guilty or not guilty. This is Brown's dilemma:
       Either I plead guilty or I plead not guilty.
       If I plead guilty, then I must pay a fine of twenty-five dollars for an offense I did not commit.
       If I plead not guilty, then I must spend another whole day in court.
       ∴Either I must pay a fine of twenty-five dollars for an offense I did not commit or I must spend another whole day in court.

In some cases, however, the only undesirable aspect of the situation is the fact that a choice is forced when one would rather not give up either alternative.

*b]*    Johnson is coming to the end of a delicious meal in a good restaurant. The waiter asks what he would like for dessert. "This is a terrible dilemma," he says with feigned distress, "because I can't decide between blueberry pie and chocolate cake." On the assumption that he cannot have both, the dilemma

---

[4]Immanuel Kant, *Critique of Pure Reason*, trans. J. M. D. Meiklejohn (New York: The Colonial Press, 1900), p. 241.

results from the fact that he must forego the cake if he chooses the pie and he must forego the pie if he chooses the cake. Either way, he must forego one or the other of his favorite desserts.

These arguments are valid; they have the following form:

c]   Either $p$ or $q$.
     If $p$, then $r$.
     If $q$, then $s$.
     ∴Either $r$ or $s$.

In the terminology of logic, any argument which has form $b$ is called a *dilemma,* whether or not the conclusion is undesirable. The dilemma is an extremely effective type of argument in controversy or debate, where it is used to try to force an opponent to accept an unwanted conclusion.

A famous example, which has a more specialized form, illustrates this use.

d]   An ancient teacher of argumentation made a contract with one of his pupils. The pupil would not have to pay for the lessons if (and only if) he did not win his first case. After the lessons were completed, the student did not take any cases. In order to receive payment, the teacher sued. The pupil defended himself with the following argument:
     Either I will win this case, or I will lose it.
     If I win this case, I will not have to pay my teacher (because he will have lost his suit for payment).
     If I lose this case, I will not have to pay my teacher (because of the terms of our agreement).
     ∴I do not have to pay.
   The teacher, however, presented this argument.
     Either I will win this case, or I will lose it.
     If I win the case, the pupil must pay me (because I will have won my suit for payment).
     If I lose the case, the pupil must pay me (because he will have won his first case).
     ∴The pupil must pay me.

It is not known how the case was decided, but these two dilemmas show that the original contract contained a hidden self-contradiction (see section 33). Both of the dilemmas in *d* have this form:

e]   Either $p$ or not-$p$.
     *If $p$, then $r$.*
     *If not-$p$, then $r$.*
     ∴*r.*

Clearly, *e* is a special case of *c*.

The ancient theological problem of evil can be posed as a dilemma. The argument runs as follows:

f]      There is evil in the world. This means that God cannot prevent evil, or else He does not want to prevent evil. If God cannot prevent evil, He is not omnipotent. If God does not want to prevent evil, He is not benevolent. Therefore, either God is not omnipotent, or else He is not benevolent.

This argument is valid; it has the form c. Theological controversies being what they are, we hasten to remark once more that validity has nothing to do with the truth of the premises. Some theologians reject the premise that there is evil in the world. Some theologians reject the premise that God is not benevolent unless He wants to prevent evil. The validity of the argument is not, however, open to question.

In section 7 we made reference, by way of example, to the problem of free will and determinism. This problem gives rise to another dilemma.

g]      Many philosophers have argued that people could not have free will if all events, including willing and acting, are completely determined by previous causes. Other philosophers, however, have said that free will would be equally impossible if some events are not entirely determined by previous causes. To whatever extent events are due to chance, they have nothing whatever to do with our will. Free will is just as incompatible with chance as it is with rigid causation. These doctrines, taken together, give rise to this dilemma.
        If determinism holds, people do not have free will.
        If determinism does not hold, people do not have free will.
        Either determinism holds or it does not.
        ∴People do not have free will.

This argument has the special form e; hence, it too is valid.

The fact that the dilemma (form c or form e) is a valid argument has an important consequence for examples like f and g. Many people would prefer to reject the conclusions of either or both of these arguments. They may believe in a God who is perfect; they do not want to admit that He is not both omnipotent and benevolent. They may place a high value on human freedom of choice and action. Since no valid argument has true premises and a false conclusion, the only way to avoid either of these conclusions is by rejecting at least one of the premises from which it is deduced.

Because of the rhetorical importance of the dilemma, a special terminology has traditionally been used. A person who cannot successfully challenge any of the premises from which an unwanted conclusion is deduced is said to be "impaled on the horns of a dilemma." A disputant who denies the first premise—the disjunctive premise containing "or"—is said to "go between the horns." The person who denies that there is really any evil in the world—that everything is for the best in the total scheme of things—is maintaining that it is false to say that God either is not able to prevent evil or does not want to do so. Going between the horns in this manner is one standard way of attacking argument f. As we shall see (example e of section 34), this kind of maneuver is not feasible for arguments that, like g are instances of form *e*. If dilemmas of this sort are to be challenged successfully, it must be by rejecting at least one of the conditional premises. This strategy is called "taking the dilemma by the horns." The dilemma of free will has often been attacked by those who deny that free will is incompatible with indeterminism and by those who deny that free will is incompatible with determinism. One strategy that holds no promise whatever for dealing with dilemmas is to accept the premises and deny the conclusion, for the validity of the argument forms can easily be demonstrated (section 10).

## 10. TRUTH TABLES AND VALIDITY

In sections 7 to 9 we discussed several deductive argument forms. Arguments like these are built out of constituent statements as parts, and the parts do not have to be further broken down to determine the validity or invalidity of the form. For example, affirming the antecedent,

*a*]    If *p*, then *q*.
        *p*.
        ∴*q*.

is valid because its first premise is a conditional statement, its second premise is the antecedent of that conditional, and the conclusion is the consequent of the same conditional. Arguments of this type are valid regardless of what statements the letters "*p*" and "*q*" stand for. The validity of the argument does not depend in any way upon the internal structure of the constituent statements "*p*" and "*q*." Similar remarks apply to denying the consequent, *reductio ad absurdum,* and the dilemma. All such arguments can be handled by an extremely efficient device known as a *truth table* (see p. 38).

Many English sentences—for example, imperatives ("Do not smoke.") and ejaculations ("Ouch!")—are neither true nor false. In the present context we are not concerned with sentences of that type. Most declarative sentences—sentences whose main function is to convey information of some sort—are either true or false, though in many cases we do not know which. These are the kinds of sentences we have in mind when we speak of statements. Truth and falsity are known as *truth values* of statements; every statement has one and only one of these truth values. In analyzing deductive arguments, we are obviously concerned with the types of sentences that are capable of assuming truth values, for we have characterized deductive validity in terms of truth values—that is, the conclusion must be true if the premises are true.

The basic idea behind the construction of truth tables is that there are certain ways of making compound statements out of simple parts so that the truth value of the compound statement is completely determined by the truth values of the component parts. The easiest example is the negation of a statement. The statement "Jefferson was the first president of the United States" can be negated by forming the statement "Jefferson was not the first president of the United States." If we begin with any true statement, its negation will be false; if we negate a false statement, the resulting statement will be true. The negation merely reverses the truth value of the statement to which it is applied.

Negation is applied to a single statement to form another statement. It is also possible to combine two statements in such ways that the truth value of the compound statement is completely determined by the truth value of the constituent parts. For example, the sentence "Abraham Lincoln was assassinated in Washington and John F. Kennedy was assassinated in Dallas" is built out of two simple statements joined together by the connective "and." The compound statement is true because it is a conjunction of two true components. The internal structure of the component statements is irrelevant to the truth value of the compound statement. *Any* compound statement of the form "*p and q*" will be true if the constituent statements "*p*" and "*q*" are both true; otherwise, if either or both component statements are false, the compound statement will also be false.

Other statement connectives, such as "or," "if . . . then . . . ," and "if and only if" can be handled similarly. All of these connectives are known as *truth-functional connectives,* for the truth value of any compound statement constructed by means of these connectives is completely determined by (is a function of) the truth values of the parts. To see how this works, let us begin by introducing some standard symbols:

| Compound statement form | Symbol | Name of form |
|---|---|---|
| not-$p$ | $\sim p$ | negation |
| $p$ and $q$ | $p \cdot q$ | conjunction |
| $p$ or $q$ | $p \lor q$ | disjunction (inclusive) |
| if $p$ then $q$ | $p \supset q$ | conditional (material) |
| $p$ if and only if $q$ | $p \equiv q$ | biconditional (material) |

We can now exhibit the meaning of each of these connectives in a convenient tabular form:

TABLE I

| $p$ | $\sim p$ |
|---|---|
| T | F |
| F | T |
| 1 | 2 |

TABLE II

| $p$ | $q$ | $p \cdot q$ | $p \lor q$ | $p \supset q$ | $p \equiv q$ |
|---|---|---|---|---|---|
| T | T | T | T | T | T |
| T | F | F | T | F | F |
| F | T | F | T | T | F |
| F | F | F | F | T | T |
| | | 3 | 4 | 5 | 6 |

These are truth tables, and they serve to define the truth-functional connectives. They can be construed in the following way. In Table I we are dealing with a connective that applies to a single statement. (We call negation a singulary "connective" by courtesy, even though it operates on only one statement.) A single statement can be either true or false; those are the only possible cases. The table tells us, for each of these cases, the result of forming the negation: A true statement, when negated, is transformed into a false statement; a false statement, when negated, is transformed into a true statement.

Table II defines the so-called binary connectives—connectives that join two statements to make a third statement. There are four possible ways in which the two truth values can be assigned to two statements; these four possibilities are displayed in the first two columns of Table II. To define the binary connectives, we need merely state the truth value of the compound statement for each possible combination of truth values of the two constituent statements. Thus, column 3 summarizes what we said about conjunctions; the conjunction is true if both components are true, but it is false in all other cases.

We noted in section 6 that conditional statements can be expressed in a variety of ways; similarly, there are words other than "and" that can be used to form conjunctions. The leading example is "but." If one says, "Abraham Lincoln was killed in Washington, but John F. Kennedy was killed in Dallas," the logical import is the same as if the word "and" had been used—both conjuncts must be true if the compound statement is to be true. "But" reveals some astonishment at the conjunction, but such surprise is an expression of a psychological attitude, not part of the informational content of the statement. Similarly, words like "although," "nevertheless," and "however" often serve, as "but" does, to state a conjunction and to heighten the contrast between the conjuncts.

We must also note emphatically that the truth-functional conjunction, which we symbolize with a dot and define in column 3 of Table II, does not correspond exactly to the English word "and." In ordinary conversation, the statement "Jane became pregnant and got married" would have a significance radically different from that of the statement "Jane got married and became pregnant." The difference arises from the fact that the English word "and" sometimes has the force of "and then." Let us suppose, without making any temporal assumptions, that both component statements, "Jane became pregnant" and "Jane got married," are true. Then, according to the truth table definition of conjunction, the conjunction of those two statements is true regardless of the order in which they are conjoined. Thus, there is a serious discrepancy between the word "and" as it is often ordinarily used and the truth-functional connective. One very important aspect of this difference is the fact that the temporally loaded "and then" sense of "and" is non-truth-functional, for the truth value of the compound statement is *not* fully determined by the truth values of the constituent parts. We use the truth-functional conjunction, as defined in the truth table, because it works neatly from a logical standpoint, but we must not forget the differences between our dot and the English word "and."

The word "or" has two distinct meanings in English: In one sense (known as the *exclusive* sense) it means "one or the other but not both." This is the meaning it has on a menu in the phrase "soup or salad," used to tell what comes with the entree. The other sense (known as the *inclusive* sense) is often rendered by the expression "and/or," which frequently appears in documents like insurance policies or wills. If, for example, a degree in law or a degree in accounting were stipulated as qualification for a position, we would not expect people who had both degrees to be automatically disqualified, as they would if "or" were meant in the exclusive sense. A glance at column 4 of Table II reveals that we have chosen the inclusive disjunction to be symbolized by the wedge, for the compound statement is true if either or both constituent statements is true, and false only if both components are false. The choice here is one of convenience. The inclusive disjunction is a useful logical operation, and the exclusive disjunction is easily symbolized in terms of others we are adopting, for example, as the negation of a biconditional.

The horseshoe-shaped symbol defined in column 5 is known as the sign of *material implication;* it is used to symbolize conditional statements, and it can be read, roughly, "if . . . then . . ." This connective is somewhat problematic, for its import differs markedly from the phrase "if . . . then . . ." as it is used in most conditional statements of ordinary discourse. In defining this connective truth-functionally, we find ourselves committed to treating as true any conditional that has a true antecedent and a true consequent—for example, "If Mars is a planet, then diamonds are composed of carbon." Such a statement would not normally be regarded as a reasonable conditional, for there seems to be no connection between the truth of the antecedent and the truth of the consequent. In this respect it contrasts sharply with our example of section 6, "If Newton was a physicist then he was a scientist," which exhibits a clear relation between antecedent and consequent. Moreover, according to the meaning given in the truth table, we must regard both the statements "If Mars is not a planet, then coal is black" and "If Mars is not a planet, then coal is white" as true material conditionals, simply by virtue of the fact that both have a false antecedent. We see from lines 3 and 4 of Table II that *any* material conditional with a false antecedent is true, regardless of its consequent. Similarly, examination of lines 1 and 3 reveals that *any* material conditional with a true consequent is true, regardless of the antecedent. Thus, "If cats bark, then two plus two equals four" and "If Beethoven was a composer, then two plus two equals four" are true material conditionals because of their true consequents. The fact that a material conditional with a false antecedent is automatically true, and the fact that a material conditional with a true consequent is likewise automatically true, are sometimes called *paradoxes of material implication*.

Given the strange properties of the material implication as defined in Table II, you might wonder why we don't abandon it altogether as hopelessly inadequate to capture the sense of "if . . . then . . ." in ordinary language. The answer is that the operation symbolized by the horseshoe has one basic characteristic that is essential to the meaning of any conditional statement—namely, the conditional is false if it has a true antecedent and a false consequent. The material implication is a truth-functional operation, and thus it cannot capture the sense of connection relating the antecedent and the consequent of more familiar conditionals. The "if . . . then . . ." of ordinary English is a stronger connective than the material implication. Nevertheless, the material conditional statement has just the feature of the ordinary conditional that insures the validity of such basic deductive argument forms as affirming the antecedent, denying the consequent, and the dilemma. We shall see in a moment how that works. We shall then see that the material conditional does, indeed, possess the basic logical core of the conditional statement.

The sign of *material equivalence*, the triple bar, is defined in column 6 of Table II, and it is used to form biconditional statements. It can be read, roughly, as "if and only if." The material equivalence inherits a good deal of the strangeness of the material implication, for it can be viewed simply as a combination of two material implications: "$p \equiv q$" has the same meaning as "$(p \supset q) \cdot (q \supset p)$," as we shall see. A material biconditional statement is true provided both components have the same truth value, and false if they have different truth values. Thus any two true statements are materially equivalent to each other, as are any two false statements, regardless of any apparent connection between the meanings of the components. "Mars is a planet if and only if the oceans contain salt" is a true biconditional; so also is "The moon shines by its own light if and only if Isaac Newton was a German."

TABLE III

| $p$ | $q$ | $\sim p$ | $\sim q$ | $p \supset q$ | $p \vee q$ | $q \cdot \sim q$ | $p \supset (q \cdot \sim q)$ |
|-----|-----|----------|----------|---------------|------------|------------------|------------------------------|
| T | T | F | F | T | T | F | F |
| T | F | F | T | F | T | F | F |
| F | T | T | F | T | T | F | T |
| F | F | T | T | T | F | F | T |
| *1* | *2* | *3* | *4* | *5* | *6* | *7* | *8* |

Let us now see how truth tables can be used to test the validity of argument forms. Table III is constructed by referring to Tables I and II. The first two columns simply give the four possible combinations of **T** and **F** for the two statements "*p*" and "*q*." We shall make it a firm policy always to list them in the same order; otherwise, mistakes would be almost inevitable. The next two columns give the truth value patterns for the negations of "*p*" and "*q*" by reversing the patterns found in the first two columns. Columns 5 and 6 are simply copied out of Table II. Column 7 results from a conjunction of columns 2 and 4; no line has **T** in both of these columns, so the result is all **F**'s. Column 8 is a conditional with column 1 as antecedent and column 7 as consequent. From Table II, column 5 (which is the same as Table III, column 5) we see that the conditional is false if it has a true antecedent and a false consequent; otherwise it is true. This fact is used to arrive at the pattern in column 8.

The premises of affirming the antecedent are "*p* ⊃ *q*" and "*p*"; their patterns are given in columns 5 and 1 respectively. Line 1 is the only line in which both premises have the value **T,** and in this line the conclusion "*q*" has the value **T** as well. Thus, affirming the antecedent is valid because there is no way that truth values can be assigned that render the premises true and the conclusion false. The validity of denying the consequent is easily shown in the same way. The premises of this form are "*p* ⊃ *q*" and "~*q*"; line 4 is the only line in which both have the value **T**. In this line, the conclusion "~*p*" also has the value **T**. Again, there is no way for the premises to be true and the conclusion false.

The same method can be used to expose the two fallacies mentioned in section 7—namely, *the fallacy of affirming the consequent* and *the fallacy of denying the antecedent*. Affirming the consequent has "*p* ⊃ *q*" and "*q*" as premises; both of these are true in lines 1 and 3 of Table III, but in line 3, the conclusion "*p*" has the value **F**. It is therefore possible, as we saw in section 7, to concoct an instance of affirming the consequent which has true premises and a false conclusion. Denying the antecedent has "*p* ⊃ *q*" and "~*p*" as premises; both are true in lines 3 and 4 of the truth table. Again, in line 3 the conclusion "~*q*" is false, which shows that this form too is invalid.

Another simple argument form, *disjunctive syllogism*, is illustrated by the following argument:

*b*]　　Either you paid your taxes or you have a guilty conscience.
　　　　You did not pay your taxes.
　　　∴You have a guilty conscience.

It has the form

*c*]　　$p \lor q$
　　　　$\sim p$
　　∴$q$

whose validity can be established by Table III. The truth value patterns of the premises are found in columns 6 and 3 respectively. Line 3 is the only line in which the value of both premises is **T**; in that line the conclusion also has the value **T**. Notice that the similar form

d]    p ∨ q
      p
      ∴~q

is invalid, as can be seen by inspecting line 1 of Table III. Even if you did pay your taxes—going back to a slight modification of *b*—it does not follow that you do not have a guilty conscience.

Column 8 can be used to evaluate one form of *reductio ad absurdum* discussed in section 8. Here, the only premise is "*p* ⊃ (*q*·~*q*)"; it has the value **T** in lines 3 and 4. The conclusion "~*p*" also has the value **T** in both of these lines. Hence it is a valid form.

The argument forms so far tested by truth tables have only two distinct constituent statements, "*p*" and "*q*." To accommodate argument forms with more than two constituent statements, we must expand the truth table in a straightforward way. Consider, for example, this argument:

e]    If you read the book you will know the plot.
      If you know the plot you will be bored by the film.
      ∴If you read the book you will be bored by the film.

This has the form

f]    p ⊃ q
      q ⊃ r
      ∴p ⊃ r

known as *hypothetical syllogism*. In order to test this argument for validity,

TABLE IV

| p | q | r | p ⊃ q | q ⊃ r | p ⊃ r |
|---|---|---|-------|-------|-------|
| T | T | T | T | T | T |
| T | T | F | T | F | F |
| T | F | T | F | T | T |
| T | F | F | F | T | F |
| F | T | T | T | T | T |
| F | T | F | T | F | T |
| F | F | T | T | T | T |
| F | F | F | T | T | T |
| *1* | *2* | *3* | *4* | *5* | *6* |

we need a truth table with enough lines to exhaust all possible combinations of **T** and **F** for three statements; eight is the required number. Columns 1 through 3 contain every possible assignment of **T** and **F** to "*p*," "*q*," and "*r*." Columns 4 and 5 contain the truth patterns for the two premises, and column 6 contains the truth pattern for the conclusion. Lines 1, 5, 7, 8 contain **T** for both premises; the conclusion also has **T** in each of these lines. Hence, the form is valid.

It is essential to be quite clear on the way the entries for columns 4 through 6 are found. Referring back to column 5 of Table II, where the conditional is defined, we see that a conditional is false if it has a true antecedent and a false consequent (line 2); otherwise it is true. In column 6 of Table IV, for example, we find that "*p* ⊃ *r*" receives the value **F** in lines 2 and 4; these are precisely the lines in which "*p*" has the value **T** and "*r*" has the value **F**. All other lines in column 6 contain **T**. Columns 4 and 5 are constructed analogously.

The method of truth tables is theoretically adequate to test any argument form whose validity depends only upon its truth-functional structure. It is fairly obvious how to extend the method to schemas that contain four or more distinct constituent statements. It is simply a matter of assigning the truth values, **T** and **F**, to all of the constituent statements in all possible ways. If a schema contains $n$ constituent statements, the truth table needed to test its validity will require $2^n$ lines. You can see that each time you add another letter, the size of the table doubles, so the method can rapidly become unwieldy. In schema *b* of section 9 we gave the general form of a dilemma; it contains four different constituent statements. You can construct the 16-line truth table needed to demonstrate its validity.

## 11. LOGICAL EQUIVALENCES

We have asserted, on a couple of occasions at least, that two statement forms are logically equivalent to one another. In section 6, for instance, we said that a conditional statement is equivalent to its contrapositive; in section 10, for a further example, we said that a material biconditional is equivalent to a conjunction of two conditional statements. Let us now use our truth tables to show how such equivalences can be demonstrated. For this purpose we construct the following table:

TABLE V

| *p* | *q* | ~*p* | ~*q* | *p* ⊃ *q* | *q* ⊃ *p* | (*p* ⊃ *q*)·(*q* ⊃ *p*) | *p* ≡ *q* | ~*q* ⊃ ~*p* |
|-----|-----|------|------|-----------|-----------|--------------------------|-----------|-------------|
| T | T | F | F | T | T | T | T | T |
| T | F | F | T | F | T | F | F | F |
| F | T | T | F | T | F | F | F | T |
| F | F | T | T | T | T | T | T | T |
| *1* | *2* | *3* | *4* | *5* | *6* | *7* | *8* | *9* |

The truth value patterns in the columns have been built up on the basis of the definitions given in Tables I and II. Column 6, for example, has a **T** in each line except the third, in which the antecedent "$q$" has the value **T** and the consequent "$p$" has the value **F**. Column 7 represents the conjunction of columns 5 and 6; it has a **T** in each line in which columns 5 and 6 both have **T**'s, and it has an **F** in every other line. Column 8 simply repeats the truth value pattern given in Table II as a definition of the biconditional form. We note that the truth value patterns in columns 7 and 8 are identical.

What does it mean when two statement forms have the same truth value patterns? It means that truth-functionally the two are equivalent to one another. Any substitutions for the letters "$p$," "$q$," "$r$," etc., which make the one into a true statement will make the other into a true statement as well, and any substitutions that make the one false will make the other false as well. This is an extremely significant fact: It means that we can interchange equivalent forms for one another anywhere in any argument and be certain that we have done nothing that would affect the validity of the argument. The reason is simple. If we have statements with equivalent forms they must have the same truth value—there is no way of assigning truth values to the constituent parts so that one is true and the other false. Since the validity of an argument form depends solely upon the fact that none of its instances can have true premises and a false conclusion, exchanging a form for an equivalent one cannot possibly transform a valid form into an invalid one. Nor can it possibly change an invalid argument form into a valid one.

Let us illustrate this important principle by a simple example. We have shown that affirming the antecedent and denying the consequent are both valid argument forms. Utilizing the equivalence between a conditional statement and its contrapositive, we can see that the validity of denying the consequent follows immediately from the validity of affirming the antecedent. Since "$p \supset q$" is equivalent to "$\sim q \supset \sim p$," the two argument forms

$a$]   $\quad p \supset q$            $\qquad\qquad\qquad$ $b$]   $\quad \sim q \supset \sim p$
$\qquad\quad \sim q$               $\qquad\qquad\qquad\qquad\qquad\quad \sim q$
$\qquad \therefore \sim p$              $\qquad\qquad\qquad\qquad\qquad\quad \therefore \sim p$

must both be valid, or they must both be invalid. But form $b$ results if we substitute "$\sim q$" for "$p$" and "$\sim p$" for "$q$" in

$c$]   $\quad p \supset q$
$\qquad\quad p$
$\qquad \therefore q$

which is the form of affirming the antecedent, and which is known to be valid.

Let us be quite sure we understand what is being done here. When we say that affirming the antecedent is a valid form, we mean that there is no way of substituting statements for the letters "$p$" and "$q$" in form $c$ (the same statement must, of course, be substituted for "$p$" in both places it appears, and the same statement must be substituted for "$q$" in both of its occurrences) that will result in an argument having true premises and a false conclusion. It does not matter how simple or how complex the statements; in particular, the statements substituted for "$p$" and "$q$" may both be negative. For example, here is a simple reformulation of argument $h$ of section 7:

$d$]     If Caesar did not take the crown, then he was not ambitious.
He did not take the crown.
∴He was not ambitious.

This exhibits the form $c$, but it also has the form $b$. Indeed, *any* argument that has form $b$ will also possess form $c$ (but not conversely—do you see why?).

We have been doing several things with argument forms. First, we have substituted *statements* for the letters in valid forms to show that the resulting *argument* is valid. Exercising due caution—see section 5—we sometimes claim that arguments are invalid when they result from substitutions in invalid forms. Second, we have substituted statement *forms* for the letters in argument forms, and in this way we have shown that additional argument *forms* are valid. To carry out this procedure, we may substitute a statement form of any degree of complexity for a given letter in the original form. That is how we showed that form $b$ is valid—by substituting statement forms for letters in form $c$. Third, we have replaced a statement form by a logically equivalent statement form—that is how we demonstrated the validity of form $a$.

The validity of the disjunctive syllogism (form $c$, section 10) can be shown by the method we just used on denying the consequent. You can carry out the demonstration by constructing a truth table showing

$e$]     "$p \vee q$" is equivalent to "$\sim p \supset q$."

When this equivalence is used to replace the first premise of disjunctive syllogism, the result is a form you can get by making a suitable substitution in affirming the antecedent (form $c$, this section).

Equivalence $e$ has another interesting consequence. In section 6, we pointed out that "unless" has the same meaning as "if not." Thus

$f$]     If you do not pass English, then you cannot graduate.

means the same as

g]     Unless you pass English, you cannot graduate.

Now, as a result of equivalence *e*, you can see that *g* means the same as

h]     Either you pass English or you cannot graduate.

Here we must be careful to note that the word "or" has its inclusive sense. Hence, the word "unless" has precisely the same meaning as "or" (in the inclusive sense). Not many native speakers of English are aware of that fact.

Statements like *f* and *g* are often used to assert *necessary conditions*—in this case, passing English is said to be a necessary condition for graduation. To say that a condition is necessary for a result means that the result will not occur if the condition is not fulfilled. When "*p*" constitutes a necessary condition for "*q*" we may symbolize the situation by "$\sim p \supset \sim q$," which, as we know, is equivalent to "$q \supset p$." In section 6 we noted that "only if" is the converse of "if"; thus "$q \supset p$" can be translated as "*q* only if *p*." This is another way of saying that "*p*" is a necessary condition for "*q*"—e.g., you will graduate only if you pass English.

To say that "*p*" constitutes a *sufficient condition* for "*q*" means merely that "*q*" will obtain if "*p*" does—in other words, it means simply "$p \supset q$."

i]     If you are decapitated, then you will die.

This is tantamount to asserting that decapitation is a sufficient condition for death. It is not, of course, a necessary condition. If decapitation were a necessary condition of death we could assert that you will die only if you are decapitated, which obviously is not the case, for there are many other causes of death. Moreover, to return to our example of a necessary condition, passing English is certainly not a sufficient condition of graduation, for you must pass many other courses as well.

At the beginning of this section we pointed out that the biconditional is equivalent to a conjunction of two conditionals, i.e.,

j]     "$p \equiv q$" is equivalent to "$(p \supset q) \cdot (q \supset p)$"

where the first conditional says "if *p* then *q*" and the second says "only if *p* then *q*." Together they say "If and only if *p* then *q*," or more idiomatically, "*p* if and only if *q*." Using the terminology just explained, the first conditional says that "*p*" is a sufficient condition for "*q*," whereas the second conditional says that "*p*" is a necessary condition for "*q*." The biconditional therefore states that "*p*" is a *necessary and sufficient condition* for "*q*." Being evenly divisible by two is, for example, a necessary and sufficient condition for a number being even.

To assert "*p* or *q*" in the exclusive sense of "or" means that one or the other but not both of these statements is true; this can be symbolized as

*k*]     $(p \lor q) \cdot \sim(p \cdot q)$,

which is to say, "*p* or *q*" in the inclusive sense of "or" with the added qualification that "*p*" and "*q*" are not both true. This same thing can be expressed by the formula

*l*]     $\sim(p \equiv q)$,

that is, by the denial of a material biconditional. It would be good practice for you to construct a truth table to demonstrate the equivalence of *k* and *l*.

## 12. TAUTOLOGIES

Our emphasis, so far, has been mainly upon arguments. It is important to recognize, however, that there are certain statement forms that represent truths of logic—forms that become true statements whenever substitutions are made that transform them into statements. One basic type of logical truth can be established by means of truth tables; the forms and the statements that result from substitutions into them are known as *tautologies*. As a classic example of a tautology, consider the famous *law of excluded middle*

*a*]     $p \lor \sim p$.

We construct a two-line truth table:

TABLE VI

| $p$ | $\sim p$ | $p \lor \sim p$ |
|---|---|---|
| T | F | T |
| F | T | T |

The truth value pattern of this formula has nothing but **T**'s in it; consequently, there is no way of assigning a truth value to the single constituent "*p*" that will make the formula false. Whatever statement we substitute for

"$p$," the form "$p \lor \sim p$" will be transformed into a true statement. Thus, "Either Newton was a physicist or Newton was not a physicist" is necessarily true, as is any other statement that has the form of the law of excluded middle.

Let us construct another truth table in order to look at some additional tautologies:

TABLE VII

| $p$ | $q$ | $p \supset q$ | $q \supset (p \supset q)$ | $\sim q \supset \sim p$ | $(p \supset q) \equiv (\sim q \supset \sim p)$ |
|-----|-----|---------------|---------------------------|-------------------------|-----------------------------------------------|
| T | T | T | T | T | T |
| T | F | F | T | F | T |
| F | T | T | T | T | T |
| F | F | T | T | T | T |
| *1* | *2* | *3* | *4* | *5* | *6* |

| $p \cdot (p \supset q)$ | $[p \cdot (p \supset q)] \supset q$ |
|-------------------------|-------------------------------------|
| T | T |
| F | T |
| F | T |
| F | T |
| *7* | *8* |

In column 4, we find another example of a tautology; it represents one of the so-called "paradoxes of material implication" (see p. 41). It says, in effect, that if "$q$" is a true statement, then any statement "$p$" materially implies it.

In section 11, we established the equivalence between a conditional statement and its contrapositive. In columns 3 and 5 of Table VII we have repeated the identical truth value patterns for these two forms; in column 6 we have worked out the truth value pattern for the biconditional joining those two forms, and we see that it is a tautology. This illustrates a general principle: *Two truth-functional statement forms are logically equivalent if and only if the biconditional between them is a tautology.*

Column 8 contains a tautology that bears a close and special relationship to the argument form affirming the antecedent. This tautology is a conditional whose antecedent is the conjunction of the two premises "$p$" and "$p \supset q$" of affirming the antecedent, and its consequent is the conclusion "$q$" of that argument form. This tautology again illustrates a fundamental general principle: *A truth-functional argument form is valid if and only if a certain conditional statement form is a tautology: namely, the conditional whose antecedent is the conjunction of the premises of that argument and whose consequent is its conclusion.*

Tautologies constitute a basic, though severely restricted, class of statements (and statement forms) whose truth can be established by logical considerations alone. This is an evident consequence of the fact that the truth pattern of a tautology consists solely of **T**'s. In section 33 we will consider the nature of logical truth in more general terms.

## 13. CATEGORICAL STATEMENTS

Having discussed truth-functional arguments, whose validity does not depend upon the internal structure of their simple constituent statements (i.e., statements represented by single letters) but only upon the ways in which they are combined, we now want to examine a fundamental group of arguments whose validity is determined by the internal structure of simple statements. These arguments are known as *categorical syllogisms.* In order to prepare the way for their discussion in the next section, we must first explain what is meant by a *categorical statement.* There are four forms of categorical statements; any statement that has one of these forms is a categorical statement. Traditionally, each of these forms has been denoted by one of the first four vowels; here is an example of each form.

a]  *A:*  All diamonds are gems.   *E:*  No diamonds are gems.
    *I:*  Some diamonds are gems. *O:*  Some diamonds are not gems.

The statements in the left column (*A* and *I*) are *affirmative;* those in the right column (*E* and *O*) are *negative.* The statements in the top row (*A* and *E*) are *universal;* those in the second row (*I* and *O*) are *particular.* The forms are as follows:

b]  *A:*  All *F* are *G.*              *E:*  No *F* are *G.*
        *Universal Affirmative*              *Universal Negative*
    *I:*  Some *F* are *G.*             *O:*  Some *F* are not *G.*
        *Particular Affirmative*             *Particular Negative*

Each categorical statement contains two *terms,* a *subject term* and a *predicate term.* In the examples *a,* "diamonds" is the subject term, and "gems" is the predicate term. In the forms *b,* "*F*" stands for the subject term, and "*G*" stands for the predicate term. Each term stands for a class of things, for example, the class of diamonds and the class of gems. Definite categorical statements result from the forms *b* if words or phrases standing for classes of things are substituted for "*F*" and "*G.*" The *content* of a categorical statement depends upon the terms that occur in the statement; the *form* of a categorical statement exhibits a definite relationship between the two classes, regardless of what classes they happen to be.

Since English is somewhat ambiguous, we must be precise about the meanings of categorical statements. The form $A$ is most troublesome. The statement "All diamonds are gems" certainly implies that there are no diamonds that are not gems; that is, if anything is a diamond, then it is a gem. This statement might be taken to imply, in addition, that there are such things as diamonds. Statements of form $A$, however, do not always carry this latter implication, even in ordinary usage. The statement "All deserters will be shot" does not imply that there will be any deserters; indeed, it may be asserted in order to prevent desertion from occurring. Its full meaning is given by the statement "If anyone deserts, then that person will be shot." This statement may be called a *universal conditional statement*. It is a conditional statement that is asserted to be true of anything whatsoever.

In treating categorical statements, especially as they occur in syllogisms, we shall adopt this interpretation for all $A$ statements. "All $F$ are $G$" will be taken as meaning, "If anything is an $F$, then it is a $G$." Thus, the statement "All diamonds are gems" will be taken to say, "If anything is a diamond then it is a gem." We shall, in addition, construe the conditional statement as a *material conditional* (see section 10), in this way building with concepts that have already been analyzed. It is, however, essential to note an important consequence of the use of the material implication in constructing the $A$ statement: *The $A$ statement does not imply that its subject term refers to any existent objects.* "All $F$ are $G$" does not assert that there is anything of the type $F$; "All diamonds are gems" does not imply that any diamonds exist, even though we all know that they do. An $A$ statement does not assert the existence of anything answering to the subject term; it is possible for $A$ statements with *empty* subject terms to be true—for example, "All nineteenth-century astronauts were male." Indeed, if we reflect for a moment upon the meaning of the material conditional statement, we see that any $A$ statement with an empty subject term *must* be true. A material conditional statement is true if it has a false antecedent; since there were no astronauts in the nineteenth century, the statement "If anyone was a nineteenth-century astronaut then he was male" must be true of everyone, for it has an antecedent that is false for everyone to whom it might be applied. As we have said, the terms of categorical statements are terms that refer to classes. A given class may or may not have members; it is perfectly meaningful to refer to classes that have none. The class of deserters may have no members, the class of thousand dollar bills in your pocket probably does not have members, and the class of nineteenth-century astronauts certainly has no members. The subject term of an $A$ statement need not have any members and still that statement may be true. The $A$ statement *does not imply* that its subject term refers to a class having members.

There are no particular difficulties in interpreting the $E$ statement. One point needs to be made concerning both the *I* and *O* statements. The word "some" is taken to mean "at least one." The statement "Some diamonds are gems" is interpreted to mean "At least one diamond is a gem." In spite of the plural form of the *I* and *O* statements, they are not construed as implying more than one.

In view of our interpretations of the four forms of categorical statements, an obvious and important relation exists among them. An *A* statement contradicts the *O* statement having the same subject and predicate terms; an *E* statement contradicts the *I* statement having the same subject and predicate terms. "All diamonds are gems" contradicts "Some diamonds are not gems"; "No diamonds are gems" contradicts "Some diamonds are gems."[5]

We have presented four rigid forms of categorical statements. As we would naturally expect, there are many other forms that are equivalent to the four we specified. The situation is similar to the one we encountered in discussing conditional statements (section 6); indeed, because the *A* statement is a universal conditional statement, many of the variations of conditional statements have counterparts as variations of *A* statements. To indicate the range of variations of *A* statements, we may list the following equivalents to the statement "All whales are mammals":

*c*]     Every whale is a mammal.
       Any whale is a mammal.
       Whales are mammals.
       If anything is a whale, it is a mammal.
       Anything that is a whale is a mammal.
       If anything is not a mammal, then it is not a whale.
       All non-mammals are non-whales.
       A thing is a whale only if it is a mammal.
       Only mammals are whales.
       Nothing is a whale unless it is a mammal.
       No whale is not a mammal.

*E* statements also have a large number of equivalents. Many of these appear when we observe that an *E* statement can be translated into an *A*

---

[5]In the traditional treatment, the four types of categorical statements were arranged in a "square of opposition" with the contradictory pairs *A-O* and *E-I* diagonally opposite one another. This square array was used to depict a number of other relations, in addition to contradiction, that obtained among categorical statements on their traditional interpretation. Under the modern interpretation, only the relation of contradiction remains, so we have not reproduced the square. For a presentation of the traditional square, see Eaton, *General Logic;* for a comparison between the traditional treatment and the modern, see Copi, *Introduction to Logic* (full bibliographic data are given at the end of this book).

    Additional contrast between the traditional and modern interpretations of the syllogism occurs in footnote 6, p. 57.

    The concept of self-contradictory statement is explained in section 33; the relation of contradiction between two statements is discussed in section 34, where it is carefully contrasted with the relation of contrariety between statements.

statement. For example, "No spiders are insects" is equivalent to "All spiders are non-insects." This *A* statement then admits all of the various translations of *A* statements just given. "No spiders are insects" has the following equivalents, among others:

*d]*    All spiders are non-insects.
      All insects are non-spiders.
      No insects are spiders.
      Nothing that is an insect is a spider.
      Nothing is a spider unless it is not an insect.
      Only non-spiders are insects.
      Only non-insects are spiders.
      If anything is a spider it is not an insect.
      If anything is an insect it is not a spider.

*I* and *O* statements do not have so many variations. We shall give a few examples. The *I* statement "Some plants are edible" has the following equivalents:

*e]*    Some edible things are plants.
      There are plants that are edible.
      There are edible plants.
      Something that is a plant is edible.
      At least one plant is edible.

The *O* statement "Some philosophers are not logicians" has the following equivalents:

*f]*    There is a philosopher who is not a logician.
      Not all philosophers are logicians.

The foregoing lists of statements equivalent to categorical statements are by no means complete, but they should give you a feeling for the sort of variety you may encounter. You should go through these lists carefully and satisfy yourself that the statements are equivalent, as claimed.

There is one further variation in the forms of categorical statements, as they are found in ordinary contexts, to which we should call attention. In all of the examples given so far, we have used a standard verb, "is" or "are," to relate the subject term to the predicate term. Sometimes a different verb form occurs, as in the statements

*g]*    Some dogs bark.
      All students have textbooks.
      No horses have wings.
      All storms create problems.

Nevertheless, they can be construed as categorical statements, for they can be paraphrased in standard form:

h]   Some dogs are animals that bark.
     All students are people who have textbooks.
     No horses are animals that have wings.
     All storms are events that create problems.

When such statements occur in categorical syllogisms (sections 14 and 15), it is best to translate them into the standard forms. This enables us to see clearly and unambiguously the relationship between the two classes that each categorical statement asserts. Such relationships among classes are *the* basis upon which the validity or invalidity of syllogisms—to which we now turn—rests.


## 14. CATEGORICAL SYLLOGISMS

*Categorical syllogisms* (which, for convenience, we shall simply call *syllogisms*) are arguments composed entirely of categorical statements. Every syllogism has two premises and one conclusion. Although each categorical statement contains two terms, a subject term and a predicate term, the whole syllogism has only three different terms. One of these terms occurs once in each premise; it is called the *middle term*. Each of the other two terms occurs once in the conclusion and once in a premise; they are called *end terms*. The following argument, consisting of three categorical statements, is a syllogism:

a]   All dogs are mammals.
     All mammals are animals.
     ∴All dogs are animals.

"Mammals" occurs once in each premise; it is, therefore, the middle term. "Dogs" occurs once in a premise and once in the conclusion, establishing itself as an end term. "Animals" occurs once in the conclusion and once in a premise. It, too, is an end term.

There are many forms of syllogisms—some valid, others invalid. Like any deductive argument, the validity of a syllogism depends only upon its form. The form of a syllogism depends upon two things: first, which of the four types of categorical statement each statement is; second, the positions of the middle term and the end terms. In a, both of the premises are A statements, and so is the conclusion. One end term, "dogs," is the subject term of the first premise and the subject term of the conclusion. The other end term, "animals," is the predicate term of the second premise and the predicate term of the conclusion. The middle term, "mammals," is the predicate term of the first premise and the subject term of the second premise. Letting "S" stand for the end term that is the subject term of the conclusion, "P" for the end term that is the predicate term of the conclusion, and "*M*" for the middle term, we may represent the form of *a* unambiguously as follows:

*b*]   $S\ A\ M$
       $M\ A\ P$
   $\therefore S\ A\ P$

The fact that each statement in the argument is a universal affirmative is indicated by the "*A*" in each line.

There are three simple rules that may be used to test the validity of any syllogism. In order to present these rules we must however, introduce the concept of *distribution*. A given term—for example, "mammals"—may occur in different categorical statements, and it may occur as the subject term or as the predicate term. When a given term occurs, it may be *distributed* or it may be *undistributed* in that occurrence. Whether a term is distributed or not *in a given occurrence* depends upon the type of statement it occurs in and whether it is the subject term or the predicate term in that statement. *A term is distributed in a categorical statement if that statement says something about each and every member of the class that term designates.*

The *A* statement "All whales are mammals" says something about every whale—namely, that it is a mammal—but it does not say anything about every mammal. Therefore, in an *A* statement, the subject term is *distributed* and the predicate term is *undistributed.*

Notice that the *A* statement does say something about the *class* referred to by its predicate term. "All whales are mammals" says that the class of mammals includes the class of whales. But it is one thing to make a statement about a class, as such, and it is quite a different thing to make a statement about each and every member of that class. A class is a collection of entities. When we speak of the class, as such, we are speaking *collectively.* When we speak of the members of a collection as individuals, we are speaking *distributively.* Some things that are true of a class as a collection are not true of its members as individuals, and some things that are true of the members of a class as individuals are not true of the class as a collection. For instance, the class of mammals is numerous; that is, it has many members. It would be nonsense, however, to say that the whale Moby Dick, a member of the class of mammals, is numerous. Likewise, it would be nonsense to say that each and every member of the class of mammals is numerous.

There are two fallacies that involve the confusion of collective and distributive statements. The *fallacy of division* consists in concluding (distributively) that every member of a class has a certain property from the premise that the class (collectively) has that property. For example,

*c*]   The Congress of the United States is a distinguished organization.
   $\therefore$Every member of Congress is a distinguished person.

The converse fallacy is the *fallacy of composition*. It is the fallacy of concluding (collectively) that a class has a property because (distributively) every member of the class has that property. For example,

d]     Each person on the football team is an excellent player.
       ∴The football team is an excellent one.

If there is an absence of teamwork, the premise of *d* might well be true even when its conclusion is false.

Every categorical statement says something about each of the classes its terms refer to, but these statements are collective. Furthermore, a categorical statement may speak distributively about some, but not necessarily all, members of a class. Sometimes, but not always, a categorical statement speaks distributively about each of the members of some class; in such cases, the term referring to that class is distributed. Consider our *A* statement again. It says collectively that the class of mammals includes the class of whales and that the class of whales is included in the class of mammals. Distributively, it says that every member of the class of whales is a mammal. It makes no distributive statement about every member of the class of mammals.

The *E* statement "No spiders are insects" has both terms *distributed*. It says that every spider is a non-insect and that every insect is a non-spider. Collectively, it says that the class of spiders is entirely excluded from the class of insects.

The *I* statement "Some plants are edible" has both terms *undistributed*. It makes no statement about every plant, and it makes no statement about every edible thing. Collectively, it says that the class of plants and the class of edible things overlap each other.

The *O* statement "Some philosophers are not logicians" says nothing about every philosopher, so its subject term is *undistributed*. Surprisingly, perhaps, it does say something about every logician. To see this, consider the equivalent statement: "There is at least one philosopher who is not a logician." The statement does not tell us exactly who that philosopher is, but it does assure us that there is one, at least, so let us agree for the moment to call him or her "Phil." Phil is a philosopher who is not a logician. It is easy to see that our *O* statement says "Every logician is distinct from Phil." Another way to put the point is this: Our *O* statement says that every logician is different from those philosophers referred to in that statement. Thus, the predicate term of an *O* statement is *distributed*. Collectively, the *O* statement says that the class of philosophers is not entirely included within the class of logicians.

Actually, it is not necessary to *understand* the concept of distribution to test syllogisms for validity; it is necessary only to *remember* which terms are distributed and which are not. This information is given in the following summary:

e]    A:   *Universal Affirmative*          E:   *Universal Negative*
Subject distributed                    Subject distributed
Predicate undistributed                Predicate distributed
I:    *Particular Affirmative*          O:   *Particular Negative*
Subject undistributed                  Subject undistributed
Predicate undistributed                Predicate distributed

These results may be further abbreviated. *The subject term of a universal statement is distributed; the predicate term of a negative statement is distributed. All other terms are undistributed.* The four letters "USNP" (standing for universal-subject, negative-predicate) may be memorized as a formula to determine the distribution of terms; a mnemonic device such as "*Uncle Sam Never Panics*" may be used to fix them in mind.

The three rules for testing the validity of syllogisms can now be stated. In a *valid syllogism*

I.   The middle term must be distributed exactly once.
II.  No end term may be distributed only once.
III. The number of negative premises must equal the number of negative conclusions.

These rules should be memorized. *Any syllogism that satisfies all three rules is valid. Any syllogism that violates one or more of these rules is invalid.* Rule I states that the middle term must be distributed in one of its occurrences and that it must be undistributed in its other occurrence. A syllogism in which the middle term is distributed twice is invalid, and so is a syllogism in which the middle term is not distributed at all. According to rule II, a syllogism cannot be valid if it contains an end term that is distributed in the premises and not in the conclusion, or if it contains an end term that is distributed in the conclusion and not in the premises. For a syllogism to be valid, it cannot have an end term that is distributed in one occurrence and not in the other. Rule III covers three cases. A syllogism may have no negative premises, one negative premise, or two negative premises. In order to be valid, a syllogism that has no negative premises must not have a negative conclusion; that is, a syllogism with two affirmative premises must have an affirmative conclusion. If a syllogism has one negative premise and one affirmative premise, it cannot be valid unless the conclusion is negative. If a syllogism has two negative premises it cannot be valid, for *by definition* a syllogism has only one conclusion, so the number of negative premises cannot be equal to the number of negative conclusions.[6]

[6]These rules reflect the modern interpretation of the categorical syllogism. This interpretation is a consequence of the decision to construe *A* statements as *universal conditional statements* (section 13). The rules are easily revised to fit the traditional (Aristotelian) interpretation as follows:

   I: The middle term must be distributed at least once.

   II: If an end term is distributed in the conclusion it must be distributed in the premises.

   III: No change.

Both sets of rules are adaptations of rules given by James T. Culbertson, *Mathematics and Logic for Digital Devices* (Princeton, N.J.: D. Van Nostrand Company, 1958), p. 99.

Let us apply the three rules to argument *a*. To do so, we rewrite the form *b* as follows, using subscripts "*d*" or "*u*" to designate a distributed or undistributed term.

*f*]    $S_d \, A \, M_u$
      $M_d \, A \, P_u$
    $\therefore S_d \, A \, P_u$

Each statement is an *A* statement, so each subject term is distributed, and each predicate term is undistributed, in accordance with *e*.

Rule I: satisfied; the middle term is distributed in the second premise but not in the first.

Rule II: satisfied; the end term *S* is distributed in both of its occurrences; the end term *P* is not distributed in either of its occurrences.

Rule III: satisfied; there are no negative premises and there are no negative conclusions.

We have shown that *a* is a valid syllogism. Here are some further syllogisms with their forms.

*g*]    All logicians are mathematicians.                  $P_d \, A \, M_u$
      Some philosophers are not mathematicians.        $S_u \, O \, M_d$
    $\therefore$Some philosophers are not logicians.          $\therefore S_u \, O \, P_d$

Since the *A* statement is universal, its subject is distributed; since it is affirmative, its predicate is undistributed. Since the *O* statement is particular, its subject is undistributed; since it is negative, its predicate is distributed.

Rule I: satisfied; the middle term is distributed in the second premise but not in the first.

Rule II: satisfied; *P* is distributed in both of its occurrences, and *S* is undistributed in both of its occurrences.

Rule III: satisfied; *g* has one negative premise and one negative conclusion.

Since *g* satisfies all three rules, it is valid.

*h*]    All Quakers are pacifists.         $M_d \, A \, P_u$
      No generals are Quakers.          $S_d \, E \, M_d$
    $\therefore$No generals are pacifists.        $\therefore S_d \, E \, P_d$

First, you should check to see that the distribution of terms has been specified correctly. Then the rules may be applied.

Rule I: violated; the middle term is distributed twice.

This proves that *h* is invalid. It is not necessary to go on to apply the other rules. To illustrate further, however, we shall apply the rules anyway.

Rule II: violated; $P$ is distributed in the conclusion but not in the premises.
Rule III: satisfied; there is one negative premise and one negative conclusion.

$i$]    All green plants (are things that) contain chlorophyll.     $S_d\ A\ M_u$
        Some things that contain chlorophyll are edible.           $M_u\ I\ P_u$
        ∴Some green plants are edible.                             $∴S_u\ I\ P_u$

Rule I: violated; the middle term is not distributed in either occurrence.

This proves that $i$ is invalid. Again, however, we apply the other rules:

Rule II: violated; $S$ is distributed in the premises but not in the conclusion.
Rule III: satisfied; there are no negative premises and no negative conclusions.

$j$]    Some neurotics are not well adjusted.              $S_u\ O\ M_d$
        Some well-adjusted people are not ambitious.       $M_u\ O\ P_d$
        ∴Some neurotics are not ambitious.                 $∴S_u\ O\ P_d$

Rule I: satisfied; the middle term is distributed in the first premise but not in the
   second premise.
Rule II: satisfied; $S$ is undistributed in both occurrences and $P$ is distributed in both
   occurrences.
Rule III: violated; there are two negative premises but only one negative
   conclusion.

Hence, $j$ is invalid. With practice, you will see at a glance when rule III is violated; in such cases you do not have to consider the other two rules. In fact, it is a good strategy to check first for a violation of rule III. If such a violation occurs you do not have to bother with distribution at all.

The examples we have used so far to illustrate the application of our rules have been given in standard logical form. Needless to say, arguments found in ordinary contexts seldom have such form. Premises may be missing, and the order of the statements may be scrambled, as we have seen in dealing with other kinds of arguments. In addition, as we would expect, variations of the categorical statements, such as we discussed in the previous section, will be encountered. Usually, then, the first step in dealing with syllogistic arguments is to translate them into complete syllogisms of standard form. This transformation involves three steps.

1.   Identify the premises and the conclusion.
2.   Translate the premises and the conclusion into categorical statements.
3.   Supply missing premises (if any are needed).

After these steps have been completed, the rules may be applied to test the syllogism for validity.

Here is the sort of thing we might find:

$k$]    Not all diamonds are gems—industrial diamonds are unsuitable for ornamental purposes.

The context or tone of voice would make it clear that the first statement is the conclusion; what comes after the dash is offered to support it. The conclusion can be translated into the $O$ statement "Some diamonds are not gems." The premise can also be rendered as an $O$ statement: "Some diamonds (namely, industrial diamonds) are not suitable for ornamental purposes." To complete the syllogism we need the premise, "All gems are suitable for ornamental purposes."

$l$]    All gems are suitable for ornamental purposes.    $P_d \, A \, M_u$
       Some diamonds are not suitable for ornamental purposes.  $S_u \, O \, M_d$
       ∴Some diamonds are not gems.    $∴S_u \, O \, P_d$

Example $l$ has the same form as $g$, which we have already found to be valid.

$m$]    Spiders can't be insects, because they are eight-legged.

The conclusion is the $E$ statement "No spiders are insects." The given premise is the $A$ statement "All spiders are eight-legged." When we supply the missing premise we have

$n$]    All spiders are eight-legged.    $S_d \, A \, M_u$
       No insects are eight-legged.    $P_d \, E \, M_d$
       ∴No spiders are insects.    $∴S_d \, E \, P_d$

Rule I: satisfied; the middle term is distributed in the second premise but not in the first.
Rule II: satisfied; both $S$ and $P$ are distributed in each of their occurrences.
Rule III: satisfied; there is one negative premise and one negative conclusion.

Hence, $n$ is valid.

$o$]    Many people think abstract painting is worthless because it does not present a likeness of any familiar object. They believe that aesthetic merit is proportional to degree of realism. This principle is completely false. We must realize that artistic merit does not depend upon realistic representation. Rather, it is a matter of structures and forms. Only pure studies in form have true artistic worth—this is the fundamental principle. It follows that a painting does not have true artistic worth *unless* it is abstract, for nothing that is not a pure study in form is abstract.

From this passage we glean the following argument:

$p$]    Only pure studies in form have true artistic worth.
       Nothing that is not a pure study in form is abstract.
       ∴A painting does not have true artistic worth unless it is abstract.

Translating into categorical statements, we get the following syllogism:

q]   All paintings that have true artistic worth are pure studies in    $S_d \, A \, M_u$
form.
All abstract paintings are pure studies in form.            $P_d \, A \, M_u$
∴All paintings that have true artistic worth are abstract.     $\therefore S_d \, A \, P_u$

We see at a glance that this syllogism is invalid because it violates rules *I* and *II*.

r]   In his famous essay "On Liberty," John Stuart Mill (1806–1873) deals with "the nature and limits of the power which can legitimately be exercised by society over the individual." He tries to establish the general principle ". . . that the sole end for which mankind are warranted, individually or collectively, in interfering with the liberty of action of any of their number, is self-protection. . . . The only part of the conduct of anyone, for which he is amenable to society, is that which concerns others. In the part which merely concerns himself, his independence is, of right, absolute." Mill then explains the method by which he intends to establish this principle. "It is proper to state that I forego any advantage which could be derived to my argument from the idea of abstract right, as a thing independent of utility. I regard utility as the ultimate appeal on all ethical questions; but it must be utility in the largest sense, grounded on the permanent interests of man as a progressive being. Those interests, I contend, authorize the subjection of individual spontaneity to external control, only in respect to those actions of each which concern the interest of other people." The principle of utility is explained and defended in another essay, "Utilitarianism." According to the principle of utility, acts are right insofar as they contribute to the general interest; that is, all and only those acts that promote the general interest are right.

If we understand self-regarding conduct to be conduct that does not affect the interests of anyone other than the agent, the following syllogism emerges:

s]   All right acts are acts that promote the general interest.        $P_d \, A \, M_u$
No act of interfering with self-regarding conduct is an act that   $S_d \, E \, M_d$
promotes the general interest.
∴No act of interfering with self-regarding conduct is right.     $\therefore S_d \, E \, P_d$

You should verify that this syllogism satisfies the three rules and is, therefore, valid. Notice that an invalid syllogism would have resulted from taking "All acts that promote the general interest are right" as the first premise. The remainder of Mill's essay "On Liberty" is devoted to proving the truth of the second premise.

Before concluding this section on syllogisms, there is one additional type of argument to be considered. We shall call it the *quasi-syllogism*. Although the quasi-syllogism is not, strictly speaking, a syllogism, it is very similar to the syllogism and is often treated as such. We shall adopt a different approach that seems more straightforward. Consider the classic example

> t]    All men are mortal.
>       Socrates is a man.
>       ∴Socrates is mortal.

This argument is certainly valid, but as it stands it is not a syllogism because neither the second premise nor the conclusion is a categorical statement. The term "Socrates" is not a class term; it is the name of a man, not the name of any class of entities. It would not make any sense to say "All Socrates are mortal" or "Some Socrates are mortal." The second premise and the conclusion can be translated into categorical statements by barbaric circumlocution, but we shall not do so. Instead, we note that the first premise is an *A* statement, and as such it is equivalent to the universal conditional "If anything is a man, then it is mortal." Whatever is true of all things is true of Socrates. We conclude from the first premise "If Socrates is a man, then Socrates is mortal." This statement, along with the second premise of *t*, gives us the following argument:

> u]    If Socrates is a man, then Socrates is mortal.
>       Socrates is a man.
>       ∴Socrates is mortal.

This argument is an instance of affirming the antecedent (section 7). Consider another example:

> v]    John Doe must be homosexual, because he favors laws that prohibit discrimi-
>       nation in employment on the basis of sexual preferences.

This argument has a missing premise. It might be made into a quasi-syllogism as follows:

> w]    All who favor laws that prohibit discrimination in employment on the basis of
>       sexual preferences are homosexual.
>       John Doe favors laws that prohibit discrimination in employment on the basis
>       of sexual preferences.
>       ∴John Doe is homosexual.

This argument can be shown to be valid by the method we used for *t*. The trouble is, the premise we supplied is surely false. However, if we supplied a somewhat more plausible premise, the argument would be made invalid.

> x]    All homosexuals favor laws that prohibit discrimination in employment on
>       the basis of sexual preferences.
>       John Doe favors laws that prohibit discrimination in employment on the basis
>       of sexual preferences.
>       ∴John Doe is homosexual.

Treating this in the manner we have adopted, we get an instance of the fallacy of affirming the consequent (section 7).

*y*]    If John Doe is homosexual, then John Doe favors laws that prohibit discrimination in employment on the basis of sexual preferences.
John Doe favors laws that prohibit discrimination in employment on the basis of sexual preferences.
∴John Doe is homosexual.

Example *v* is exactly like example *z* of section 7, and we could have treated it in the same manner by supplying a conditional premise directly instead of first introducing a categorical premise. There is, however, some merit in treating arguments of this sort as quasi-syllogisms. Generally speaking, the only grounds we would have for asserting a conditional statement like "If John Doe favors laws that prohibit discrimination in employment on the basis of sexual preferences, then John Doe is homosexual" is to derive it from the corresponding universal conditional. For this reason, it is realistic to translate *v* into a quasi-syllogism.

## 15. VENN DIAGRAMS AND CLASS LOGIC

Although the rules given in the last section for testing the validity of syllogisms are quite easy to remember and apply, they may have had an air of hocus-pocus about them. They work, but it is hard to see why. In this section we shall present the Venn diagram technique.[7] It has great intuitive clarity (for which reason you may prefer it to the rules for checking the validity of syllogisms), and it can be applied to other types of arguments as well as categorical syllogisms.

As noted in the last section, the subject and predicate terms of categorical statements may be taken to refer to classes. The categorical statement itself can then be construed as a statement about the relationship between the two classes. Thus, the *A* statement "All whales are mammals" says that the class of whales is contained within the class of mammals. Similarly, the *E* statement "No spiders are insects" says that the class of spiders is entirely excluded from the class of insects. The *I* statement "Some diamonds are expensive" asserts that the class of diamonds overlaps the class of expensive things—that is, that the two classes have at least one member in common. Finally, the *O* statement "Some animals are not carnivorous" states that the class of animals is not entirely included within the class of carnivores—that is, that there is at least one animal that lies outside of the latter class.

These relations can all be shown diagrammatically, starting with a basic standard diagram of two overlapping circles—one for each class—enclosed in a box (Fig. 1). The numerals have been added temporarily, to provide easy reference to the four distinct regions, but they are not part of the standard diagram. Let the interior of the left-hand circle stand for the class *F*, and let the interior of the right-hand circle stand for the class *G*. The

---

[7]Named for the nineteenth-century English logician John Venn.

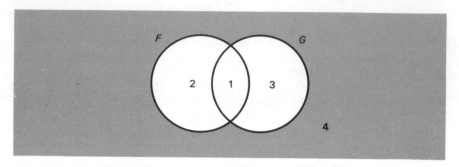

Figure 1

area of overlap of the two circles (region 1) stands for those things that belong to both classes, the portion of the left-hand circle that falls outside the right-hand circle (region 2) stands for the things that belong to class $F$ but not to class $G$, and the part of the right-hand circle that falls outside the left-hand circle (region 3) stands for those things that belong to the class $G$ but not to $F$. If $F$ is the class of students and $G$ the class of females, then region 1 represents female students, region 2 represents non-female students, and region 3 represents female non-students. The remainder of the area of the box—that part that falls outside both circles (region 4)—represents those things that are neither students nor females. The entire box represents what is known as the *universe of discourse*—the realm of entities we are talking about—in this case, people.

The diagram in Fig. 1 does not make any assertion at all about the existence or nonexistence of members of the classes for which the circles stand—it makes no commitment whatever about the existence of females, students, female students, female non-students, non-female students, or non-female non-students. The basic diagram is simply a standard starting point to which we can add information about the inclusion, exclusion, or overlap of classes. If we want to assert that a class has no members, we may do so by crossing out the region in the diagram that represents that class. Hence, if we wish to diagram the statement "All whales are mammals," we

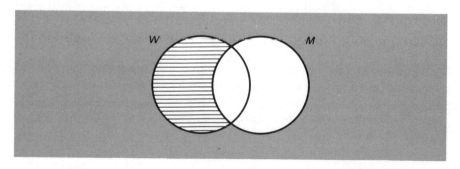

Figure 2

may cross out the area that stands for things that are whales but not mammals (Fig. 2): This is the standard diagram of an *A* statement.

To represent the assertion "No spiders are insects," we simply cross out the region that stands for things that are both spiders and insects:

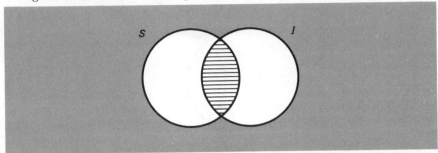

**Figure 3**

This is the standard diagram of an *E* statement. Notice that each diagram starts from the same basic diagram and then proceeds to assert that some area or other stands for a class that is empty.[8] This does not imply that the regions not crossed out do have members; the diagram makes no commitment one way or the other. Consequently, this way of diagramming corresponds to our interpretation of the *A* statement as a universal (material) conditional. There is nothing in the diagram that makes an assertion that the subject class has members; the diagram leaves that matter completely open.

To assert that a region represents a class that does have members, we place an "x" within it. Thus, to diagram the statement "Some diamonds are expensive," we place an "x" in the area standing for things that are both diamonds and expensive (Fig. 4), thereby asserting that there is at least one such thing:

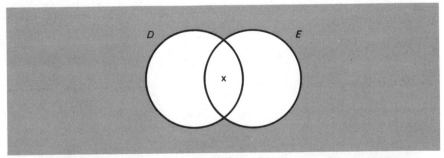

**Figure 4**

[8]In constructing the diagram for the *A* statement we do *not* begin by drawing the circle for the subject term inside the circle for the predicate term. Likewise, in constructing the diagram for the *E* statement, we do *not* begin by drawing the two circles completely separated from one another with no area of overlap. We always begin with the same basic diagram, indicating inclusion and exclusion by appropriate crossings-out. The reason for insisting upon the standard basic diagram is that it makes the checking of syllogisms easier and more accurate.

This is the standard diagram of an *I* statement.

To diagram the statement "Some animals are not carnivorous," we put our "x" within the circle that stands for animals but in the portion of it that lies outside the circle standing for carnivores:

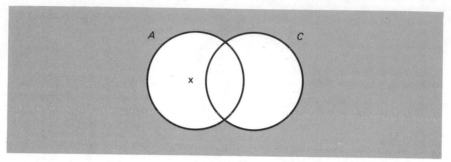

Figure 5

This is the standard diagram of an *O* statement. We now have standard diagrams for each type of categorical statement.

The categorical syllogism is an argument that involves three categorical statements and three distinct terms—the middle term "*M*" and two end terms "*S*" and "*P*." In order to deal with the syllogism, we construct a basic diagram that contains three overlapping circles (Fig. 6). The way they are drawn enables us to represent every possible relation of inclusion, exclusion, or overlap among the three classes for which they stand. The basic diagram looks like this (again, with numerals temporarily added to refer to the separate regions):

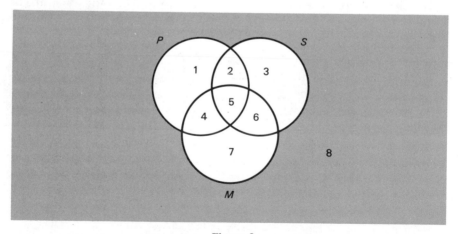

Figure 6

The three circles have been drawn to create eight distinct regions; it is essential that they always be drawn in that way. It is an easy and disastrous error to draw the circles so that region 5 is missing.

The basic three-circle diagram (Fig. 6), like its two-circle counterpart (Fig. 1), is completely noncommittal concerning the emptiness or non-emptiness of any of the classes represented therein. It is the basic framework into which we can put assertions about the relationships among the three classes mentioned in the syllogism. And this is precisely what we do to test the validity of a syllogism. The syllogism is an argument containing two premises. We begin by diagramming the statements made by these premises. Then we look to see whether the content of the conclusion has been placed in the diagram in the process. The rationale for this general procedure is the second fundamental characteristic of valid deduction (section 4):

*All of the information or factual content in the conclusion was already contained, at least implicitly, in the premises.*

To see how that works, let us reconsider example *n* of section 14:

a]   All spiders are eight-legged.        *S A M*
     No insects are eight-legged.         *P E M*
     ∴No spiders are insects.             ∴*S E P*

In the Venn diagram technique we can forget about the distribution of terms, for the diagram takes care of that matter automatically. We may begin by diagramming the first premise (Fig. 7). Because that premise asserts a relationship between the classes *S* and *M*, we may pay attention only to the two circles representing those classes, and we may ignore the circle representing *P*. Since that premise states that all *S* are *M*, we cross out that portion of the *S*-circle that lies outside the *M*-circle (regions 2 and 3 in the basic diagram [Fig. 6]).

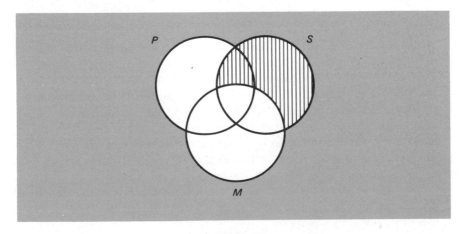

Figure 7

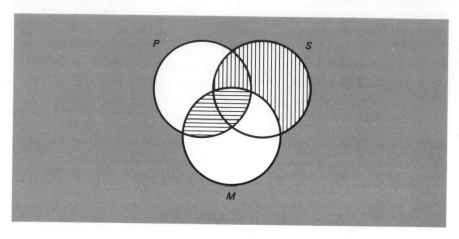

**Figure 8**

Next, we diagram the content of the second premise (Fig. 8). Since that premise says that no $P$ is $M$, we cross out that portion of the $P$-circle and the $M$-circle that overlap one another (regions 4 and 5 in the basic diagram [Fig. 6]). In this step we are focusing on the $P$-circle and the $M$-circle, ignoring the $S$-circle for the moment because the class $S$ is not mentioned in the second premise.

We have now inserted into the diagram all of the information supplied by the two premises of the argument, and we can simply inspect the result to see whether the conclusion has been diagrammed in the process. The conclusion says that no $S$ is $P$—that is, it says that the area of overlap between the $S$-circle and the $P$-circle (regions 2 and 5 of the basic diagram) is empty. We see that this area is, indeed, crossed out in Fig. 8. In diagramming the two premises we have diagrammed the conclusion; consequently, the syllogism is valid.

Do not be confused by the fact that some other regions besides areas 2 and 5 are crossed out. The conclusion "No $S$ is $P$" asserts that the area of overlap between the two classes $S$ and $P$ is empty, and this is shown by the fact that regions 2 and 5 are crossed out. The conclusion says absolutely nothing about the emptiness or nonemptiness of the other regions, in particular regions 3 and 4, which were crossed out in the course of diagramming the premises. It does not matter what happens to them. Look back at the standard two-circle diagram of the $E$ statement (Fig. 3); the area of overlap is crossed out, but the remaining areas are unmarked. Because the $E$ statement says nothing about them, the fact that they are partly crossed out in our three-circle diagram has no bearing on the validity of the argument.

The foregoing example had two universal premises; let us now try an example with a particular premise (example *g* of section 14):

*b*]     All logicians are mathematicians.                         *P A M*
         Some philosophers are not mathematicians.        *S O M*
         ∴Some philosophers are not logicians.              ∴*S O P*

As always, we begin with the basic diagram (Fig. 6) and proceed by diagramming the premises. Since the first premise says that all *P* are *M*, we cross out all of the *P*-circle that falls outside the *M*-circle, ignoring the *S*-circle while doing so. Next, we diagram the second premise, which says that some *S* is not *M*. This requires us to place an "x" inside the *S*-circle but outside the *M*-circle. This "x" must go in region 3 of the basic diagram. Obviously, we cannot put an "x" in a crossed-out region; crossing out signifies an empty region, whereas putting an "x" into a region asserts that it is not empty. To assert that the same region is both empty and not empty is a flat contradiction. Hence, the "x" cannot be placed in region 2. Moreover, the "x" should not be placed in regions 5 or 6, for we want to say that some *S* is not *M*, and those two regions are within the *M*-circle.

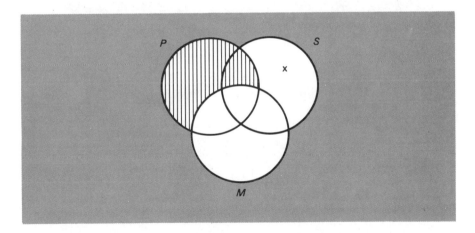

**Figure 9**

Having completed the crossing-out for the first premise, and having placed the "x" for the second premise, we now inspect the diagram to see whether it yields the desired conclusion. Focusing attention on the *S*- and *P*-circles, we see that there is an "x" in a portion of the *S*-circle that lies outside the *P*-circle. The diagram does assert that some *S* is not *P*, thereby showing that the conclusion follows logically from the premises.

In writing down a syllogism, it is obviously irrelevant, from the stand-point of validity, which premise is stated first. It *does* sometimes matter, from the standpoint of convenience, which premise is diagrammed first. If a syllogism has one particular premise and one universal premise, it is always advisable to diagram the universal premise first. Go back to example *b* and see what would have happened had we tried to diagram the particu-lar premise first. Since none of the regions would have been crossed out, we would not have known whether to put the "x" in region 2 or region 3.

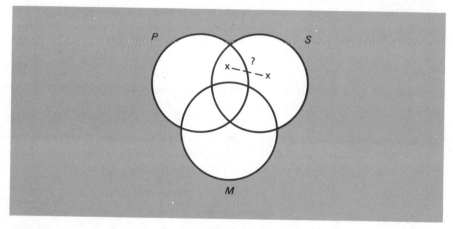

**Figure 10**

We could have handled that problem by using a "floating x"—by placing an "x" in each region and connecting the two with a dotted line to which a question mark is attached. In diagramming the universal premise, we would then have seen that the "x" must go into region 3, because region 2 must be crossed out. But it is much easier, and less apt to lead to confusion, to diagram the universal premise first.

You might wonder what to do if both premises are particular. You *can* diagram both premises by using the "floating x" device, but you will always find that the syllogism is invalid. Without a universal premise to cross out some regions and thereby force the "x" into a definite compartment, there can be no valid conclusion. As a matter of fact, *no syllogism with two particular premises can be valid.*[9] The easiest way to deal with such syllogisms is just to remember that fact, but if you do go ahead and diagram them you will get the right answer.

Both of the preceding examples have been valid syllogisms; let us now look at some invalid ones.

[9]This rule can be derived from rules I through III of section 14.

*c]*     All professional rock musicians (are persons who) have green hair.
         No presidents of banks are professional rock musicians.
         ∴No presidents of banks have green hair.

Starting with the basic diagram, we cross out all of the *M*-circle that lies
outside the *P*-circle; this takes care of the first premise. Then, by virtue of
the second premise, we cross out all of the area common to the *S*-circle and

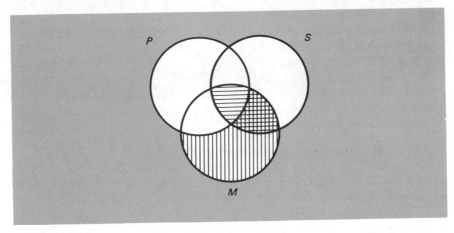

**Figure 11**

the *M*-circle. It does not matter that region 6 is crossed out twice, once by
each premise, for that is only to repeat that the area is empty. When,
however, we examine the relation between the *S*- and *P*-circles, we see that
the region they share in common is not entirely crossed out, so the conclusion "No *S* is *P*" does not follow validly.

   Here is another example:

*d]*     Some people with high earnings are smart investors.
         All professional athletes have high earnings.
         ∴Some smart investors are professional athletes.

Even though the universal premise comes second, we follow our earlier
hint and diagram it first, crossing out the part of the *P*-circle that lies
outside the *M*-circle. We then proceed to try to place an "x" in the area of
overlap between the *S*- and *M*-circles, but we find that there are two regions
in which it might be placed (regions 5 and 6 of the basic diagram). In this
case we use the "floating x" to register our doubt. When we try to read the
conclusion, we find that our "x" might be in the region that is common to

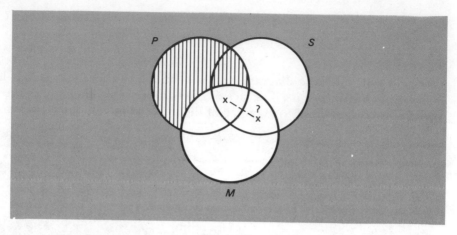

**Figure 12**

the S- and P-circles, but it might be in that part of the S-circle that lies outside the P-circle. It may be true that some S are P, but it may not; the conclusion is not necessitated by the premises, so by characteristic I of valid deductive arguments (section 4), the argument cannot be valid.

We have now provided two distinct ways of testing syllogisms for validity. Is either method more adequate? Not as a test of validity of syllogisms. The choice between them is a matter of personal preference. The Venn diagrams have a great deal of intuitive appeal, once you get the hang of them, and the rules seem arbitrary by contrast. My own preference, nevertheless, is for the rules, because it is easier to carry three simple rules in my head than it is to carry a pencil and notebook (to draw diagrams) in my pocket.

Before abandoning the diagrams, however, we should take account of the fact, noted at the beginning of this section, that Venn diagrams can be used to handle nonsyllogistic arguments. Consider the following example:

e]    Everyone convicted of conspiracy will be imprisoned or fined.
      Some who are convicted will be fined.
      No one will be imprisoned and fined.
      ∴Not all who are convicted of conspiracy will be imprisoned.

This argument is obviously not a categorical syllogism, for it has one premise too many, and the first premise is not a categorical statement. The Venn diagrams will, nevertheless, provide an easy check on its validity. Three classes are involved—those convicted of conspiracy, those who are imprisoned, and those who are fined—so we begin with the standard three-circle diagram. To diagram the first premise, we cross out that portion of the C-circle that falls outside both the I- and F-circles. All three circles are involved, for the first premise mentions all three classes. Recalling an earlier hint, we skip the second premise (which is particular) and go on to the

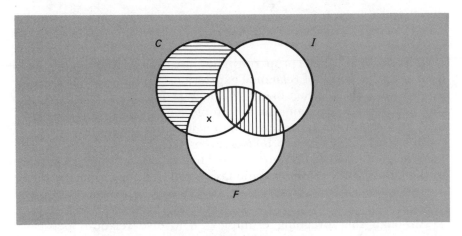

**Figure 13**

third premise (which is universal). In accordance with the third premise, we cross out the region in which the *I*-circle and the *F*-circle overlap. Then, by virtue of the second premise, we place an "x" in the only available area shared by the *F*- and *C*-circles. Finally, inspecting the diagram, we see that it does sustain the conclusion that some who are convicted of conspiracy will not be imprisoned, which is equivalent to the statement offered as the conclusion of *e*.

This example hints at the powers and limitations of the Venn diagram technique. The Venn diagrams are far more versatile than the syllogistic rules. They can be used throughout the logic of classes, a logic that is far more general and important than the logic of categorical syllogisms. The chief limitation on the Venn diagrams concerns the number of basic classes involved. As we have seen, they work admirably for arguments involving only two or three classes. They are much trickier for four classes (circles have to be replaced by ellipses), and for five or more they are positively unwieldy. That does not deprive them of their status as an outstandingly useful item in the logician's tool kit.

## 16. THE LOGIC OF RELATIONS

In dealing with the categorical syllogism and the simple logic of classes, we were treating statements about things and their properties—for example, "Anything that has the property *F* also has property *G*" or "At least one thing has both of the properties *F* and *G*." The fact that we often talked about classes *F* and *G* instead of properties *F* and *G* is inconsequential, for each such property determines a class, namely, the class of things having that property—for example, the property *intelligent* delineates the class of intelligent things. It is only in much more esoteric reaches of logic that we need worry seriously about whether each property does, in fact, determine a class.

Things not only have properties; they also bear relations to one another. Our language is full of relational expressions: "John *loves* Jane," "This car is *more expensive than* that one," "World War I was *earlier than* World War II," and so forth. Relations are not simple combinations of properties. Jack may be shorter than Jim, even though neither of them is short—they might both be basketball players who top seven feet. John and Jane may each be married, but whether they are married to each other is the crucial question if they want to file a joint income tax return. Because so many important considerations involve relations, it will be advisable to look briefly at their logic.

Although the foregoing examples all involve relations between two things—so-called *binary relations*—other relations obtain among larger numbers of objects. The word "between," for example, as it occurs in "*Arizona* is between *California* and *New Mexico*," denotes a relationship among three things—a so-called *ternary relation*—as does the word "gave" in "*Bill* gave *Thelma* an *engagement ring*." The statement "*Bob* sold *his car* to *Hal* for *three hundred dollars*" involves a four-place or *quaternary relation*. In principle, it would be possible to have five-place, six-place, etc., relations. Having acknowledged the existence of these more complex relations, however, we shall now confine our attention to binary relations.

It is easy to describe some important characteristics of binary relations, but a little symbolism will be helpful. When we want to say that a relation $R$ holds between two objects $a$ and $b$, we simply write "$aRb$." If, for instance, "$a$" stands for Harry, "$b$" for Peter, and "$R$" for the relation *father of*, then "$aRb$" translates as "Harry is the father of Peter."

The *converse* of a relation $R$ is a relation $\check{R}$ that holds between the objects $b$ and $a$ (*in that order*) whenever the relation $R$ holds between $a$ and $b$ (*in that order*)—that is, "$b\check{R}a$" is true whenever "$aRb$" is true. Thus, for example, *less than* is the converse of *greater than*, *parent of* is the converse of *child of*, and *is loved by* is the converse of *loves*. However, *father of* is not the converse of *son of*; can you see why?

Some relations are *symmetrical*—that is, whenever the relation holds between two objects $a$ and $b$ it also holds between $b$ and $a$. The relation *sibling of* is symmetrical; if Bill is a sibling of Jean, then Jean must be a sibling of Bill. Other familiar examples of symmetrical relations are *at the same time* (Susan finished her exam at the same time Dick finished his), *equals* (the number of men in the logic class equals the number of women), and *married to* (John is married to Jane). A symmetrical relation is identical to its converse. The relation *father of* is *asymmetrical;* if Harry is the father of Peter, then Peter cannot be the father of Harry. The relation *brother of* has neither of these characteristics; if Scott is a brother of Kim, Kim may or may not be a brother of Scott (depending upon whether Kim is a boy or a girl). Such relations are called *nonsymmetrical. Loves,* alas, is also a nonsymmetrical relation.

Using the letters "*x*," "*y*," "*z*" as variables that can stand for any objects, and importing the truth-functional connectives from earlier sections, we can offer the following definitions:

*a*]     *R* is a *symmetrical* relation if $xRy \supset yRx$.
      *R* is an *asymmetrical* relation if $xRy \supset \sim(yRx)$.
      *R* is a *nonsymmetrical* relation if it is neither symmetrical nor asymmetrical.

A relation is said to be *reflexive* if objects always bear that relation to themselves; for example, any number is *equal to* itself, any triangle is *congruent to* itself, and one is *as intelligent as* oneself. A relation that an object never bears to itself is *irreflexive;* for example, *greater than* is an irreflexive relation because nothing can be greater than itself. Relations that are neither reflexive nor irreflexive are said to be *nonreflexive. Loves* is a nonreflexive relation, since some people love themselves and others do not. These concepts, also, can be formally defined:

*b*]     *R* is a *reflexive* relation if $xRx$.
      *R* is an *irreflexive* relation if $\sim(xRx)$.
      *R* is a *nonreflexive* relation if it is neither reflexive nor irreflexive.

It is easily shown that an asymmetrical relation cannot be reflexive, for suppose the relation *R* is asymmetrical, i.e.,

$$xRy \supset \sim(yRx).$$

Then, since the foregoing is true for any *y* (including whatever "*x*" stands for),

$$xRx \supset \sim(xRx).$$

But this is a *reductio ad absurdum* (section 8), for the assumption that *R* is reflexive leads to the conclusion that it is not.

Another important characteristic of relations is *transitivity.* Consider, for example, the relation *older than.* If Aunt Agatha is older than Aunt Matilda, and if Aunt Matilda is older than Cousin Nellie, then Aunt Agatha must be older than Cousin Nellie. A relation is transitive provided that, like the *older than* relation, whenever it holds between one thing and another and also between the other and some third thing, it always holds between the first and the third. (I have deliberately stated this definition without using the variables "*x*," "*y*," "*z*," in order to show how awkward and contrived the formulations become; from here on we will use the more perspicuous formulas containing variables and other symbols. Furthermore—a point that was not clear in the verbal formulation—the variables "$x$," "$y$," "$z$," etc., need not refer to different entities. In the next paragraph we have an example in which "$x$" and "$z$" refer to the same individual.)

The relation *mother of* is *intransitive;* if $x$ is mother of $y$ and $y$ is mother of $z$, then $x$ cannot be mother of $z$. The relation *friend of* is *nontransitive;* if $x$ is a friend of $y$ and $y$ is a friend of $z$, then $x$ may or may not be a friend of $z$. The relation *brother of* is also nontransitive; if Jack is a brother of Jim and Jim is a brother of Joe, then Jack is a brother of Joe; nevertheless, though Jack is a brother of Jim and Jim is a brother of Jack, it does not follow that Jack is a brother to himself.

We can define these concepts formally:

$c$]     $R$ is a *transitive* relation if $(xRy{\cdot}yRz) \supset xRz$.
     $R$ is an *intransitive* relation if $(xRy{\cdot}yRz) \supset {\sim}(xRz)$.
     $R$ is a *nontransitive* relation if it is neither transitive nor intransitive.

Transitivity is used to define two extremely important types of relations. Ordering relations such as *greater than, earlier than,* and *more intelligent than* are transitive and asymmetrical; as we noted above, they must also be irreflexive. If, moreover, every two distinct entities $x$ and $y$ are related $xRy$ or $yRx$, then the transitive and asymmetrical relation $R$ establishes a simple order among the entities it relates, similar to the order established among numbers by the relation *greater than.*

Relations of the second type—known as *equivalence relations*—are transitive and symmetrical (and, we must add to avoid trivial exceptions, reflexive). The relation of congruence among triangles, learned in elementary geometry, is an equivalence relation. Any triangle *abc* is congruent to itself; if triangle *abc* is congruent to triangle *def,* then *def* is congruent to *abc;* and, if triangle *abc* is congruent to triangle *def* and triangle *def* is congruent to triangle *ghi,* then *abc* is congruent to *ghi.* An equivalence relation breaks up a domain into a set of nonoverlapping equivalence classes. All triangles congruent to one another belong to one equivalence class and are equivalent to one another with respect to the relation of congruence, but triangles that are not congruent to one another belong to different equivalence classes. All the triangles that belong to one of these equivalence classes, defined by the relation of congruence, are alike with respect to size and shape.

Another familiar example of an equivalence relation—this one holds among classes—is the relation *having the same number of members.* Under this relation all classes having two members are equivalent to one another—a pair of shoes, a team of horses, a married couple, a set of twins—and these are all nonequivalent to classes having three, four, etc., members. Don't be distressed by the fact that these equivalence classes are classes of classes.

Such classes are perfectly respectable, and it is sometimes very useful to talk about them.

If we perform a slight redefinition of the term "sibling" to allow one person to be a sibling of oneself, then the relation *sibling of* becomes an equivalence relation—namely, the relation of *having the same parents.* A given equivalence class, under this relation, is simply a group of children of common parents.

Ordering relations and equivalence relations can be fruitfully combined to provide a basis for quantitative measurement. To establish a method of measuring weight, for example, we might choose an equal arm balance as the basic instrument of measurement. The equivalence relation *having the same weight* then holds between objects that balance each other precisely; this relation defines equivalence classes of objects that are equal in weight. Next, we introduce an ordering relation *heavier than,* which applies to a pair of objects when one goes down and the other goes up as they are placed in the opposite pans of the balance. Although this ordering relation does not provide a complete ordering of all the objects we are dealing with—it does not order objects that are equal in weight—it does establish a simple ordering of the equivalence classes defined by the first relation. Once these two relations have been brought to bear, we need only choose some object to be the standard unit of weight, and a complete scale of numerical measurement emerges. (The definitions just given of "equal in weight" and "heavier than" are *operational definitions*—see section 32.)

The foregoing properties of relations—especially symmetry, asymmetry, and transitivity—are often employed in arguments, usually in unstated premises. Most of the time this causes no problem. For example,

*d*]    Alice Green earns more money than her husband William.
∴William Green does not earn more money than his wife Alice.

When we recognize that the relation *earns more money than* is asymmetric, we see that the argument, which can be spelled out as follows, is deductively valid.

*e*]    Alice Green earns more money than her husband William.
If *x* earns more money than *y*, then *y* does not earn more money than *x* (by definition *a*).
∴William Green does not earn more money than his wife Alice.

This argument is so obvious that it hardly needs stating. Suppose, however, that because of his lower earnings, William feels inferior to Alice. One might conclude that Alice does not feel inferior to William; indeed, one might conclude that she feels superior to her husband. Two mistakes are involved here. First, the argument

*f]*     William feels inferior to Alice.
       If *x* feels inferior to *y*, then *y* does not feel inferior to *x* (i.e., *feels inferior to* is an asymmetric relation).
       ∴Alice does not feel inferior to William.

is deductively valid, but it contains a false premise. The relation *feels inferior to* is not asymmetric. It is entirely possible—in fact, it probably happens frequently between two people—that each feels inferior to the other. But that is a matter of psychological fact, not a matter of logic.

The second mistake involves a misconception regarding the converse of a relation. It probably goes something like this:

*g]*     William feels inferior to Alice.
       The relation *superior* is the converse of *inferior*.
       ∴Alice feels superior to William.

The problem is that the first premise involves not the relation *is inferior to* but rather *feels inferior to*. The converse of *feels inferior to* is the relation *is considered superior by;* thus, the only conclusion that can be drawn from the first premise is that Alice is considered superior by William. Since *is considered superior by* is by no means the same as *feels superior to*, *g* cannot plausibly be made into a valid argument.

Let us consider another rather transparent argument.

*h]*     Arnold is stronger than Bruce.
       Bruce is stronger than Charles.
       ∴Arnold is stronger than Charles.

This time we are relying upon the fact that *stronger than* is a transitive relation. More explicitly,

*i]*     Arnold is stronger than Bruce.
       Bruce is stronger than Charles.
       If *x* is stronger than *y* and *y* is stronger than *z*, then *x* is stronger than *z* (by definition *c*).
       ∴Arnold is stronger than Charles.

It is safe to assume that *is stronger than* is a transitive relation, but there can be somewhat trickier cases. Here is one from the 1982 matches at Wimbledon:

*j]*     Billie Jean King beat Tracy Austin at tennis.
       Chris Evert Lloyd beat Billie Jean King at tennis.
       ∴When next they play tennis with one another, Chris Evert Lloyd will beat Tracy Austin.

Those who have much familiarity with individual or team sports would not be inclined to regard *j* as a strong argument, for it is fairly obvious that *wins against* is not a transitive relation. Better players sometimes lose to players who are not as good, and stronger teams sometimes lose to weaker teams. Thus,

*k*]  King beats-at-tennis Austin.
    Lloyd beats-at-tennis King.
    If *x* beats-at-tennis *y* and *y* beats-at-tennis *z*, then *x* beats-at-tennis *z*.
    ∴Lloyd beats-at-tennis Austin.

is a valid deductive argument, but its third premise is not really plausible. Whether *feels inferior to* (example *f*) is an asymmetric relation, and whether *beats-at-tennis* (example *k*) is a transitive relation, are questions of fact, not of logic. Logic does, however, have a bearing upon the foregoing sorts of arguments, for it provides precise definitions of such concepts as symmetry and transitivity, and it helps us see clearly what premises are required to make such arguments deductively valid.

Not all questions about transitivity are as simple to answer as the one about winning at sports; indeed, it is easy to make false assumptions about the transitivity of relations. Let us conclude this discussion by looking at a couple of examples that have some significant consequences.

*l*]  Suppose you have a batch of paint, and you mix another batch that is indistinguishable from it in color. Suppose further that you mix a third batch that is indistinguishable from the second in color. It might be tempting to suppose that the third batch will be indistinguishable in color from the first batch. Experience shows, unfortunately, that the relation of perceptual color matching is not a transitive relation; sample one may match sample two, and sample two may match sample three, but sample one may fail to match sample three. If you mix three batches of paint you must make sure that all three samples match one another by pairs—that is, you must not assume the transitivity of perceptual color matching—if you want to avoid noticeable color differences.

There are many such examples of perceptual indistinguishability relations that turn out to be nontransitive, and hence do not constitute genuine equivalence relations. Indeed, in our example of equality of weight, we had to assume an *ideal* balance that would discriminate perfectly between objects of unequal weight. With any *real* balance, we would face the same problem we encountered with color matching.

Another significant area in which transitivity sometimes breaks down is the realm of individual choice and preference.

*m*]  You might easily suppose that the relation of preference is a transitive ordering relation, that a person who prefers *x* to *y* and *y* to *z* will surely prefer *x* to *z*. But this supposition is not always correct. Given a choice between owning a particular book and attending an opera, John might choose to attend the opera. Given, moreover, the choice between attending an opera and having dinner in a fine restaurant, he might choose the delicious meal. The same individual might, however, when presented with a choice between possessing the book and enjoying the dinner, choose to own the book. This is not to say that it is reasonable to have preferences nontransitively ordered, but it can happen.

Notice, in fact, that John can get into trouble if he meets an unscrupulous operator who is aware of the nontransitivity of his preferences. Suppose John has a book and I have an opera pass that John would prefer to have; in fact, he is willing to give me the book plus one dollar for the pass. (If he really prefers the pass to the book, he will pay something to exchange the one for the other.) Suppose, moreover, that I have a meal ticket that will entitle the holder to an exquisite dinner, and that John would prefer the meal ticket to the opera pass. In fact, he is willing to give me the opera pass plus one dollar in exchange for the meal ticket. Now I present him with the choice between the book (which he traded to me earlier) and the meal ticket, and true to the nontransitivity of his preferences, he gives me the meal ticket plus one dollar for the book. The net result is that John has his book back, I have possession of the opera pass and meal ticket that I had in the beginning, but I am three dollars richer than before. It is not likely that anyone would allow oneself to be victimized in such a transparent way, but people do have nontransitive preference rankings, and our imaginary barter shows that there is something quite irrational about them.

## 17. QUANTIFIERS: THE FALLACY OF "EVERY" AND "ALL"

When we analyzed $A$ statements in section 13, we said that the statement "All whales are mammals" could be rendered "If anything is a whale, then it is a mammal." Had we felt inclined, we could have gone on to analyze the latter statement, "For any object $x$, if $x$ is a whale, then $x$ is a mammal," using the letter "$x$" as a variable in expressing our universal material conditional statement. Using standard logical notation, we could then have abbreviated the phrase "for any object $x$" as "$(x)$," calling it a *universal quantifier*. Abbreviating "$x$ is a whale" as "$Wx$" and "$x$ is a mammal" as "$Mx$," and using the horseshoe symbol as the sign of material implication, we could have symbolized the $A$ statement

a]      $(x)[Wx \supset Mx]$

The $E$ statement "No spiders are insects" could then have been symbolized

b]      $(x)[Sx \supset {\sim}Ix]$

We did not introduce all of this notation in treating the categorical syllogism, for nothing much would have been gained at that point. Ordinary English, with a few abbreviations, worked quite well.

In the last section, we found that the introduction of variables "$x$," "$y$," "$z$" was virtually indispensable, especially for the purpose of keeping track of several different entities that bear relations to one another. Thus, we used our truth-functional connectives and some variables to define such concepts as reflexivity, symmetry, and transitivity. Had we added universal quantifiers, we could have defined transitivity as follows:

$c]$      Relation $R$ is transitive $=_{df} (x)(y)(z)[(xRy \cdot yRz) \supset xRz]$

It is useful to introduce another quantifier, the *existential quantifier*, which can be used immediately to symbolize $I$ statements. Using obvious abbreviations, the statement "Some diamonds are expensive" can be written

$d]$      $(\exists x)[Dx \cdot Ex]$

where the existential quantifier "$(\exists x)$" may be read "There exists at least one object $x$ such that" or "For some object $x$." The $O$ statement "Some animals are not carnivorous" can likewise be symbolized

$e]$      $(\exists x)[Ax \cdot {\sim} Cx]$

We now have simple symbolic renditions of each type of categorical statement.

We noted in section 13 that $A$ and $O$ statements are contradictories of one another. Consequently, the $O$ statement is equivalent to the negation of the corresponding $A$ statement; i.e., "Some animals are not carnivorous" is equivalent to "Not all animals are carnivorous." Hence,

$f]$      ${\sim}(x)[Ax \supset Cx]$

must be equivalent to $e$. You can make a truth table to establish the equivalence of "$Ax \cdot {\sim} Cx$" to "${\sim}(Ax \supset Cx)$," thereby showing that $e$ and $f$ are both equivalent to

$g]$      $(\exists x) \sim [Ax \supset Cx]$

The symbol "$\sim (x)$" is thus seen to have the same import as "$(\exists x){\sim}$"; a similar argument, starting from the equivalence of an $A$ statement to the negation of the corresponding $O$ statement, shows that "${\sim}(\exists x)$" is tantamount to "$(x){\sim}$."

The formalism of quantifiers is rather pointless in dealing with categorical syllogisms and the simple logic of classes, because one variable is all we need to formulate any argument. It is only when we get to the logic of relations that the quantifiers become really useful, for in this context we need to keep track of several variables. This can be illustrated by some very simple relational statements.

*h*]     $(x)(y)\ xLy$       Everybody loves everyone.

*i*]     $(\exists x)(\exists y)\ xLy$       Somebody loves someone.

These two statements are quite straightforward, but things become somewhat trickier if we have a mixture of universal and existential quantifiers in the same statement. Consider the statements

*j*]     $(\exists x)(y)\ xLy$       Someone loves everybody.

*k*]     $(y)(\exists x)\ xLy$       Everyone is loved by somebody.

These differ from one another in the order of the two quantifiers, and differ radically in meaning. According to *j*, there is some one individual who (like Albert Schweitzer perhaps) loves all human beings (including, incidentally, oneself). Statement *k*, in contrast, says that every person is loved by someone or other (one's mother perhaps), but different people may be loved by different individuals. In no way does *k* imply that any single person loves all people.

Analogous remarks apply to statements

*l*]     $(\exists y)(x)\ xLy$       Someone is loved by everybody.

*m*]     $(x)(\exists y)\ xLy$       Everyone loves somebody.

Statement *l* asserts that there is one person who is the object of love for all people, whereas *m* says merely that each person loves somebody or other, without implying that any one individual is the recipient of all that affection.

Each of the statements, *h* to *m*, differs in meaning from every other member of that group. Statements *j* to *m* illustrate a very important point: *In statements that involve a mixture of existential and universal quantifiers, the order of the quantifiers is essential to the meaning.* Failure to keep this principle in mind can lead to a rather common fallacy, which may aptly be called the *fallacy of "every" and "all."*

Statement *l* might be translated from symbols into fairly idiomatic English as "Someone is loved by *all* people," and *m* might be rendered as "*Every* person loves someone." Obviously, *l* does not follow logically from *m*, for *m* does not say that it is one and the same individual that is loved by everyone, whereas this is precisely what *l* asserts. In general, it is a fallacy to reason from "every" to "all." If we are reasoning about concrete things, this fallacy is not apt to occur. Given that every member of the country club drives a sports car, we are not inclined to conclude that all members drive the same one. Let us state the fallacious argument explicitly.

*n*]   Every member of the country club has a sports car to drive.
∴There is a sports car that all members of the country club drive.

The premise asserts that a certain relation, namely, the relation of driving, holds between members of two classes, namely, the class of people who belong to the country club and the class of sports cars. It says that every member of the former class has the relation to some member or other of the latter class. The conclusion states that the same relation holds between members of the same two classes. It says that all members of the former class have that relation to some single member of the latter class. The form of the argument may be given as follows:

*o*]   For every *F* there is some *G* to which it has the relation *R*.
∴There is some *G* to which all *F* have the relation *R*.[10]

This form is shown diagrammatically in Fig. 14.

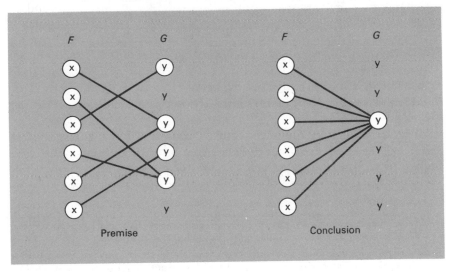

Figure 14

The *x*'s are the individual members of the class *F* and the *y*'s are the individual members of the class *G*. A line connecting an "*x*" and a "*y*" represents the relation *R* holding between that member of *F* and that member of *G*. Notice that the premise does not require that every member of *G* stand in relation to a member of *F*, nor does it exclude the possibility that a given member of *G* may stand in relation to more than one member of *F*. It is evident that form *d* is invalid; the premise diagram can hold even if the conclusion diagram does not.

[10]In the examples dealing with the love relation, both *F* and *G* would be the class of humans.

Consider the third proof for the existence of God given by St. Thomas Aquinas.

p]     The third way is taken from possibility and necessity, and runs thus. We find in nature things that are possible to be and not to be, since they are found to be generated, and to corrupt, and consequently, they are possible to be and not to be. But it is impossible for these always to exist, for *that which is possible not to be at some time is not.* Therefore, *if everything is possible not to be, then at one time there could have been nothing in existence.* Now, if this were true, even now there would be nothing in existence, because that which does not exist only begins to exist by something already existing. Therefore, if at one time nothing was in existence, it would have been impossible for anything to have begun to exist; and thus even now nothing would be in existence—which is absurd. Therefore, not all beings are merely possible, but there must exist something the existence of which is necessary.[11]

This is an excellent example of *reductio ad absurdum,* but we are not particularly concerned with the whole argument. We are interested in the italicized part of the sub-deduction. It may be written

q]     For every thing, there is a time at which it does not exist.
       ∴There is a time at which all things do not exist.

Clearly, q has the form o. The two classes involved are the class of things and the class of times. The relation is the relation of a thing *not existing at* a time.

The same fallacy sometimes occurs in philosophical arguments designed to prove the existence of an underlying substance. Substance is sometimes taken to be something that remains identical throughout change. The argument for the existence of substance, thus conceived, follows this line.

r]     Change is a relative notion. It requires that, throughout each change, there must be something that remains constant; otherwise we would not be justified in speaking of one thing changing, for there would simply be two completely distinct things. For example, one changes in many ways as one grows from infancy to maturity, but there must be something that is constant and unchanging, for otherwise there would be no ground for regarding the infant and the mature person as the *same* individual. The world is full of change at all times. *Since each change requires something constant and unchanging, there must be something that is constant throughout all change.* This thing is substance.

The beginning of this passage is the justification for the premise of the italicized argument. This argument may be rendered:

s]     For every change there is something remaining constant through that change.

[11]*The "Summa Theologica" of St. Thomas Aquinas,* Part I, trans. Fathers of the English Dominican Province, 2nd and rev. ed. (London: Burns Oates & Washbourne Ltd.; New York: Benziger Brothers, 1920), pp. 25f. Reprinted by permission. Italics added.

∴There is something (substance) which remains constant through all changes.

Again the argument has form *o*. In this case the two classes are changes and things; the relation is *remaining constant during*.

## 18. DEDUCTIVE LOGIC

Modern deductive logic is often called *symbolic logic* or *mathematical logic* because it employs a symbolic apparatus much like that found in mathematics. In our treatment of basic argument types, we have found it helpful to introduce some special symbols. The notation we have used is quite standard, although there is some variation in usage. Some authors use an ampersand (&) instead of a dot as the symbol of conjunction; sometimes an arrow is used instead of a horseshoe as the sign of material implication, and a double arrow (↔) instead of a triple bar for material equivalence. Such variation is trivial and easily accommodated.[12]

Anyone who has taken even elementary algebra in high school can appreciate the value of the special symbolic apparatus. Given the use of letters as variables and a few operation symbols, relatively intractable "story problems" can be translated into easily manageable equations that can be solved by applying certain clearly specified rules of operation. Problems in deductive logic can be handled analogously—and just as in elementary algebra, we often find that the hardest part is the translation of the problem from everyday English into the language of symbolic logic. For this reason we have taken considerable trouble to discuss different ways of formulating a particular kind of statement (e.g., the conditional statement) in ordinary language.

One advantage of special symbols is brevity; "$(\exists x)$" is much briefer than "There exists at least one object $x$ such that. . . ." A further advantage is

---

[12]A much more radical departure is found in the so-called Polish notation. In this system, "$\sim p$" is written "$Np$," "$p \cdot q$" is written "$Kpq$," "$p \lor q$" is written "$Apq$," "$p \supset q$" is written "$Cpq$," and "$p \equiv q$" is written "$Epq$." For example, the formula "$[(p \cdot (p \supset q)] \supset q$" would be written "$CKpCpqq$"; beginning with the innermost implication we write "$Cpq$," then we conjoin this to "$p$," writing "$KpCpq$," and finally we make this the antecedent of the main implication by writing the final formula "$CKpCpqq$." This notation has the advantage that it can be typed on any standard typewriter, without the need for special keys, and it dispenses entirely with parentheses and brackets for the purpose of grouping parts of formulas. The notation we have adopted is, however, the most widely used, and (to me) it exhibits the logical structure of formulas more clearly (though this may be no more than a result of my early training with the non-Polish notation).

Some electronic calculators use a similar idea to simplify the execution of a series of operations. It is called "RPN" for "reverse Polish notation." Suppose you want to add or multiply two numbers. Instead of entering one number, then the operation, and then the other number, you enter the two numbers first and then specify the operation. This is just the reverse of the Polish logical notation explained in the preceding paragraph; there we entered the operation first and followed it with the statements to which it is applied. Let us use "A" for "add" and "M" for "multiply." Suppose we want to add $x$ to $y$ and multiply the result by $z$. We would enter "$xyAzM$." The calculator would give us $(x + y) \times z$.

precision. It is of crucial importance to distinguish, for example, between the inclusive and exclusive senses of the word "or." It is essential to understand the logical affinity of "and" and "but" as well as their psychological difference. Likewise, we must distinguish the truth-functional meaning of "and" from its temporal "and then" sense. The words of English are ambiguous and equivocal; for logical purposes we need a precise language. A still more significant advantage of the symbolic language is its perspicuity. We are not merely developing a shorthand notation, nor are we merely trying to make ordinary language more precise. We are trying to display clearly the logical structure of statements and arguments. It is important, for instance, to see that the *A* statement can be construed as a universal material conditional, even if such a construction is neither briefer nor more precise than alternative formulations. When we defined the truth-functional material implication, we deliberately departed from the everyday "if . . . then . . ." in order to have an operation that embodies the logical core of conditional statements.

By far the greatest advantage of the symbolic system lies in the fact that it employs a relatively small number of exactly defined symbols that can be manipulated according to a few simple and precisely formulated rules. Affirming the antecedent is an excellent example; it says that you may assert a statement of a given form (namely, the consequent of a conditional) if you already have available as premises statements of other forms (namely, the conditional itself as well as its antecedent). There are other rules such as substitution and generalization, but we shall not discuss them in detail. If you are interested in seeing the development and elaboration of a full-blown logical system, you would do well to consult the references at the end of the book.

The symbolic apparatus we have introduced comes surprisingly close to being adequate for a complete basic logical system. We might want to have proper names as well as variables for individual objects. We probably would want to have the logical identity in order to assert, by denying their identity, that two individuals are distinct. And we would certainly need relation symbols for ternary, quaternary, etc. relations. But such supplementation is modest in comparison with what we already have available. With logical systems of this basic kind—so-called *first-order logic*[13]—it is possible to analyze and evaluate arguments of amazing complexity and subtlety, far beyond any of the examples we have dealt with in the preceding sections.

---

[13]Logical systems of this kind are considered *first-order* because they contain symbols that refer to individual objects and their properties, and quantifiers that apply to individual objects. They contain neither symbols that refer to properties of properties of individuals nor quantifiers that apply to properties of individuals. In first-order logic we can readily handle such statements as "All Boy Scouts are trustworthy," "All Boy Scouts are loyal," "All Boy Scouts are helpful," etc., but we cannot symbolize "No Boy Scouts have any faults" because this statement refers to *all properties* of Boy Scouts. It states that no property of any Boy Scout is a fault (a bad property).

# CHAPTER THREE

# Induction

Inductive arguments, unlike deductive arguments, provide conclusions whose content exceeds that of their premises. It is precisely this characteristic that makes inductive arguments useful; at the same time, it gives rise to extremely difficult philosophical problems in the analysis of the concept of inductive support. In spite of these difficulties we can—without becoming involved in great philosophical subtleties—set out and examine some important forms of inductive argument and some common inductive fallacies. Beginning with the simplest kind of inductive generalization, we shall consider a number of different types of inductive arguments, including analogy, causal reasoning, and the confirmation of scientific hypotheses. Arguments of these sorts underlie almost all of our knowledge, from the most basic levels of common sense to rather sophisticated realms of science.

## 19. INDUCTIVE CORRECTNESS

The fundamental purpose of arguments, inductive or deductive, is to establish true conclusions on the basis of true premises. We want our arguments to have true conclusions if they have true premises. As we have seen, valid deductive arguments necessarily have that characteristic. Inductive arguments, however, have another purpose as well. They are designed to establish conclusions whose content goes beyond the content of the premises. To do this, inductive arguments must sacrifice the necessity of deductive arguments. Unlike a valid deductive argument, a logically correct inductive argument may have true premises and a false conclusion. Nevertheless, even though we cannot guarantee that the conclusion of an inductive argument is true if the premises are true, still, the premises of a correct inductive argument do support or lend weight to the conclusion. In other words, as we said in section 4, if the premises of a valid deductive argument are true, the conclusion must be true; if the premises of a correct inductive argument are true, the best we can say is that the conclusion is probably true.

As we also pointed out in section 4, deductive arguments are either completely valid or else totally invalid; there are no degrees of partial validity. We shall reserve the term "valid" for application to deductive arguments; we shall continue to use the term "correct" to evaluate inductive arguments. There are certain errors that can render inductive arguments either absolutely or practically worthless. We shall refer to these errors as *inductive fallacies*. If an inductive argument is fallacious, its premises do not support its conclusion. On the other hand, among correct inductive arguments there are degrees of strength or support. The premises of a correct inductive argument may render the conclusion extremely probable, moderately probable, or probable to some extent. Consequently, the premises of a correct inductive argument, if true, constitute reasons, of some degree of strength, for accepting the conclusion.

There is another difference between inductive and deductive arguments that is closely related to those already mentioned. Given a valid deductive argument, we may add as many premises as we wish without destroying its validity. This fact is obvious. The original argument is such that, if its premises are true, its conclusion must be true; this characteristic remains no matter how many premises are added as long as the original premises are not taken away. By contrast, the degree of support of the conclusion by the premises of an inductive argument can be increased or decreased by additional evidence in the form of additional premises. Since the conclusion of an inductive argument may be false even though the premises are true, additional relevant evidence may enable us to determine more reliably whether the conclusion is, indeed, true or false. Thus, it is a general characteristic of inductive arguments, which is completely absent from deductive arguments, that additional evidence may be relevant to the degree to which the conclusion is supported. Where inductive arguments are concerned, additional evidence may have crucial importance.

In the succeeding sections of this chapter we shall discuss several correct types of inductive argument and several fallacies. Before beginning this discussion, it is important to mention a fundamental problem concerning inductive correctness. The philosopher David Hume (1711–1776), in *A Treatise of Human Nature* (1739–1749) and *An Enquiry Concerning Human Understanding* (1748), pointed to serious difficulties that arise in trying to prove the correctness of inductive arguments. At the present time there is still considerable controversy about this problem—usually called "the problem of the justification of induction." Experts disagree widely about the nature of inductive correctness, about whether Hume's problem is a genuine one, and about the methods of showing that a particular type of inductive argument is correct.[1] In spite of this controversy, there is a reasonable amount of agreement about which types of inductive argument are correct. We shall not enter into the problem of the justification of induction; rather, we shall attempt to characterize some of the types of inductive argument about which there is fairly general agreement.

## 20. INDUCTION BY ENUMERATION

By far the simplest type of inductive argument is *induction by enumeration*. In arguments of this type, a conclusion about *all* of the members of the class is drawn from premises that refer to *observed* members of that class.

*a*] Suppose we have a barrel of coffee beans. After mixing them up, we remove a sample of beans, taking parts of the sample from different parts of the barrel. Upon examination, the beans in the sample are all found to be grade A. We then conclude that all of the beans in the barrel are grade A.

This argument may be written as follows:

*b*]     All beans in the observed sample are grade A.
∴All beans in the barrel are grade A.

The premise states the information about the observed members of the class of beans in the barrel; the conclusion is a statement about all of the members of that class. It is a generalization based upon the observation of the sample.

It is not essential for the conclusion of an induction by enumeration to have the form "All *F* are *G*." Frequently, the conclusion will state that a certain percentage of *F* are *G*. For example,

*c*] Suppose we have another barrel of coffee beans, and we take a sample from it as in *a*. Upon examination, we find that 75 percent of the beans in the sample are grade A. We conclude that 75 percent of all of the beans in the barrel are grade A.

This argument is similar to *b*.

[1]My dialogue, "An Encounter with David Hume," in Joel Feinberg, ed., *Reason and Responsibility*, 3rd ed. (New York: Wadsworth Publishing Co., 1975) attempts to set forth in elementary terms Hume's problem of the justification of induction and place it in a modern context. See also my *Foundations of Scientific Inference* (Pittsburgh, Pa.: University of Pittsburgh Press, 1967) for an introductory treatment of this and other problems lying at the basis of inductive logic.

*d*]    75 percent of the beans in the observed sample are grade A.
∴75 percent of the beans in the barrel are grade A.

Both *b* and *d* share the same form. Since "all" means "100 percent," the form of both arguments may be given as follows:

*e*]    *Z* percent of the observed members of *F* are *G*.
∴*Z* percent of *F* are *G*.

This is the general form of induction by enumeration. If the conclusion is "100 percent of *F* are *G*" (i.e., "All *F* are *G*") or "0 percent of *F* are *G*" (i.e., "No *F* are *G*"), it is a *universal generalization*. If *Z* is some percentage other than 0 or 100, the conclusion is a *statistical generalization*.

Here are some additional examples of induction by enumeration.

*f*]    A public opinion pollster questions 5,000 people in the United States to ascertain their opinions about the desirability of a constitutional amendment prohibiting abortion. Of those questioned, 62 percent are opposed. The pollster concludes that approximately 62 percent of the people in the United States oppose adoption of such an amendment.

*g*]    In a certain factory, there is a machine that produces can openers. An inspector examines one-tenth of all the can openers produced by this machine. In this sample, the inspector finds that 2 percent of the can openers are defective. The management concludes, on the basis of this information, that 2 percent (approximately) of the can openers produced by the machine are defective.

*h*]    A great deal of everyday commonsense learning from experience consists in making inductions by enumeration. All observed fires have been hot; we conclude that all fires are hot. Every instance of drinking water when one is thirsty has resulted in the quenching of thirst; future drinking of water when thirsty will result in the quenching of thirst. Every lemon so far tasted has been sour; future lemons will taste sour.

It is evident that induction by enumeration can easily yield false conclusions from true premises. For example,

*i*]    Europeans had, for centuries before the discovery of Australia, observed countless swans, and all that they had ever seen were white. They concluded, quite reasonably, that all swans are white. This inductive generalization turned out to be false, for black swans were found in Australia.

We should not be surprised that such failures of induction by enumeration sometimes occur, for this possibility is characteristic of all types of inductive argument. All we can do is try to construct our inductive arguments in a way that will minimize the chances of false conclusions from true premises. In particular, there are two specific ways to lessen the chances of error in connection with induction by enumeration; that is, there are two inductive fallacies to be avoided. They will be taken up in the next two sections.

## 21. INSUFFICIENT STATISTICS

The *fallacy of insufficient statistics* is the fallacy of making an inductive generalization before enough data have been accumulated to warrant the generalization. It might well be called "the fallacy of jumping to a conclusion."

a] In examples *a* and *c* of the preceding section, suppose the observed samples had each consisted of only four coffee beans. These surely would not have been enough data to make a reliable generalization. On the other hand, a sample of several thousand beans would be large enough for a much more reliable generalization.

b] A public opinion pollster who interviewed only ten people could hardly be said to have enough evidence to warrant any conclusion about the general climate of opinion in the nation.

c] A person who refuses to buy an automobile of a certain make because he knows someone who owned a "lemon" is probably making a generalization, on the basis of exceedingly scanty evidence, about the frequency with which the manufacturer in question produces defective automobiles.

d] People who are prone to prejudice against racial, religious, or national minorities are often given to sweeping generalizations about all of the members of a given group on the basis of observation of two or three cases.

It is easy to see that the foregoing examples are all too typical of mistakes made every day by all kinds of people. The fallacy of insufficient statistics is a common one indeed. It is closely related to the *post hoc* fallacy (see section 29).

It would be convenient if we could set down some definite number and say that we always have enough data if the examined instances exceed this number. Unfortunately, this cannot be done. The number of instances that constitute sufficient statistics varies from case to case, from one area of investigation to another. Sometimes two or three instances may be enough; sometimes millions may be required. How many cases are sufficient can be learned only by experience in the particular area of investigation under consideration.

There is another factor that influences the problem of how many cases are needed. Any number of instances constitutes *some* evidence; the question at issue is whether we have sufficient evidence to draw a conclusion. This depends in part upon what degree of reliability we desire. If very little is at stake—if it does not matter much if we are wrong—then we may be willing to generalize on the basis of relatively few instances. If a great deal is at stake, then we require much more evidence.

## 22. BIASED STATISTICS

It is important not only to have a large enough number of instances but also to avoid selecting them in a way that will prejudice the outcome. If inductive generalizations are to be reliable, they must be based upon representative samples. Unfortunately, we can never be sure that our samples are genuinely representative, but we can do our best to avoid unrepresentative ones. The *fallacy of biased statistics* consists of basing an inductive generalization upon a sample that is known to be unrepresentative or one that there is good reason to suspect may be unrespresentative.

a]     In example *a* of section 20; it was important to mix up the beans in the barrel before selecting our sample; otherwise there would be danger of getting an unrepresentative sample. It is entirely possible that someone might have filled the barrel almost full of low-quality beans, putting a small layer of high-quality beans on top. By mixing the barrel thoroughly we overcome the danger of taking an unrepresentative sample for a reason of that kind.

b]     Many people disparage the ability of the weather forecaster to make accurate predictions. Perhaps the forecaster has a legitimate complaint when she says, "When I'm right no one remembers; when I'm wrong no one forgets."

c]     Racial, religious, or national prejudice is often bolstered by biased statistics. An undesirable characteristic is attributed to a minority group. Then all cases in which a member of the group manifests this characteristic are carefully noted and remembered, whereas those cases in which a member of the group fails to manifest the undesirable characteristic are completely ignored.

d]     Francis Bacon (1561–1626) gives a striking example of biased statistics in the following passage: "The human understanding when it has once adopted an opinion (either as being the received opinion or as being agreeable to itself) draws all things else to support and agree with it. And though there be a greater number and weight of instances to be found on the other side, yet these it either neglects and despises, or else by some distinction sets aside and rejects; in order that by this great and pernicious predetermination the authority of its former conclusions may remain inviolate. *And therefore it was a good answer that was made by one who when they showed him hanging in a temple a picture of those who had paid their vows as having escaped shipwreck, and would have him say whether he did not now acknowledge the power of the gods,—'Aye,' asked he again, 'But where are they painted that were drowned after their vows?'* And such is the way of all superstition, whether in astrology, dreams, omens, divine judgments, or the like; wherein men, having a delight in such vanities, mark the events where they are fulfilled, but where they fail, though this happen much oftener, neglect and pass then by."[2]

[2]Francis Bacon, *Novum Organum,* aphorism xlvi. Italics added.

What Bacon noticed centuries ago still happens frequently today:

e] The *Pittsburgh Post-Gazette,* on June 22, 1982, carried a front-page story about a couple who had won a large prize in the Pennsylvania lottery. "Dorothy Thomas had discovered earlier in the day that she and her husband were the winners of last week's Pennsylvania Lotto game and its $5.5 million prize, the largest sum ever won in a lottery in the United States.

"Mrs. Thomas literally consulted the stars in selecting the six winning numbers.

" 'I just picked the birth dates for our four kids, my husband and myself,' she said.

"For the record, it was a combination of two Capricorns and one each Gemini, Libra, Taurus and Virgo. . . . *So much for the disrepute of astrology and its practitioners.*" (Italics added.)

f] In 1936 the *Literary Digest* conducted a pre-election poll to predict the outcome of the Roosevelt-Landon contest. About ten million ballots were sent out and over two-and-a-quarter million were returned. The *Literary Digest* poll did not commit the fallacy of insufficient statistics, for the number of returns constitutes an extremely large sample. However, the results were disastrous. The poll predicted a victory for Landon and forecast only 80 percent of the votes Roosevelt actually received. Shortly thereafter, the magazine and its poll, which had cost about a half-million dollars, folded. There were major sources of bias. First, the names of people to be polled were taken mainly from lists of telephone subscribers and lists of automobile registrations. Other studies showed that 59 percent of telephone subscribers and 56 percent of automobile owners favored Landon, whereas only 18 percent of those on relief favored him. Second, there is a bias in the group of people who voluntarily returned questionnaires mailed out to them. This bias probably reflects the difference in economic classes which was operating in the first case. Even in those cases in which the *Literary Digest* used lists of voter registrations, the returns showed a strong bias for Landon.[3]

The most blatant form of the fallacy of biased statistics occurs when one simply closes one's eyes to certain kinds of evidence, usually evidence unfavorable to a belief one holds. Examples *b* and *c* illustrate the fallacy in this crude form. In other cases, especially *f*, subtler issues are involved. However, there is one procedure generally designed to lessen the chances of getting a sample that is not representative. The instances examined should differ as widely as possible, as long as they are relevant. If we are concerned to establish a conclusion of the form "Z percent of F are G," then our instances, to be relevant, must all be members of F. One way to attempt to avoid a biased sample is to examine as wide a variety of members of F as possible. In addition, if we can know what percentage of all the members of F are of various kinds, we can see to it that our sample reflects the makeup of the whole class. This is what many public opinion polls try to do.

[3]See Mildred Parten, *Surveys, Polls, and Samples* (New York: Harper & Row, Publishers, Inc., 1950), pp. 24f and 392f. Adapted by permission.

g] In order to predict the outcome of an election, a public opinion poll will interview a certain number of rural voters and a certain number of urban voters; a certain number of upper-class, middle-class, and lower-class voters; a certain number of voters from the different sections of the country; etc. In this way a variety of instances is accumulated, and furthermore, this variety in the sample reflects the percentages in the makeup of the whole voting population.

We have discussed the fallacies of insufficient statistics and biased statistics as errors to be avoided in connection with induction by enumeration. Essentially the same sort of fallacy can occur with any sort of inductive argument. It is always possible to accept an inductive conclusion on the basis of too little evidence, and it is always possible for inductive evidence to be biased. We must, therefore, be on the lookout for these fallacies in all kinds of inductive arguments.

## 23. STATISTICAL SYLLOGISM

If often happens that a conclusion established by one argument is used as a premise in another argument. In example *a* of section 20 we concluded, using induction by enumeration, that all the coffee beans in a certain barrel are grade A. Using that conclusion as a premise of a *quasi-syllogism* (section 14), we may conclude that the next coffee bean drawn from the barrel will be grade A.

a] All beans in the barrel are grade A.
The next bean to be drawn from the barrel is a bean in the barrel.
∴The next bean to be drawn from the barrel is grade A.

In this example, the conclusion of the previous induction by enumeration is a universal generalization. However, if the conclusion of the previous induction is a statistical generalization, we obviously cannot construct the same type of *deductive* argument. In this case, we can construct an *inductive* argument of the type called *statistical syllogism* (because of a resemblance to categorical syllogism). In example *c* of section 20 we concluded, using induction by enumeration, that 75 percent of the coffee beans in a certain barrel are grade A. We can use this conclusion as a premise and construct the following argument:

b] 75 percent of the beans in the barrel are grade A.
The next bean to be drawn from the barrel is a bean in the barrel.
∴The next bean to be drawn from the barrel is grade A.

Obviously, the conclusion of argument *b* could be false even if the premises are true. Nevertheless, if the first premise is true and we use the same type of argument for each of the beans in the barrel, we will get a true conclusion in 75 percent of these arguments and a false conclusion in only 25 percent of them. On the other hand, if we were to conclude from these premises that the next bean to be drawn will not be grade A, we would get false conclusions in 75 percent of such arguments and true conclusions in only 25 percent of them. Clearly it is better to conclude that the next bean will be grade A than to conclude that it will not be grade A. (Even if we are not willing to assert that the next bean will be grade A, we could reasonably be prepared to bet on it at odds somewhere near three to one.)

The form of the statistical syllogism may be represented as follows:

$c$]      $Z$ percent of $F$ are $G$.
         $x$ is $F$.
         $\therefore x$ is $G$.

The strength of the statistical syllogism depends upon the value of $Z$. If $Z$ is very close to 100, we have a very strong argument; that is, the premises very strongly support the conclusion. If $Z$ equals 50, the premises offer no support for the conclusion, for the same premises would equally support the conclusion "$x$ is not $G$." If $Z$ is less than 50, the premises do not support the conclusion; rather, they support the conclusion "$x$ is not $G$." If $Z$ is close to zero, the premises offer strong support for the conclusion "$x$ is not $G$."

The first premise of a statistical syllogism may be stated in terms of an exact numerical value for $Z$, but in many cases it will be a less exact statement. The following kinds of statement are also acceptable as first premises in statistical syllogisms:

$d$]      Almost all $F$ are $G$.
         The vast majority of $F$ are $G$.
         Most $F$ are $G$.
         A high percentage of $F$ are $G$.
         There is a high probability that an $F$ is a $G$.

You may feel uneasy about arguments like $b$ in which the conclusion is given without qualification; perhaps you feel that the conclusion should read, "The next bean to be drawn from the barrel is *probably* grade A." In order to deal with this problem, reconsider argument $a$, which might be rendered less formally:

$e$]      Since all of the beans in the barrel are grade A, the next bean to be drawn
         from the barrel *must be* grade A.

Obviously, there is no necessity in the mere fact of the next bean being grade A. As we noted earlier, a verb form like "must be" serves to indicate that a statement is the conclusion of a deductive argument. The necessity it indicates is this: *If* the premises are true, the conclusion *must be* true. The conclusion of the deductive argument is "The next bean to be drawn from the barrel *is* grade A", not "The next bean to be drawn from the barrel *must be* grade A." "Must be" signifies a certain relationship between premises and conclusion; it is not part of the conclusion by itself. Similarly, argument *b* might be informally stated,

*f]*   Since 75 percent of the beans in the barrel are grade A, the next bean to be drawn from the barrel is *probably* grade A.

In this case, the term "probably" indicates that an *inductive* conclusion is being given. Just as "must be" signifies a deductive relation between premises and conclusion in *e,* so does "probably" signify an inductive relation between premises and conclusion in *f.* Just as "must be" is not part of the conclusion itself, so is "probably" not part of the conclusion itself.

This point can be further reinforced. Consider the following statistical syllogism:

*g]*   The vast majority of 35-year-old American men will survive for three more years.
Henry Smith is a 35-year-old American man.
∴Henry Smith will survive for three more years.

Suppose, however, that Henry Smith has an advanced case of lung cancer. Then we can set forth the following statistical syllogism as well:

*h]*   The vast majority of people with advanced cases of lung cancer will not survive for three more years.
Henry Smith has an advanced case of lung cancer.
∴Henry Smith will not survive for three more years.

The premises of *g* and *h* could all be true; they are not incompatible with each other. The conclusions of *g* and *h* contradict each other. This situation can arise only with inductive arguments. If two valid deductive arguments have compatible premises, they cannot have incompatible conclusions. The situation is not noticeably improved by adding "probably" as a qualifier in the conclusions of *g* and *h*. It would still be contradictory to say that Henry Smith probably will, and probably will not, survive for three more years.

Given two arguments like *g* and *h*, which should we accept? Both arguments have correct inductive form and both have true premises. However, we cannot accept both conclusions, for to do so would be to accept a self-contradiction. The difficulty is that neither *g* nor *h* embodies all the relevant evidence concerning the survival of Henry Smith. The premises of *g* state only part of our evidence, and the premises of *h* state only part of our evidence. However, it will not be sufficient simply to combine the premises of *g* and *h* to construct a new argument:

*i*] The vast majority of 35-year-old American men will survive for three more years.
The vast majority of people with advanced cases of lung cancer will not survive for three more years.
Henry Smith is a 35-year-old American man with an advanced case of lung cancer.
∴ ?

From the premises of *i* we cannot draw any conclusion, even inductively, concerning Henry Smith's survival. For all we can conclude, either deductively or inductively, from the first two premises of *i*, 35-year-old American men may be an exceptional class of people with respect to lung cancer. The vast majority of them may survive lung cancer, or the survival rate may be about 50 percent. No conclusion can be drawn. However, we do have further evidence. We know that 35-year-old American men are not so exceptional; the vast majority of 35-year-old American men with advanced cases of lung cancer do not survive for three more years. Thus, we can set up the following statistical syllogism:

*j*] The vast majority of 35-year-old American men with advanced cases of lung cancer do not survive for three more years.
Henry Smith is a 35-year-old American man with an advanced case of lung cancer.
∴Henry Smith will not survive for three more years.

Assuming that the premises of *j* embody all the evidence we have that is relevant, we may accept the conclusion of *j*.

We can now see the full force of the remark in section 19 to the effect that additional evidence is relevant to inductive arguments in a way in which it is not relevant to deductive arguments. The conclusion of a deductive argument is acceptable if (1) the premises are true and (2) the argument has a correct form. These two conditions are not sufficient to make the conclusion of an inductive argument acceptable; a further condition must be added. The conclusion of an inductive argument is acceptable if (1) the premises are true, (2) the argument has a correct form, and (3) the premises of the argument embody all available relevant evidence. This last requirement is known as the requirement of total evidence. Inductive arguments that violate condition 3 commit the *fallacy of incomplete evidence*.

## 24. ARGUMENT FROM AUTHORITY

A frequent method of attempting to support a conclusion is to cite some person, institution, or writing that asserts that conclusion. This type of argument has the form

*a*]    *x* asserts *p*.
      $\therefore p$.

As this form stands, it is clearly fallacious. Nevertheless, there are correct uses of authority as well as incorrect ones. It would be a sophomoric mistake to suppose that every appeal to authority is illegitimate, for the proper use of authority plays an indispensable role in the accumulation and application of knowledge. If we were to reject every appeal to authority, we would have to maintain, for example, that no one is ever justified in accepting the judgment of a medical expert concerning an illness. Instead, one would have to become a medical expert oneself, and one would face the impossible task of doing so without relying on the results of any other investigators. Instead of rejecting the appeal to authority entirely, we must attempt to distinguish correct from incorrect appeals.

As a matter of fact, we frequently do make legitimate uses of authority. We consult textbooks, encyclopedias, and experts in various fields. In these cases the appeal is justified by the fact that the authority is known to be honest and well informed in the subject under consideration. We often have good grounds for believing that the authority is usually correct. Finally—and this is a crucial point—the expert is known to have based his or her judgment upon objective evidence which could, if necessary, be examined and verified by any competent person. Under these conditions, we shall say that the authority is *reliable*. The appeal to a reliable authority is legitimate, for the testimony of a reliable authority *is* evidence for the conclusion. The following form of argument is correct:

*b*]    *x* is a reliable authority concerning *p*.
      *x* asserts p.
      $\therefore p$.

This form is not deductively valid, for the premises could be true and the conclusion false. Reliable authorities do sometimes make errors. It is, however, inductively correct, for it is a special case of the statistical syllogism. It could be rewritten as follows:

*c*]    The vast majority of statements made by *x* concerning subject *S* are true.
      *p* is a statement made by *x* concerning subject *S*.
      $\therefore p$ is true.

There are a number of ways in which the argument from authority can be misused.

1. *The authority may be misquoted or misinterpreted.* This is not a logical fallacy but a case of an argument with a false premise; in particular, the second premise of *b* is false.

*d*]    The authority of Einstein is sometimes summoned to support the theory that
      there is no such thing as right or wrong except insofar as it is relative to a

particular culture. It is claimed that Einstein proved that everything is relative. As a matter of fact, Einstein expounded an important physical theory of relativity, but his theory says nothing whatever about cultures or moral standards. This use of Einstein as an authority is a clear case of misinterpretation of the statements of an authority.

When a writer cites an authority, the accepted procedure is to document the source so that the readers can, if they wish, check the accuracy of transmission.

2. *The authority may have only glamour, prestige, or popularity;* even if he or she has competence in some related field of learning, that does not constitute a requirement that such an "authority" must fulfill.

*e*] Testimonials of movie stars and athletes are used to advertise breakfast cereals.

The aim of such advertising is to transfer the glamour and prestige of these people to the product being advertised. No appeal to evidence of any kind is involved; this is a straightforward emotional appeal. It is, of course, essential to distinguish emotional appeals from logical arguments. Although some athletes who make claims about the nutritional superiority of breakfast foods may have considerable knowledge of human physiology and nutrition, by no means all of them do. What is more important, whether they have knowledge of this sort or not, such expertise is not a qualification for making these endorsements, and the advertising appeal is to athletic prowess rather than scientific knowledge. Insofar as any argument is involved in such testimonials, it is fallacious, for it has the form *a* rather than the form *b*. Likewise, when an appeal to authority is made to support a conclusion (rather than to advertise a product), it may be merely an attempt to transfer prestige from the authority to the conclusion.

*f*] As the president of Consolidated Amalgamated said in a recent speech, the Fifth Amendment to the Constitution, far from being a safeguard of freedom, is a threat to the very legal and political institutions that guarantee us our freedoms.

An industrial magnate like the president of Consolidated Amalgamated is a person of great prestige but one who can hardly be expected, by virtue of that position, to be an expert in jurisprudence and political theory. Transferring personal prestige to a conclusion is not the same as giving evidence that it is true. This misuse of the argument from authority is clearly an appeal to emotion.

3. *Experts may make judgments about something outside their special fields of competence.* This misuse is closely akin to the preceding one. The first premise required in *b* is "*x* is a reliable authority concerning *p*." Instead, a different premise is offered, namely, "*x* is a reliable authority concerning something" (which may have nothing to do with *p*).

g]   Einstein is an excellent authority in certain branches of physics, but he is not thereby a good authority in other areas. In the field of social ethics he made many pronouncements, but his authority as a physicist does not carry over.

Again, a transfer of prestige is involved. Einstein's great prestige as a physicist is attached to his statements on a variety of other subjects.

4. *Authorities may express opinions about matters concerning which they could not possibly have any evidence.* As we pointed out, one of the conditions of reliable authorities is that their judgments be based upon objective evidence. If $p$ is a statement for which $x$ could not have evidence, then $x$ cannot be a reliable authority concerning $p$. This point is particularly important in connection with the pronouncements of supposed authorities in religion and morals.

h]   Moral and religious authorities have often said that certain practices, such as sodomy, are contrary to the will of God. It is reasonable to ask how these persons, or any others, could possibly have evidence about what God wills. It is not sufficient to answer that this pronouncement is based upon some other authority, such as a sacred writing, a church father, or an institutional doctrine. The same question is properly raised about these latter authorities as well.

In this example, also, there is great danger that the appeal to authority is an emotional appeal rather than an appeal to any kind of evidence. In any case, the point is that appeals to authority cannot be supported indefinitely by further appeals to other authorities. At some stage the appeal to authority must end, and evidence of some other sort must be taken into account.

5. *Authorities who are equally competent,* as far as we can tell, *may disagree.* In such cases there is no reason to place greater confidence in one than in the other, and people are apt to choose the authority that gives them the answer they want to hear. Ignoring the judgment of opposed authorities is a case of biasing the evidence. When authorities disagree it is time to reconsider the objective evidence upon which the authorities have supposedly based their judgments.

A special form of the argument from authority, known as the *argument from consensus,* deserves mention. In arguments of this type a large group of people, instead of a single individual, is taken as an authority. Sometimes it is the whole of humanity, sometimes a more restricted group. In either case, the fact that a large group of people agrees with a certain conclusion is taken as evidence that it is true. The same considerations that apply generally to arguments from authority apply to arguments from consensus.

i]   There cannot be a perpetual motion machine; competent physicists are in complete agreement on this point.

This argument may be rendered as follows:

*j*]    The community of competent physicists is a reliable authority on the pos-
        sibility of perpetual motion machines.
        The community of competent physicists agrees that a perpetual motion ma-
        chine is impossible.
        ∴A perpetual motion machine is impossible.

The argument from consensus is seldom as reasonable as *j*. More often it is
a blatant emotional appeal.

*k*]    Every right-thinking American knows that national sovereignty must be pro-
        tected against the inroads of international organizations like the United
        Nations.

The force of the argument, if it merits the name, is that a person who
supports the United Nations is not a right-thinking American. There is a
strong emotional appeal for many Americans to be members of the group
of right-thinking Americans.

The classic example of an argument from consensus is an argument for
the existence of God.

*l*]    In all times and places, in every culture and civilization, people have believed
        in the existence of some sort of deity. Therefore, a supernatural being must
        exist.

Two considerations must be raised. First, is there any reason for regarding
the whole of humanity as a theological authority, even if the alleged agreement exists? Second, on what evidence has the whole of mankind come to
the conclusion that God exists? As we have seen, reliable authorities must
base their judgment upon objective evidence. In view of this fact, the argument from consensus cannot be the only ground for believing in the existence of God, for if it were, it would be logically incorrect.

To sum up, arguments of form *b* are inductively correct, and those of
form *a* are fallacious. Fallacious appeals to authority are usually appeals to
emotion rather than appeals to evidence.

## 25. ARGUMENT AGAINST THE PERSON

The *argument against the person*[4] is a type of argument that concludes that a
statement is false because it was made by a certain person. It is closely
related to the argument from authority, but it is negative rather than
positive. In the argument from authority, the fact that a certain person

[4]The argument against the person is closely related to, but not identical with the traditional
*argumentum ad hominem*. This departure from tradition is motivated by the symmetry between
the argument from authority and the argument against the person, and by the fact that the
argument against the person is reducible to statistical syllogism.

asserts $p$ is taken as evidence that $p$ is true. In the *argument against the person*, the fact that a certain person asserts $p$ is taken as evidence that $p$ is false.

In analyzing the argument from authority, we saw that it could be put into an inductively correct form, a special case of the statistical syllogism. To do so, it was necessary to include a premise of the form "$x$ is a reliable authority concerning $p$." We discussed the characteristics of reliable authorities. The argument against the person can be handled similarly. To accomplish this end we need an analogous premise involving the concept of a *reliable anti-authority*. A reliable anti-authority about a given subject is a person who almost always makes false statements about that subject. We have the following inductively correct argument form:

*a*]   $x$ is a reliable anti-authority concerning $p$.
       $x$ asserts $p$.
       ∴Not-$p$ (i.e., $p$ is false).

Like the argument from authority, this is also a special case of the statistical syllogism. It could be rewritten:

*b*]   The vast majority of statements made by $x$ concerning subject $S$ are false.
       $p$ is a statement made by $x$ concerning subject $S$.
       ∴$p$ is false.

It must be emphasized that a reliable anti-authority is not merely someone who fails to be a reliable authority. A person who is not a reliable authority cannot be counted upon to be right most of the time. This is far different from being consistently wrong. An unreliable authority is a person who cannot be counted upon at all. The fact that such a person makes a statement is evidence for neither its truth nor its falsity.

Schema $a$ is, as we have said, inductively correct, but whether it has any utility depends upon whether there are any reliable anti-authorities. It will be useless if we can never satisfy the first premise. Although there are not many cases in which we can say with assurance that a person is a reliable anti-authority, there does seem to be at least one kind of reliable anti-authority, namely, scientific *cranks*.[5] They can be identified by several characteristics.

1. They usually reject, in wholesale fashion, all of established science or some branch of it.
2. They are usually ignorant of the science they reject.
3. The accepted channels of scientific communication are usually closed to them. Their theories are seldom published in scientific journals or presented to scientific societies.

[5]For interesting discussions of many scientific cranks, see Martin Gardner, *Fads and Fallacies in the Name of Science* (New York: Dover Publications, Inc., 1957).

4. They regard opposition of scientists to their views as a result of the prejudice and bigotry of scientific orthodoxy.
5. Their opposition to established science is usually based upon a real or imagined conflict between science and some extrascientific doctrine—religious, political, or moral.

A "scientific" theory propounded by a person who has the foregoing characteristics is very probably false.

Great scientific innovators propose theories that are highly unorthodox and they meet with strenuous opposition from the majority of scientists at the time. Nevertheless, they are not cranks, according to our criteria. For instance, highly original scientific theorists are, contrary to characteristic 2, thoroughly familiar with the theories they hope to supersede. Furthermore, we must note, deductive validity has *not* been claimed for schema *a*. The fact that a statement is made by a reliable anti-authority does not prove conclusively that it is false. We cannot claim with certainty that no scientific crank will ever produce a valuable scientific result.

Although the argument against the person does have the inductively correct form *a*, it is frequently misused. These misuses are usually substitutions of emotional appeal for logical evidence. Instead of showing that someone who makes a statement is a reliable anti-authority, the misuser vilifies the person by attacking that person's personality, character, or background. The first premise of *a* is replaced by an attempt to arouse negative feelings. For example,

*c*] In the 1930s the Communist party in Russia rejected the genetic theories of Gregor Mendel, an Austrian monk, as "bourgeois idealism." A party orator who said "The Mendelian theory must be regarded as the product of a monkish bourgeois mind" would be guilty of a fallacious use of the argument against the person.

Clearly, the national, social, and religious background of the originator of a theory is irrelevant to its truth or falsity. Being an Austrian monk does not make Mendel a reliable anti-authority in genetics. The condemnation of the Mendelian theory on these grounds is an obvious case of arousing negative emotions rather than providing negative evidence. It is also an instance of the *genetic fallacy* (section 3). A subtler form of the same fallacy may be illustrated as follows:

*d*] Someone might claim that there is strong psychoanalytic evidence in Plato's philosophical writings that he suffered from an unresolved oedipal conflict and that his theories can be explained in terms of this neurotic element in his personality. It is then suggested that Plato's philosophical theories need not be taken seriously because they are thus explained.

Even if we assume that Plato had an Oedipus complex, the question still remains whether his philosophical doctrines are true. They are not *ex-*

*plained away* on these psychological grounds. Having an Oedipus complex does not make anyone a reliable anti-authority.

Just as the argument from consensus is a special form of the argument from authority, similarly there is a *negative argument from consensus* which is a special form of the argument against the person. According to this form of argument, a conclusion is to be *rejected* if it is accepted by a group that has negative prestige. For example,

e]      Chinese Communists believe that married women should have the right to use their own family names.
∴Married women should be compelled to adopt the family names of their husbands.

This argument is clearly an attempt to arouse negative attitudes toward some aspects of women's liberation.

There is one fundamental principle that applies both to the argument from authority and to the argument against the person. If there is, objectively, a strong probability relation between the truth or falsity of a statement and the kind of person who made it, then that relation can be used in a correct inductive argument. It becomes the first premise in a statistical syllogism. Any argument from the characteristics of the person who made a statement to the truth or falsity of the statement, in the absence of such a probability relation, is invariably incorrect. These fallacious arguments are often instances of the *genetic fallacy* (section 3). Example *c* of section 3, as well as example *c* of this section, illustrates this point.


## 26. ANALOGY

*Analogy,* a widely used form of inductive argument, is based upon a comparison between objects of two different types. This is how it works. Objects of one kind are known to be similar in certain respects to objects of another kind. Objects of the first kind are known to have a certain characteristic; it is not known whether objects of the second kind have it or not. By analogy we conclude that, since objects of the two kinds are alike in some respects, they are alike in other respects as well. Therefore, objects of the second kind also have the additional property that those of the first kind are already known to possess. For example,

a]      Canadian medical researchers conducted experiments upon rats to determine the effects of saccharin upon humans. They found that a significantly greater percentage of rats that had been given large quantities of saccharin developed cancer of the bladder than did those that had not been given any saccharin. By analogy, many experts have concluded that, since rats and humans are physiologically similar in various respects, saccharin poses a threat of bladder cancer to humans who use it as an artificial sweetener. It is for this reason that your favorite diet soft drink carries a warning.[6]

This kind of argument may be schematized as follows:

b]     Objects of type $X$ have properties $G, H$, etc.
       Objects of type $Y$ have properties $G, H$, etc.
       Objects of type $X$ have property $F$.
       ∴Objects of type $Y$ have property $F$.

In argument $a$, rats are objects of type $X$, and humans are objects of type $Y$. $G$, $H$, etc., are the physiological properties rats and humans have in common. $F$ is the property of developing bladder cancer upon consumption of large quantities of saccharin. (The fact that only some, but not all, rats developed bladder cancer does not undermine the analogy; saccharin increases the chances of bladder cancer in rats, and so it is a reasonable inference that it will have the same effect upon humans.)

Like other kinds of inductive arguments, analogies may be strong or weak. The strength of an analogy depends principally upon the similarities between the two types of objects being compared. Any two kinds of objects are alike in many respects and unlike in many others. The crucial question for analogical arguments is this: Are the objects that are being compared similar in ways that are *relevant* to the argument? To whatever extent there are *relevant similarities*, the analogy is *strengthened*. To whatever extent there are *relevant dissimilarities*, the analogy is *weakened*. Rats and humans are very dissimilar in many ways, but the question at issue in $a$ is a physiological one, so that the physiological similarities are important and the nonphysiological dissimilarities are unimportant to the particular argument.

It is not easy to state with precision, in a general way, what constitutes relevance or irrelevance of similarities or differences. The question is, what kinds of similarities or differences are likely to *make a difference* to the phenomenon under consideration? Our common sense tells us that the fact that both rats and humans are mammals is apt to be an important similarity where the physiological effects of saccharin are concerned. We might well wonder whether the fact that rats are four-legged animals whereas humans are two-legged could be relevant. We might be fairly confident that the possession of tails by rats and the lack of them in humans is irrelevant. We can be pretty sure that the fact that male rats do not wear neckties whereas some human males do is totally irrelevant. Of course, the scientists who conduct physiological experiments have a considerable body of background knowledge and experience that enables them to make informed judgments regarding relevance and irrelevance. Experimentation with lab-

[6]For an excellent analysis of this example, see Ronald N. Giere, *Understanding Scientific Reasoning* (New York: Holt, Rinehart & Winston, 1979), chap. 12.

oratory animals is an established procedure in the biomedical sciences; its values and limitations are well known.

Here are some additional analogies.

c] Archaeologists, excavating a site where prehistoric people lived, find a number of stones that are similar in shape, and which could not have acquired that shape unless they had been fashioned by humans. Although these stones do not have attached handles, the archaeologists notice that they have about the same shape as axheads used by primitive people today. It is inferred, by analogy, that these stones served the prehistoric people as axheads. The handles are missing because the wood has rotted away.

Archaeologists who make analogical inferences of this sort must attempt to evaluate both the similarities between the ancient stones and the modern axheads and also the similarities between the prehistoric culture and the primitive culture in which stone axes are used today.

d] Some pacifists have argued, along the following lines, that war can never be a means for bringing about peace, justice, or brotherhood. If you plant wheat, wheat comes up. If you plant corn, you get corn. If you plant thistles, you don't expect to get strawberries. Likewise, if you plant hatred and murder, you can't expect to get peace, justice, and brotherhood. "Fighting for peace is like fornicating for chastity" seems to be a concise formulation of this argument.

The enormous dissimilarities between the kinds of "planting" in this example make a very weak analogy.

The *design argument*—probably the most widely used argument for the existence of God—is often given explicitly in the form of an analogy.

e] "I [Cleanthes] shall briefly explain how I conceive this matter. Look around the world: contemplate the whole and every part of it: you will find it to be nothing but one great machine, subdivided into an infinite number of lesser machines, which again admit of subdivisions, to a degree beyond what human senses and faculties can trace and explain. All these various machines, and even their most minute parts, are adjusted to each other with an accuracy, which ravishes into admiration all men, who have ever contemplated them. The curious adapting of means to ends, throughout all nature, resembles exactly, though it much exceeds, the productions of human contrivance; of human design, thought, wisdom, and intelligence. Since therefore the effects resemble each other we are led to infer, by all the rules of analogy, that the causes also resemble; and that the Author of Nature is somewhat similar to the mind of men; though possessed of much larger faculties, proportioned to the grandeur of the work, which he has executed. By this argument . . . alone, do we prove at once the existence of a Deity, and his similarity to human mind and intelligence."[7]

[7]David Hume, *Dialogues Concerning Natural Religion*, Part II.

The evaluation of this analogy is a complex matter which we shall not undertake. Hume's *Dialogues* provide an extremely illuminating analysis of this argument. In the same place, Hume gives some additional examples.

f] ". . . whenever you depart, in the least, from the similarity of cases, you diminish proportionately the evidence; and may at last bring it to a very weak *analogy*, which is confessedly liable to error and uncertainty. After having experienced the circulation of the blood in human creatures, we make no doubt that it takes place in Titius and Maevius; but from its circulation in frogs and fishes, it is only a presumption, though a strong one, from analogy, that it takes place in men and other animals. The analogical reasoning is much weaker, when we infer the circulation of the sap in vegetables from our experience, that the blood circulates in animals; and those, who hastily followed that imperfect analogy, are found, by more accurate experiments, to have been mistaken."[8]

Analogical arguments abound in philosophical literature. We shall conclude by mentioning two additional examples of great importance.

g] Plato's dialogues contain an abundance of analogical arguments; the analogy is one of Socrates' favorite forms. In *The Republic*, for example, many of the subsidiary arguments that occur along the way are analogies. In addition, the major argument of the whole work is an analogy. The nature of justice in the individual is the main concern of the book. In order to investigate this problem, justice in the state is examined at length—for this is justice "writ large." On the basis of an analogy between the state and the individual, conclusions are drawn concerning justice in the individual.

h] Analogy has often been used to deal with the philosophical problem of *other minds*. The problem is this. One is directly aware of one's own state of consciousness, such as a feeling of pain, but one cannot experience another person's state of mind. If we believe, as we all do, that other people have experiences similar in many ways to our own, it must be on the basis of inference. The argument used to justify our belief in other minds is regarded as an analogy. Other people behave as if they experience thought, doubt, joy, pain and other states of mind. Their behavior is similar to our own manifestations of such mental states. We conclude by analogy that these manifestations are due, in others as in ourselves, to states of consciousness. In this way we seek to establish the existence of other minds besides our own.

The argument by analogy illustrates once more the important bearing upon inductive arguments of information in addition to that given in the premises. To evaluate the strength of an analogy it is necessary to determine the relevance of the respects in which the objects of different kinds are similar. Relevance cannot be determined by logic alone—the kind of relevance at issue in analogical arguments involves factual information.

[8]*Ibid.*

Biological knowledge must be brought to bear to determine what similarities and differences are relevant to a biological question such as example *a*. Anthropological information is required to determine the relevant similarities and differences with respect to an anthropological question such as example *c*. These arguments, like most inductive arguments, occur in the presence of a large background of general knowledge, and this general knowledge must be brought into consideration to evaluate the strength of analogies. Failure to take it into account is a violation of the requirement of total evidence.

## 27. CAUSAL ARGUMENTS

Our general background of scientific and commonsense knowledge includes information about a great many causal relations. Such knowledge serves as a basis for inferences from what we directly observe to events and objects that are not available for immediate observation, it enters into causal explanations, and it is a necessary adjunct to rational action. For example,

*a*]    A body is fished out of the river, and the medical examiner performs an autopsy to determine the cause of death. By examining the contents of the lungs and stomach, analyzing the blood, and inspecting other organs, she finds that death was caused, not by drowning, but by poison. Her conclusion is based on extensive knowledge of the physical effects of various substances, such as arsenic and water.

This is a case of inferring the causes when the effects have been observed. Conversely, there are cases in which effects are inferred from observed causes.

*b*]    A ranger observes lightning striking a dry forest. On the basis of his causal knowledge, he infers that a fire will ensue.

Causal knowledge also enables us to exercise some degree of control over events that occur in the world. Sometimes, for example, it is within our power to bring about a cause that will, in turn, produce a desired effect.

*c*]    The highway department spreads salt on icy roads to cause the ice to melt, thereby reducing the risk of highway accidents.

In other cases, our aim is to prevent occurrences of an undesirable sort. Causal knowledge makes this possible as well.

*d*]    Careful investigations are conducted to ascertain the causes of airline crashes in order to prevent such accidents from happening in the future. In a recent case, for example, an airplane taking off from Washington National Airport failed to gain sufficient altitude to clear a bridge and crashed into the Potomac River. Preliminary investigation suggested that the cause was a buildup of ice on the surfaces of the wings. Since airplanes derive their lift from the passage of air over wings having the shape of airfoils, an accumulation of ice that radically alters the shape of the wing surfaces can deprive the airplane of its lift. It is not, incidentally, the weight of the ice that causes the problem; it is the change in shape of the cross-section of the wing that is at fault. More careful de-icing immediately before take off could prevent accidents of this type in the future.

In example *c*, as in *b*, there is an inference from cause to effect on the basis of a knowledge of causal relations. In example *d*, as in *a*, the inference is from effect to cause. Moreover, in each of the foregoing examples we have an explanation of the effect. The victim died *because* poison was ingested, the fire broke out *because* lightning struck, the ice on the road melted *because* salt was spread upon it, and the airplane crashed *because* ice had collected on its wings.

Regardless of the purposes of such inferences, the reliability of the conclusions depends upon the existence of certain causal relations. If, for purposes of logical analysis, we transform these inferences into arguments, we must include premises stating that the appropriate causal relations hold. Consider the following argument:

*e]*    Mrs. Smith was frightened by bats during her pregnancy.
∴Mrs. Smith's baby will be "marked."

As it stands, this argument is neither deductively valid nor inductively correct, for it needs a premise stating that there is a causal relation between being frightened and having a "marked" baby.

*f]*    If an expectant mother is frightened, it will cause her baby to be "marked."
Mrs. Smith was frightened by bats during her pregnancy.
∴Mrs. Smith's baby will be "marked."

Now the argument is logically correct; in fact, it is deductively valid. Let us give a similar reconstruction of example *b*.

*g]*    If a bolt of lightning strikes a dry forest, it will ignite the dry wood and cause a fire to start.
A bolt of ligtning has just struck a dry forest.
∴A fire will start.

This argument is also deductively valid.

It will be useful for our discussion of causality to note that arguments *f* and *g* have premises of two different kinds. The first is a *general* causal assertion about what happens *whenever* a condition of a certain kind occurs.

In example *f,* the first premise makes a claim (which is, of course, false) about what happens when a pregnant woman is frightened. It is stated in a conditional form, but to emphasize the fact that it is not just an ordinary material conditional, the causal relation is explicitly mentioned. The second premise is a particular statement about something that happened to a particular person. Example *g* has premises of the same two types, but in this latter example, the general premise is at least plausible.

In all of the examples that have been considered so far, it has been supposed that the general causal relations were given, and attention was focused upon the particular cause. In example *a,* there are many possible causes of death; the medical examiner wants to know which one was present in this particular case. In example *d,* again, there are many possible causes of an airplane crash, but the investigators want to know which one was responsible for this particular crash.

One striking difference between examples *f* and *g* is the fact that the former has an obviously false general premise, whereas the general premise in the latter might well be true. We have reiterated many times that logic is concerned, not with the truth or falsity of the premises, but with the logical structure of the arguments. Nevertheless, it is clear that the reliability of such causal arguments depends upon the existence of causal relations of the sort described by the general causal premise. Given the enormous practical and theoretical importance of knowledge of such causal relations, we must consider the logical character of the kinds of arguments that can be used to establish them. The main purpose of many scientific investigations is to establish just such *general causal relations.* An interesting historical case illustrates the point.

*h*]     During the years 1844–1848, Ignaz Semmelweis was a member of the medical staff of the First Maternity Division of the Vienna General Hospital. He was alarmed to discover that a high percentage of women who had their babies in that division became ill with a serious disease, known as "childbed fever," and many of them died. In 1844, 8.2 percent of the new mothers— that is, 260 women—died; in 1845, the death rate was 6.8 percent; and in 1846, 11.4 percent succumbed to the disease. In the Second Maternity Division, located next to the First, the death rate was surprisingly low by comparison—2.3 percent, 2.0 percent, and 2.7 percent for the corresponding years. After careful investigation, Semmelweis ascertained that the problem was connected with the fact that the women in the First Division—unlike those in the Second—were examined by medical students and physicians who came there directly from the autopsy room, where they had been performing dissections of cadavers. Although the germ theory of disease had not been established at that time, Semmelweis concluded that the disease was caused by the transfer of "putrid matter" on the hands of the examiners from the corpses to the mothers. He believed that the foul odor of this material was a sign of some harmful component, and he knew that chlorinated lime was commonly used to eliminate the odor of decaying matter. Thus he recommended a program of careful hand-washing in chlorinated lime (which, we

know today, is a powerful disinfectant) for the examiners. When this program
was instituted, the death rate declined to that of the Second Division. This is
another case in which knowledge of a causal relation helped to prevent an
undesirable effect.[9]

This example illustrates the fundamental distinction between the problem
of ascertaining which particular cause was operative and the problem of
establishing a general causal relation. In the case of the airplane crash, the
investigators are aware of the fundamental physical relationship between
the shape of the wing and the lift produced when it moves through air, as
well as many other general causal relations that might have been involved.
We may say that the general *causal laws* are known. In this case the problem
is to find out which particular cause happened to be operative. In the case
of childbed fever, in contrast, Semmelweis did not know any general causal
relationship that would connect a particular fact with the effect that concerned him. In this situation it was the ascertainment of the general causal
law that was needed.

It would be nice if, at this point, we could produce some rules for the
discovery of general causal relations, but as we recall from section 3, Discovery and Justification, logic simply cannot provide any such thing. The
best we can hope to do is to furnish methods for the evaluation of arguments designed to justify the claim that a general causal relation exists. A
set of methods that serve this purpose is available.


## 28. MILL'S METHODS

The basic methods for establishing general causal relations that we shall
study were propounded in the middle of the nineteenth century by the
English philosopher John Stuart Mill. He offered five methods; we shall
discuss four of them. They constitute an excellent point of departure for
the topic with which we are concerned. After presenting them in their
traditional forms, we shall suggest important modifications to bring them
up to date.

The first is known as the *method of agreement*. Consider the following
example:

a]     Suppose you operate a fruit store, and you find that some oranges that look
       fine on the outside are pulpy and juiceless. You try to learn what causes this
       condition. You find that it sometimes happens to navel, Valencia, and other
       varieties of oranges, and sometimes not. You find that it sometimes happens

---

[9]A fascinating discussion of this example can be found in Carl G. Hempel, *Philosophy of
Natural Science* (Englewood Cliffs, N.J.: Prentice-Hall, Inc. [*Foundations of Philosophy Series*],
1966), chap. 2.

to oranges that have been hauled by truck and sometimes to those that have been transported by train. It happens sometimes to those grown in Florida and sometimes to those from California. You have several different wholesale suppliers, and it sometimes happens to oranges that come from each of them. The one thing they always have in common is that they were subjected to freezing temperatures. You conclude that being frozen is the cause of the defect.

The general idea behind Mill's method of agreement is this. There is a certain effect whose cause you wish to ascertain. You look for instances of this effect arising in as wide a variety of circumstances as you can find. In this case the effect is the dryness in the oranges. The variety of circumstances refers to the different varieties of oranges, the different modes of transport, the different suppliers, and the different states in which they were grown. The one thing these various cases have in common is the fact that they were subjected to freezing temperatures. We might schematize the method of agreement as follows:

$b$]     $ABCD \rightarrow X$
     $ABCE \rightarrow X$
     $ABDF \rightarrow X$
     $ACDG \rightarrow X$
          where $X$ is the effect whose cause is sought, and $A, B, C, D, E, F, G,$ are
          the various circumstances.
     Since $A$ is the only circumstance common to all of the different instances, it is
     concluded that $A$ is the cause of $X$.

The method of agreement must be used with considerable caution. There is an old joke that illustrates the danger:

$c$]     A man wants to find out what causes him to get drunk. One night he drinks
     scotch and soda, another night he drinks bourbon and soda, another night he
     drinks rye and soda, etc. He concludes that the soda is causing his
     intoxication.

What is the problem? The use of Mill's methods (not just the method of agreement) requires us to make certain assumptions. In the first place, we presume that there is some cause of the phenomenon we are investigating, and that we have identified it as one of the items in our schematization. In example $a$, it was crucial that being subjected to freezing temperatures was among the factors considered. If it had not been included in the list, Mill's method of agreement could never have revealed it as the cause. This shows, incidentally, why Mill's method of agreement is not a method for discovering causes. We have to think of the various conditions that might be causally relevant. If we have included the item in the list, Mill's method of agreement could pick it out of the list of possible candidates. Moreover, as example $c$ shows, causal factors do not come labeled in nature. If we do not realize that alcohol is a possible cause of intoxication and is contained in all different varieties of whiskies, the method of agreement cannot possibly locate the real cause.

Mill's second method is known as the *method of difference*. Consider the following example:

d]     You wonder whether drinking coffee in the evening keeps you awake at night. In order to answer this question you perform a small experiment. On two successive Wednesdays you try to do everything the same except for one thing. You attend the same classes during the day, you have exactly the same meals, you do the same amount of studying in the evening, and you watch the same television shows. On one of these two days you have several cups of coffee after dinner, but on the other you cut out the evening coffee. On the night following the evening coffee drinking you have a great deal of trouble getting to sleep, but on the night after omitting the evening coffee you fall asleep immediately after going to bed. You conclude that drinking coffee in the evening does interfere with your sleep.

The basic idea behind the method of difference is this: We seek the cause of a particular phenomenon—in this case sleeplessness. We try to find, or we deliberately set up, two similar situations—one in which the effect is present, the other in which the effect is absent. Suppose it turns out that all factors, except one that might be causally relevant to the effect in question, are the same in both cases, but that one factor is present in the case in which the effect occurs and absent in the case in which the effect does not occur. Under these circumstances, we conclude that the factor that is present in the one case and absent in the other is a cause of the phenomenon under investigation. The method of difference is so called because the factor present in the one case and absent in the other *makes the difference* between the occurrence and nonoccurrence of the effect.

The method of difference can be represented by the following schema:

e]          $ABCD \rightarrow X$
        $(not\text{-}A)\ BCD \rightarrow not\text{-}X$

If this schema is applied to example *d*, "*X*" stands for sleeplessness, "*A*" represents the consumption of coffee in the evening, and "*B*," "*C*," and "*D*" stand for such factors as attending the same classes during the day, having the same food to eat during the day, and spending the evening engaged in the same activities. The conclusion is that drinking coffee in the evening does cause a problem in going to sleep at night.

Before going on to consider the next of Mill's methods, it will be worthwhile to pause for a brief comparison of the methods of agreement and difference. The method of agreement should seem rather familiar, for it is very much like induction by enumeration (section 20). We notice that in many cases *A* is followed by *X*, and we conclude inductively that in all cases,

*A* will be followed by *X*. The fact that we insist that other factors such as *B*, *C*, *D*, . . . must be varied from one case to another is designed to avoid committing the fallacy of biased statistics (section 22). We say, roughly, that in a large number of instances found in a wide variety of different circumstances *A* has, without exception, been followed by *X;* therefore, in all likelihood, future instances of *A* will be followed by instances of *X*.

The method of difference does not seem to resemble the method of agreement at all closely. When we apply the method of difference, we show that *B*, *C*, *D*, . . . cannot be causes of *X*, for those factors can be present even when *X* is absent. Therefore, we reason, neither *B* nor *C* nor *D* can produce *X*. This method of approaching causal relations is often called *induction by elimination*. Neither the evening's study and television, for example, nor the food you had for dinner are the causes of difficulty in going to sleep, for that problem was absent on one of the nights when those factors were present. The elimination of *B*, *C*, *D*, . . . can be regarded as deductive, for we have counterexamples to the statements that *B* is always followed by *X*, *C* is always followed by *X*, etc. It does *not* follow deductively that *A* is always followed by *X*. The use of the method of difference, like the use of the method of agreement, requires us to suppose that the phenomenon we are investigating has a cause, and that the cause has been included as one of the items represented in the schema. At best, then, *A* is only established inductively as the causal factor we were seeking.

Toward the end of section 11, we defined the concepts of *sufficient condition* and *necessary condition*. We can introduce an analogous (but different— they must not be confused) distinction between *sufficient cause* and *necessary cause*. If *A* always produces *X*, we say that *A* is a sufficient cause of *X*. If exposure to freezing temperatures always results in pulpy juiceless oranges, then exposure to freezing temperatures is a sufficient cause of pulpy juicelessness. We say that *A* is a necessary cause of *X* if *X* cannot occur in the absence of *A*. Having an adequate supply of water is a necessary cause for the growth of high-quality oranges; if there is not enough water, the oranges will not be good. Indeed, as we can see from this latter consideration, exposure to freezing temperatures is not a necessary cause of pulpy juicelessness, for that same effect can be a result of an inadequate amount of water.

In many everyday situations, what we would normally regard as a cause is a necessary cause. Turning the switch is necessary to turn on your desk lamp, for example, but it certainly is not sufficient. Turning the switch will not make the light go on if the bulb has burnt out or if the lamp is not plugged in.

It is very easy to see that not all sufficient *conditions* are sufficient *causes*, and not all necessary *conditions* are necessary *causes*. When we defined sufficient conditions, it will be recalled, we simply used the *material* conditional

$p \supset q$ (p. 47), which is true in all cases except that in which $p$ is true and $q$ is false. The material conditional "If Mars is a planet, then grass is green" is true—Mars being a planet is a sufficient condition of grass being green—but by no stretch of the imagination could it be considered a sufficient *cause*. In a parallel fashion, we defined necessary conditions in terms of the *material* conditional $\sim p \supset \sim q$. The material conditional "If coal is not black, then Alaska is not a state" is true—coal being black is a necessary condition of Alaska being a state—but it obviously is not a necessary *cause*. There is no causal connection whatever between the motion of Mars and the color of grass, and none between the color of coal and the statehood of Alaska. No one would be likely to become confused in such cases.

If we are talking about cause-effect relations, it is particularly important to be clear about the distinction between necessary and sufficient conditions on the one hand and necessary and sufficient causes on the other. If, for example, lighting a fuse is a sufficient cause of the explosion of a bomb, then it is also a sufficient condition for that explosion. Because of the relation of contraposition (p. 24), if $p$ is a sufficient condition of $q$, then $q$ is a necessary condition of $p$. *You should recall the definition of* contraposition *and make sure you understand why this relationship between sufficient and necessary conditions holds.* By virtue of this fact, then, the explosion of the bomb is a necessary *condition* of the lighting of the fuse. But the explosion certainly cannot be considered any kind of cause of the lighting of the fuse; it is, instead, an effect. Similarly, if planting seeds in the spring is a necessary cause of harvesting corn in July, it is also a necessary condition. But the corn harvested in July is surely not a sufficient *cause* of the seed being sewn in April.

With these words of caution about not confusing necessary and sufficient conditions with necessary and sufficient causes firmly in mind, let us return to Mill's methods of agreement and difference. Consider, once again, the example of coffee drinking and sleeplessness, which we used to illustrate the method of difference. You will recall that it was called a method of induction by elimination, for it ruled out *as possible sufficient causes* of sleeplessness all factors, other than evening coffee drinking, that were mentioned. Thus, if there is a sufficient cause of sleeplessness among the circumstances mentioned, evening consumption of coffee must be it. Sleeplessness failed to occur in one of the cases in which each of the other factors was present. Notice, however, that none of these factors—other than evening coffee drinking—was ruled out as a necessary cause, for we did not even consider what would happen if any of them was absent. We might claim to have a slight amount of evidence that evening coffee drinking is a necessary cause of sleeplessness, for we did find one case in which this condition was absent and sleeplessness was also absent, but we would need to consider many more cases in many different circumstances in order to have any reasonable confidence in that conclusion. Perhaps you could say, on the basis of *further* evidence about your own sleeping patterns, whether difficulty in getting to sleep occurs only after you have been drinking coffee during the evening.

Let us now take another look at the example of pulpy juiceless oranges which we used to illustrate the method of agreement. In that case, we said that we had used something akin to induction by enumeration to establish freezing as as a sufficient cause of the defect. It is worth noting, however, that each of the factors mentioned in our schema—other than exposure to freezing temperatures—was ruled out as a necessary cause. Being shipped by truck, for example, is not a necessary cause, for some of the pulpy juiceless oranges were transported by train. Similarly, neither the variety of orange, nor the wholesaler from whom they were obtained, nor the state in which they were grown could possibly be a necessary cause. However, as I noted previously, it is not very plausible, in view of additional information that we have, to suppose that exposure to freezing temperatures is the only cause that can produce the defect we are considering.

Although the methods of agreement and difference can be represented by means of neat and simple schemas, I am inclined to believe that most serious investigations of causal relations are somewhat more complicated. As Mill realized, it is possible to combine the two methods to construct a much more sophisticated method. He called it the *joint method*. Consider the following example:

*f*]   It has been found that behind all airplanes, whether jet or propeller driven, there is severe air turbulence. This can be a serious danger to smaller airplanes, especially in the vicinity of major airports where larger aircraft arrive and depart frequently. It is known as *wing-tip turbulence*, for it consists of a pair of vortices (something like small tornadoes) following behind the tips of the wings. A small private airplane attempting to land soon after a large commercial jetliner could be thrown completely out of control if it encountered the wing-tip turbulence of the jet. The crucial factor in wing-tip turbulence, it has been discovered, is whether the aircraft is actually airborne. Before an airplane leaves the ground—so that it is being supported by the landing gear rather than the wings—there is no wing-tip turbulence, and as soon as it touches down in landing—so that again it is supported by the ground rather than the air—the turbulence ceases.

We may investigate this phenomenon in the following way. Begin by considering a wide variety of cases in which the turbulence is present. It occurs with different types of aircraft—large or small planes, jet or propellor planes, different altitudes, different weather conditions, with engine power on or gliding, etc. We find that in all such cases, if the aircraft is being supported by its wings, the turbulence is present. This is an application of the method of agreement, entirely similar in structure to example *a*. Now, we do the same thing again, but in this phase of the investigation we consider a wide variety of cases in which the phenomenon is absent. We find that they all agree in the circumstance that the weight of the aircraft is not supported by the wings (normally because it is on the ground). This constitutes a second application of the method of agreement. In this part of the investigation it is the fact that the craft is not airborne that is always present when the wing-tip turbulence does not occur. So, we have used the method of agreement twice.

When we compare the two uses of the method of agreement, we find that we are essentially using the method of difference. Taken together, all of the cases in which the phenomenon of wing-tip turbulence is present are exactly similar to all of the cases, taken together, in which that phenomenon is absent, except for the fact that in the latter set of cases there is one difference—the aircraft is not airborne.

The joint method, which this example illustrates, can be schematized as follows:

g]   $ABCD \rightarrow X$     *(not-A) BCD* $\rightarrow$ *not-X*
     $ABCE \rightarrow X$     *(not-A) BCE* $\rightarrow$ *not-X*
     $ABDF \rightarrow X$     *(not-A) BDF* $\rightarrow$ *not-X*
     $ACDG \rightarrow X$     *(not-A) CDG* $\rightarrow$ *not-X*

Note that each of the two columns is an instance of the method of agreement, and each one of the four horizontal rows is an instance of the method of difference. This is why it is called the joint method.

As I said, it seems to me that the methods of agreement and difference are usually oversimplifications of what actually occurs when causal relations are being investigated. In the case of the defective oranges, for example, we would naturally compare a variety of instances in which the dry pulpy condition did not occur as well as a variety of instances in which it did occur. So example *a* would naturally be expanded into an application of the joint method. Similarly, if you were interested in determining whether coffee drinking caused you difficulty in going to sleep at night, you would not make just one comparison of two days, as much alike as possible except for the evening consumption of coffee. You would make the same sort of comparison on a number of different kinds of days—days when you had classes and days on which you had no classes, days when you had meals in the school cafeteria and days on which you ate elsewhere, days on which you stayed home in the evening and days when you went out, etc. Again, the example we introduced to illustrate the method of difference is readily expanded into an instance of the joint method. Schemas *b* and *e*, which represent the methods of agreement and difference, respectively, are mainly useful, I think, in showing what goes into the joint method. The joint method is by far the most important of the three.

The fourth of Mill's methods is known as the *method of concomitant variation.* Here is an interesting historical example of its use:

h]   A mercury barometer can be made in the following way. Take a long glass tube—say 36 inches in length—closed at one end. Fill it with mercury, invert it, and submerge the open end in a dish of mercury. Some of the mercury will run out of the tube, leaving a space of about six inches at the top. In other words, a column of mercury about 30 inches high will remain in the tube. This type of barometer was invented around 1643 by Evangelista Torricelli. Soon after, to prove that the air pressure on the mercury in the dish is what causes the mercury to stay at that height in the tube, Robert Boyle placed a Torricelli barometer in a large container to which he attached a vacuum pump. As the air was pumped out of the container, the level of the mercury in the tube dropped until it finally reached the level of the mercury in the dish. The fact that the mercury is caused to rise in the tube by the pressure of the air is demonstrated by showing that the height of the mercury in the tube varies concomitantly with the changes in air pressure brought about by evacuating the container in which the barometer had been placed. Before the time of Torricelli and Boyle, the behavior of the liquid in such a tube was explained by saying that "nature abhors a vacuum." Today, we often use inches of mercury as a measure of atmospheric pressure.

Using the method of concomitant variation, we show that one condition is causally related to another by showing that when one of them is varied the other varies in a corresponding way. This method is familiar from many everyday uses.

i]     We know that there is a causal relation between the speed of an automobile and the amount of pressure applied to the accelerator; the more you push down on the gas pedal, the faster the car goes.

Sometimes there is an inverse relation; an increase in one variable results in a decrease in the other. For instance,

j]     The amount of time a piece of meat is cooked is causally related to its color. The longer it is cooked, the less red it becomes.

Although Mill's methods give us important insights into reasoning about causal relations and the kinds of arguments that are helpful in this regard, there are some further refinements that must be added if we are to bring the discussion up to date. In particular, we must take account of the fact that statistical considerations often play an indispensable role in studies of causal relations. We shall return to this point in the next section after discussing a basic causal fallacy. The controlled experiment, which will be introduced in section 29, is a natural extension of Mill's methods and a powerful antidote for several causal fallacies.

## 29. CAUSAL FALLACIES AND CONTROLLED EXPERIMENTS

Now that we have discussed some standard types of arguments used in connection with investigations of causal relations, it is time to turn our attention to some common mistakes in reasoning about causes—in other words, causal fallacies. The first of these had traditionally been called *post hoc; ergo, propter hoc* (which may be translated, "after this; therefore, because of this"); we shall call it the *post hoc fallacy*. This is the fallacy of concluding that X was caused by A just because X followed A. Popular medical ideas are often based upon this fallacy.

*a*]     Uncle Harry felt a cold coming on, so he took several stiff shots of whiskey.
         That cleared it up in a hurry.

In this case drinking whiskey is supposed to be the cause of the recovery, but all we have observed is that the cold cleared up *after* he took it. The fact that colds generally last only a few days, regardless of treatment—indeed, many incipient colds never develop—makes it easy to attribute curative powers to all sorts of things that are actually worthless. The fallacy is psychologically reinforced, of course, if the conclusion is a pleasant one, that is, if Uncle Harry is happy to have any excuse to take a few stiff shots.

The *post hoc* fallacy is often combined with the fallacy of insufficient statistics, as it is in *a*. However, it need not be.

*b*]     It is reported that the ancient Chinese believed that a lunar eclipse occurred
         when a dragon tried to devour the moon. They set off fireworks to scare the
         dragon away, leaving the moon behind. Their attempts were successful, for
         the moon always reappeared. They concluded that there was a causal rela-
         tionship between shooting off fireworks and the reappearance of the moon.

This example involves many instances, so it is not a case of insufficient statistics, as in *a;* nevertheless, it exemplifies the *post hoc* fallacy.

The *post hoc* fallacy consists in ascribing a causal relation on the basis of inadequate evidence; it leads to the error of mistaking a coincidence for a causal relation. The problem of distinguishing between genuine causal relations and mere coincidences is a tricky one, and it has vast practical importance. The widespread practice of psychotherapy provides a good example.

*c*]     Many people undertake lengthy and expensive psychotherapy in order to be
         freed of troublesome psychological problems, and many of the people who
         undergo such treatment experience noticeable lessening or complete disap-
         pearance of their neurotic symptoms. One might therefore argue that psy-
         chotherapy is responsible for the improvement. It is well known, however,
         that many neurotic symptoms disappear spontaneously, regardless of treat-
         ment. The question, then, is whether the symptoms went away because of the
         treatment, or whether they would have gone away anyhow.

The *post hoc* fallacy has a strong psychological appeal in this context. If an individual undertakes psychotherapy and experiences noticeable improve-ment, it is natural to attribute the improvement to the treatment. Most people would prefer to believe that the outcome resulted from their expen-diture of time, effort, and money in psychotherapy rather than to entertain seriously the possibility that the improvement would have occurred regardless. In addition, the therapist is likely to reinforce the conviction, for the vast majority of psychotherapists sincerely want to believe that they are doing worthwhile work. And when the former patients talk to their friends they are apt to report, "I went to Dr. Jones for two years, and he helped me a great deal," or "I spent four years in psychoanalysis, and I benefitted enormously from it."

The problem of the causal efficacy of psychotherapy obviously has great import for anyone contemplating spending much time and thousands of dollars on extensive psychiatric treatment. Moreover, the federal government has recently commissioned a large study of just this question, because it is concerned about the advisability of expending federal funds on psychiatric aid for such groups as veterans and medicare patients.

The fundamental technique used to ascertain whether a causal relation—rather than a mere coincidence—does obtain is the controlled experiment.[10] Let us see how that works.

Hardly a week goes by without some story appearing in the newspaper about a suspected causal relationship—very often one that involves our health. During the past twenty to thirty years, we have been told that heavy cigarette smoking *causes* lung cancer, that exposure to radiation *causes* leukemia, that use of oral contraceptives *causes* thrombosis (blood clots), and that saccharin *causes* cancer of the bladder (in rats, at least). The striking feature of all of these claims is that they fall far short of constituting either sufficient or necessary causes. Neither *all* nor *only* heavy smokers contract lung cancer, neither *all* nor *only* those who have been subjected to unusually strong radiation contract leukemia, etc. Indeed, in example *h* of section 27 (the investigation of childbed fever by Semmelweis), the same was true. In fact, that example is typical of causal studies. The basic situation involves two groups; in the Semmelweis example, there were the women in the First Maternal Division and the women in the Second Maternal Division. The fundamental fact was that childbed fever occurred in a noticeably higher percentage of cases in the one group than in the other. By using an approach that has some resemblance to Mill's joint method, Semmelweis established the connection between the contaminated hands of the examiners and the occurrence of childbed fever. However, it was not that every woman examined by a student or physician who had been performing dissections contracted childbed fever, or that every woman who was not examined by such persons avoided the disease. What did happen was that the frequency of the disease differed markedly between the two groups.

In order to see clearly what is going on in the Semmelweis study, it will be helpful to introduce a schema analogous to the one we used (schema *g*, section 28) to explain Mill's joint method:

---

[10]For an excellent introductory survey of the nature of controlled experiments, their uses, and their limitations, see Giere, *Understanding Scientific Reasoning*, chap. 11–12.

$d$]  $ABCD \rightarrow X$          $(not\text{-}A)\ BCD \rightarrow not\text{-}X$
     $ABCE \rightarrow not\text{-}X$       $(not\text{-}A)\ BCE \rightarrow not\text{-}X$
     $ABDF \rightarrow X$         $(not\text{-}A)\ BDF \rightarrow X$
     $ACDG \rightarrow X$        $(not\text{-}A)\ CDG \rightarrow not\text{-}X$

This schema is, of course, quite incomplete, for it is meant to represent a large number of cases in which $A$ is present and a large number of cases in which $A$ is absent. Although $X$ is not present in every case in which $A$ is present, nor absent in each case in which $A$ is absent, it does indicate that $X$ is present in a distinctly larger percentage of cases in which $A$ is present than it is when $A$ is absent.

Schema $d$ can appropriately be called the schema of the *controlled experiment*. It represents the most basic method for investigating causal relationships. The idea is this: If $A$ is to be considered the cause of $X$, the presence of $A$ must make a difference to the occurrence of $X$. Only in a few exceptional cases do we have the sort of situation found in example $f$ of section 28, where $X$ occurs if and only if $A$ is present; in the usual case, the presence of $A$ merely serves to enhance the probability that $X$ will occur.

To determine whether psychotherapy has any curative value (example $c$) it is necessary to compare the proportions of people who improve during treatment (or shortly thereafter) with the spontaneous remission rate. More precisely, we should examine two groups of people: a group that receives psychotherapy (the *experimental group*) and one that does not (the *control group*). These two groups should be as similar to one another as possible. The types of psychological problems, and their severity, should be the same in the two groups. Each group should contain the same proportion of males and females. The ages of the members of the two groups should match closely. The setup should be similar to that represented by the schema for Mill's joint method (schema $g$ of the preceding section). There is, however, no presumption that every person in the experimental group (those who receive treatment) will show improvement and that none of the people in the control group (those who do not receive treatment) will get better. In fact, then, it is schema $d$ of this section that best represents what is to be done here. If it should turn out that the rates of improvement in the two groups are the same, this would be strong evidence against the claim that psychotherapy has causal efficacy in bringing about cures.

The use of experimental controls is further illustrated by the problem of cold remedies. Perhaps no one seriously believes that whiskey really works; however,

$e$]  For some time there has been a controversy about the value of vitamin C for the prevention and/or cure of colds. Various studies seemed to show that it has no such therapeutic value, but Linus Pauling, a Nobel-laureate chemist, has argued strongly for the efficacy of vitamin C.[11] Regardless of who is right, the matter has to be settled in the following way. Two similar groups of individuals are selected. One group is given vitamin C; the other is not. It is essential, of course, that the subjects not know whether they are getting the vitamin C, for great is the power of suggestion. The correct procedure is to give a placebo (a substance known to have no medicinal value) to the control group. Indeed, even the persons who administer the medication should not know which subjects are receiving the vitamin C and which the placebo, for they might unwittingly convey some hint to the subjects in the experiment.

This experimental procedure is called *double-blind,* for neither the subject nor the person who gives out the pills knows which is which. We observe both groups to see whether the experimental group has a smaller frequency of colds or colds of less duration and severity. If the group that has been taking vitamin C is noticeably better off, this supports the claim that vitamin C really does help in the prevention, amelioration, or cure of colds. If the two groups are about the same, the evidence is against the causal efficacy of vitamin C.

The ancient Chinese could have conducted an experiment by refraining from the use of fireworks during one or more eclipses to learn whether their noise actually caused the reappearance of the moon. Of course, they might not have wanted to take that kind of chance on losing the moon forever. This illustrates one of the serious practical problems associated with controlled experiments. Who wants to be a member of the group that has more cavities?

The *post hoc* fallacy is one that is committed often, and it has a great deal of popular appeal in many contexts. Many superstitions probably arise from it. Example *e* of section 22—the case of the woman who explained her winning of the lottery in terms of astrological considerations—is an excellent illustration of this point. She won the $5.5 million *after* choosing numbers on the basis of dates of birth of members of her family. The fact that she chose the numbers in that way had no *causal* relevance to the fact that her ticket was drawn. Another typical example was mentioned in *e* and *f* of section 27, where I referred to the belief that the appearance of a birthmark on a baby is a result of something frightening that the mother experienced while she was pregnant. If the birthmark is shaped even vaguely like a bat, and if the mother saw a bat during her pregnancy, then a causal connection is inferred. Such are the origins of many "old wives' tales."

Human beings seem generally to have an overwhelming desire to provide a causal explanation for any important or striking occurrence. In earlier days (before Isaac Newton), even highly educated people "explained" an epidemic of the plague on the basis of the appearance of a

---

[11]Linus Pauling, *Vitamin C and the Common Cold* (San Francisco, Calif.: W. H. Freeman and Co., 1970).

large comet shortly before. Now we have a fairly good scientific under-standing of both comets and the plague. More recently, unusually severe weather has been "explained" in terms of detonations of nuclear bombs. (I am not for a moment suggesting that atmospheric nuclear tests have no harmful effects, but only that severe weather is probably not one of them.) It is, of course, desirable to try to find explanations for occurrences that interest us. The mistake is to jump to conclusions about causal relations on the basis of extremely inadequate evidence.

In dealing with the *post hoc* fallacy, we have been concerned with the problem of distinguishing cases in which a genuine causal relationship exists from cases in which there is merely some sort of coincidence. Howev-er, even if we have established the fact that a causal relationship exists, we may still possibly make an error about the type of causal relationship it is. Given that A and B are causally related, there are three basic relationships that might obtain: A causes B, B causes A, or both A and B have a common cause C. The next causal fallacy consists of mistaking one kind of causal

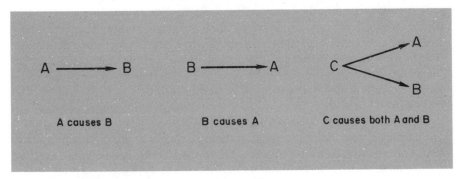

**Figure 15**

relation for another. It takes the form of concluding that A causes B on the basis of the fact that A and B are causally related. We shall call it the *fallacy of confusing an effect with a cause.*

There are two main ways in which this fallacy can occur. First, even when there is a direct causal relationship between two events, it is possible to regard the cause as the effect and the effect as the cause.

♫   A young woman who was working for a master's degree, reading a study of sexual behavior, learned that intellectuals generally prefer to have the lights on during sexual intercourse, and nonintellectuals generally prefer to have the lights off. Since her master's examinations were about to occur, she insist-ed upon having the lights on in the hope that it would improve her chances of passing the examinations.

Common sense tells us that she was confusing an effect with a cause. Other cases are not quite so obvious.

g]    A nineteenth-century English reformer noted that every sober and indus-
      trious farmer owned at least one or two cows. Those who had none were
      usually lazy and drunken. He recommended giving a cow to any farmer who
      had none, in order to make him sober and industrious.

Our immediate reaction to this example might be to say that the farmers
who were lazy and drunken must have lost whatever cows they had because
of those character defects, but that is not necessarily the actual situation. It
is possible that some of them never had any cows in the first place. It may
be, in other cases, that adverse circumstances over which they had no
control caused them to lose their animals, and that their laziness and drinking resulted from the feeling of helplessness that ensued. We would need
to have a good deal more information about the actual situation in order to
choose between these alternatives. If, however, a controlled experiment
had been performed at the time, it might have provided an answer to the
question. By selecting two groups of cowless farmers who were lazy and
drunken, and by giving a cow to each member of one group but none to
any member of the other group, it would have been possible to see whether
there was an increase in sobriety and industry among the farmers who
received cows as compared to those who did not. Those who received cows
might have renewed their hopes and worked hard to take advantage of the
new opportunity, or they might have sold the cow without much delay in
order to buy additional supplies of strong drink.

   We were fairly sure, in example f, that a cause had been confused with an
effect, but if there were any serious doubt, the issue could be settled by
means of a controlled experiment. Among a class of students taking a given
type of examination, we might get some volunteers to take part in an
experiment. Those in the control group would agree to keep the lights out
during intercourse; those in the experimental group would agree to have
the lights on. We must, of course, use some random method to choose
which volunteers go into which group. To let the volunteers decide would
obviously undermine the very purpose of the study. Comparison of the
examination scores should furnish the evidence needed to determine what
is the cause and what is the effect.

   Let us turn to the second way in which the fallacy of confusing an effect
with a cause can occur. Two events may be causally related even though
neither is the cause of the other; instead, both may be effects of a third
event, which is the cause of both of them (see Fig. 15). For example,

h]    Storm conditions can cause the reading on the barometer to fall and the river
      to rise. The falling barometric reading does not cause the rising of the river.
      The rising of the river does not cause the barometric reading to go down.

The error that may occur is to suppose that one of the effects of the
common cause is the cause of the other, all the while ignoring the third

event, which is the common cause of both. No one would be likely to make this mistake in the case of the barometer and the river, but in other cases it does occur.

i]  John, a freshman in college, stutters badly and is very shy with girls. His roommate suggests that he take speech correction lessons so that he will be cured of stuttering and, as a result, will feel less uneasy with girls. The roommate believes that stuttering is the cause of shyness with girls. According to many professional psychologists, however, both the stuttering and the shyness may be symptoms of another underlying psychological problem.

As example i shows, the fallacy of confusing an effect with a cause can have serious practical consequences. It sometimes leads people to confuse symptoms with underlying causes.

j]  In newspapers and magazines we are frequently reminded that genital herpes has reached epidemic proportions. No cure for this disease is known, though there is an effective treatment for the painful sores that are its main symptom. However, removing the symptom does not remove the disease. The sores can recur in persons who have the disease, and they can transmit it to sexual partners or—in the case of expectant mothers—to their newborn babies (in normal deliveries while the disease is active).

This example shows, incidentally, that knowing what causes a phenomenon does not necessarily make it possible for use to prevent it. The virus that causes genital herpes has been identified, but no cure has yet been found. This is not to say the treatment of symptoms is unimportant—quite the contrary. It is just that we should not suppose that relieving the symptoms is the same thing as curing the disease.

In closing this discussion of causal reasoning, I want to offer some words of warning. First, the concept of causality is extremely difficult, and it is surrounded with long-standing philosophical controversy. I have deliberately tried to avoid entanglement with deep philosophical issues. Instead, the discussion has been conducted at a fairly commonsense level. We do not need to enter into great philosophical subtleties in order to deal with the basic forms of argument and the simple causal fallacies.

Second, the causal relationships that exist in the real world are usually more complicated than the simple cause-effect relation.

k]  An automobile accident may be a result of a combination of circumstances. The road, for example, may have been wet because of rain. One of the cars might have had faulty brakes. One of the drivers might have been distracted by an unruly child. Vision at the intersection might have been restricted by an untrimmed bush.

In most cases, as in the foregoing example, there are many different causal factors involved. Oftentimes, moreover, there are complicated causal interconnections. The familiar feedback loop provides a simple example.

*l]*     Many homes are heated by a furnace that is controlled by a thermostat; the
         thermostat is set to keep the house at a certain temperature—say 68 degrees.
         When the house temperature falls below that point, the thermostat is acti-
         vated and it turns the furnace on. The furnace then heats the house. When
         the temperature reaches the desired level, the thermostat turns the furnace
         off. The fact that the furnace is not operating allows the temperature in the
         house to fall, and then the thermostat again turns the furnace on. The ther-
         mostat turns the furnace on *in order to* keep the house at the desired 68 degree
         temperature. It seems as if the achievement of the correct temperature is
         what causes the furnace to turn on or off.

Feedback loops are sometimes confusing because they can give the appearance of involving two events, each of which is the cause of the other,
and each of which is the effect of the other. The temperature in the house
seems to control the furnace, by means of the thermostat, and the operation of the furnace determines the temperature in the house.

Although some philosophers have found subtle reasons to doubt that
causes can never follow their effects, it will be safe to make the commonsense assumption in the sorts of examples we are discussing that causes do
not come after their effects. It is true that the furnace operates in order to
bring the house temperature up to 68 degrees, but the fact that the temperature *later* rises to that point is not the cause of the furnace beginning to
operate *now*. The furnace turns on now because the temperature *has already*
fallen below 68 degrees. The fact that the furnace is operating now will
cause the house temperature to rise in the near future. That, in turn, will
cause the thermostat to turn the furnace off. Because the furnace is off, the
temperature in the house will again fall below 68 degrees, and another
similar cycle will take place. But each event in the sequence is caused by a
prior event; in no case does a later event cause an earlier one.

If events happen in a clear temporal succession, it is usually easy to avoid
the mistake, exemplified in *f*, of taking the effect to be the cause and the
cause to be the effect. The same consideration enabled us to sort out the
cause-effect relations in *l*. Example *g*—which concerns the farmers and
their cows—is more difficult, because we have not been given any such
temporal information, and also because a large number of causal factors
may be involved. Moreover, the situation may be further complicated by
the presence of feedback loops. A farmer's drinking may, for example,
irritate his wife and produce family tensions which, in turn, lead him to
drink even more. Or his pessimistic outlook may reinforce the pessimism of
his neighbors who are in the same situation, and their response may serve
to deepen his feelings of discouragement.

Even in such complex cases, an experimental approach is often helpful.
If a circumstance *A* is a causal factor in bringing about an event *B*, then a
change in *A* may bring about a change in *B*. This is an important application of Mill's method of concomitant variation. If *A* is even a partial cause

of *B*, and if *A* is varied, then we may be able to observe a variation in *B*. If, however, *B* is a cause of *A*, then a variation in *A* will not bring about any change in *B*.

There is one important kind of variation which Mill did not mention explicitly in connection with his method of concomitant variation, namely, variation in the *frequency* with which a phenomenon occurs. As we have seen, this sort of *statistical* variation plays a prominent role in controlled experiments. By varying one condition in the childbed fever investigation—i.e., handwashing in chlorinated lime—Semmelweis produced a variation in the frequency with which childbed fever occurred in the First Maternity Division. By varying the amount of saccharin ingested by experimental animals, scientists produced varying frequencies of bladder cancer. If humans are exposed to varying amounts of radiation, as were the residents of Hiroshima and Nagasaki in World War II, the incidence of leukemia is found to vary.

As I said, causal relations often are extremely complex. Unless we have some idea of what is related to what, we cannot get far in our efforts to establish general causal laws. We need to be able to make some reasonable guesses even to get started, and a fair amount of background information is usually required in order to come up with any plausible candidates. Such guesses are known as *hypotheses*. If we have some causal hypotheses, the methods that have been discussed in sections 28 and 29 provide basic tools for testing these notions. In the next section, we shall move on to a more general discussion of the use and testing of causal hypotheses—and hypotheses of other sorts as well.

## 30. HYPOTHESES

People, nowadays, hold a wide range of attitudes toward science. Some extol the benefits that come from breathtaking technological advances; others decry the nuclear weapons and ecological dangers that intrude so insistently upon the present scene. It is not our business, in this book, to pass judgment upon the *fruits* of modern science; our concern is with the nature of scientific *knowledge*. We must begin by making a clear distinction between *pure science* as a knowledge-seeking venture and *applied science* as the practical application of such knowledge. It is one thing to understand nuclear fusion, the process by which the sun produces incredible amounts of radiant energy; it is quite another to decide to put that knowledge to use in the construction of hydrogen bombs. We must be careful not to confuse science with technology. For better or for worse, science seems unquestionably to provide the most comprehensive and most systematic knowledge we have about our world. We shall attempt to analyze the kind of reasoning involved in establishing such knowledge. It is only when we look at the way induction is used in science that we can fully appreciate the power and importance of inductive reasoning.

It is a commonplace that the essence of science rests in its ability to establish, on the basis of observational evidence, far-reaching hypotheses about nature. Our task in this section will be to examine the kinds of inductive argument that occur when observational evidence is used to confirm or disconfirm scientific hypotheses. These arguments are often complex and subtle in detail, but they exhibit an overall logical structure that is simple enough to be examined profitably in a relatively short treatment. At the same time, it is important to realize that we shall be treading on controversial territory, for the full analysis of arguments of this sort is one of the most vexing problems of contemporary inductive logic.[12]

From the outset, we should be clear about the meaning of the word "hypothesis." Various distinctions are sometimes made among hypotheses, theories, and laws. For our purposes, it will be safe to ignore these distinctions and use the term "hypothesis" broadly enough to comprehend all of them. In our usage, then, Kepler's *laws* of planetary motion and Einstein's *theory* of relativity will qualify as hypotheses. As we shall use the term, a statement is functioning as a hypothesis if it is taken as a premise, in order that its logical consequences can be examined and compared with facts that can be ascertained by observation. When the comparison is favorable, that is, when a consequence of the hypothesis turns out to be true, it is a *confirmatory instance* of the hypothesis. When a consequence turns out to be false, it is a *disconfirmatory instance* of the hypothesis. A hypothesis is *confirmed* if it is adequately supported by inductive evidence. There are degrees of confirmation; a hypothesis may be highly confirmed, moderately confirmed, or slightly confirmed. Likewise, there are degrees to which a hypothesis is confirmed by a confirmatory instance. A given confirmatory instance may add considerable support or only slight support to a hypothesis; indeed, in certain special cases a confirmatory instance may not actually confirm the hypothesis at all. These are matters we shall investigate.

Statements of many different types may occur as hypotheses; for instance, some hypotheses are universal generalizations and some hypotheses are statistical generalizations.

*a*]  According to Hooke's law, the force required to produce a distortion in an elastic object (such as a steel spring) is directly proportional to the amount of distortion. A particular spring has been observed to elongate by one inch when a force of five pounds is applied. A force of ten pounds is now applied. It follows that the spring will be elongated by two inches. If the spring is, indeed, elongated by two inches, this constitutes a confirmatory instance of Hooke's law.

---

[12]See Wesley C. Salmon, *The Foundations of Scientific Inference* (Pittsburgh, Pa.: University of Pittsburgh Press, 1967), chap. VII.

*b*]     If a fair coin is tossed repeatedly, heads and tails occur randomly and equally
        often in the long run. It can be shown that there is a probability of 0.95 that
        100 tosses of such a coin will contain between 40 and 60 heads. Consider the
        hypothesis that a particular coin is fair. Several experiments are made with
        this coin, each experiment consisting of 100 tosses. In each case, the number
        of heads is between 40 and 60. Under suitable conditions, these results would
        confirm the hypothesis that the coin is fair.

These examples are similar in certain respects, but there are important
differences. The hypothesis in *a* is a universal generalization; it permits us
to *deduce* that the spring will be elongated by two inches. The hypothesis in
*b* is a statistical generalization; in this case, the conclusion that 40 to 60
heads will be obtained is *inductive*. The deduction in *a* can be put into the
form of affirming the antecedent (section 7); the induction in *b* can be
represented as a statistical syllogism (section 23).

Having suggested that there are important similarities between the confirmation of statistical and universal hypotheses, we shall forego further
discussion of the confirmation of statistical hypotheses. Mathematical statistics provides powerful methods for dealing with problems of this kind.[13]
From here on, we shall confine our attention to the confirmation of hypotheses in terms of their deductive consequences. This kind of argument
is often called the *hypothetico-deductive method;* it is exemplified by *a*. As it is
frequently characterized, the hypothetico-deductive method consists of (1)
setting up a hypothesis, (2) deducing consequences from the hypothesis,
and (3) checking by observation to see whether these consequences are
true. Calling the deduced consequences *observational predictions,* we have the
following schema:

*c*]     Hypothesis
        ∴Observational prediction

The argument from the hypothesis to the observational prediction is supposed to be deductive; the argument from the truth of the observational
prediction to the truth of the hypothesis is supposed to be inductive.

The first thing to notice is that the hypothesis of *a*, Hooke's law, is a
general statement about the behavior of elastic bodies under the influence
of deforming forces. As such, it does not, by itself, entail the occurrence of
any particular events. The hypothesis is not the only premise in the deduction. It does not follow from the hypothesis alone that the spring will be
elongated by two inches; in addition, premises are needed to say how stiff
the spring is and how much force is being applied. These are the conditions
under which Hooke's law is being tested, and the premises that state these

[13]Giere, *Understanding Scientific Reasoning*, chap. 11, provides an excellent introductory treatment of statistical hypothesis testing.

facts are called *statements of initial conditions*. In every case, not just example *a*, the deduction of observational predictions for the confirmation of a general hypothesis requires premises formulating initial conditions. Schema *c* is incomplete; if the deduction is to be valid it must take the following form:

*d*]     Hypothesis (Hooke's law).
         Statements of initial conditions (a force of five pounds elongates the spring by one inch; a force of ten pounds is being applied).
         ∴Observational prediction (the spring will be elongated by two inches).

In the simple example *a* there is no trouble in ascertaining the initial conditions, and there is no trouble in finding out whether the observational prediction is true. In more complicated examples, these matters would present more difficulty.

*e*]     Using his general theory of relativity as a hypothesis, Einstein deduced that light rays passing near the sun would be bent. During the solar eclipse of 1919, observations were made that proved to be in close agreement with the predicted deflection. Einstein's theory was dramatically confirmed by these findings.

Example *e*, like example *a*, has the form *d*. In this case, however, the verification of the statements of initial conditions and the verification of the deduced observational prediction are much more complicated. For instance, the amount of the deflection depends upon the mass of the sun, so the statements of initial conditions must include a statement about the mass of the sun. This cannot be ascertained by direct observation; it must be calculated by using well-established theoretical methods. Similarly, the deflection of the light ray cannot be observed directly; it must be inferred by well-established methods from the relative positions of certain spots on photographic plates.

The inferences used in *e* to establish the statements of initial conditions involve *auxiliary hypotheses*. The inference used to determine the truth of the observational prediction involves other auxiliary hypotheses. In this respect, example *e* is quite typical. These auxiliary hypotheses are hypotheses that have previously and independently been confirmed by scientific investigation. Among the auxiliary hypotheses used to establish the truth of the observational prediction are hypotheses concerning the photochemical effects of light upon photographic emulsions and optical hypotheses concerning the behavior of light passing through telescopes. The auxiliary hypotheses can be used because they have been highly confirmed, but this does not assure absolutely that they can never be disconfirmed by future scientific findings.

Since we are dealing with the logical structure of the hypothetico-deductive method, let us examine schema *d* under some simplifying assumptions.

To begin with, let us assume that any auxiliary hypotheses used to establish statements of initial conditions, or to establish the truth or falsity of the observational prediction, are true. Indeed, let us further assume that the statements of initial conditions are true and that we have correctly determined the truth or falsity of the observational prediction. Under these assumptions, we have a valid deductive argument with only one premise, a hypothesis, whose truth is in question. Suppose, now, that the argument has a false conclusion. What can we say about the questionable premise?

The answer to this question is easy. A valid deductive argument with a false conclusion must have at least one false premise. Since the hypothesis is, according to our assumptions, the only premise that could possibly be false, we must conclude that the hypothesis is false. In this case, the hypothesis is conclusively disconfirmed. We have an instance of denying the consequent (section 7).

*f*]     If the hypothesis is true, then the prediction is true (since we are assuming the statements of initial conditions are true).
The prediction is not true
∴The hypothesis is not true.

The conclusiveness of this disconfirmation rests, of course, upon our simplifying assumptions. The only way a hypothesis can validly be maintained in the face of a disconfirming instance is either by rejecting a statement of initial conditions or by deciding that the observational prediction came true after all. Either of these alternatives might, of course, involve rejection of one or more auxiliary hypotheses. By our simplifying assumptions we ruled out both of these possibilities. In practice, however, there are cases in which we would retain the hypothesis and modify our judgments about initial conditions or about the falsity of the observational prediction. There are famous examples in the history of science that illustrate the successful adoption of this course.

*g*]     Prior to the discovery of the planet Neptune, it was found that Uranus moved in an orbit that differed from the orbit predicted on the basis of Newton's theory and the initial conditions involving the known bodies in the solar system. Instead of rejecting Newton's theory, Adams and Leverrier postulated the existence of the planet Neptune to account for the perturbations of Uranus. Neptune was subsequently discovered by telescopic observation. Revised initial conditions, incorporating facts about Neptune, made possible the deduction of the correct orbit of Uranus. A similar procedure later led to the discovery of Pluto.

This procedure is not always so successful.

*h*]     Leverrier attempted to account for known perturbations in the orbit of Mercury by postulating a planet Vulcan which has an orbit smaller than that of Mercury. Every attempt to locate Vulcan failed. It was only when Newton's theory was superseded by Einstein's general theory of relativity that Mercury's orbit was more satisfactorily explained. Observed facts concerning the motion of Mercury turned out, in the view of most theorists, to be a genuine disconfirmation of Newton's theory.

One important moral to be drawn from the foregoing examples is this. An apparent disconfirmation of a hypothesis is not satisfactorily dealt with until we have good grounds for making a correct prediction. If the hypothesis is rejected, it must be replaced by a hypothesis for which there is other evidence. For example, general relativity is not confirmed merely by its ability to account for the orbit of Mercury. Its ability to predict the results of observations during solar eclipse (example e) is independent evidence. If the statements of initial conditions are amended, there must be independent evidence that the revised statements are correct. For example, the planet Neptune had to be located telescopically. If auxiliary hypotheses are to be revised, there must be independent evidence for the correctness of the revised hypotheses.

Example g shows, incidentally, that hypotheses need not be universal statements. When Adams and Leverrier attempted to explain the perturbations of Uranus, they made the hypothesis that a previously undiscovered planet exists. This hypothesis, in conjunction with Newton's theory and other initial conditions, permitted deduction of the observed positions of Uranus. The truth of Newton's theory was assumed, and the observed facts were taken to confirm the hypothesis that Neptune exists. Having noted that singular statements may be treated as hypotheses, we shall continue to focus attention upon the confirmation of universal hypotheses.

The second question we must consider is far more difficult. Given a valid deductive argument with only one premise (a hypothesis) whose truth is in question, and given that this argument has a true conclusion, what can we conclude about the questionable premise? *Deductively,* we can draw no conclusion whatever. The following argument is an instance of the fallacy of affirming the consequent (section 7):

i]    If the hypothesis is true, then the prediction is true.
      The prediction is true.
      ∴The hypothesis is true.

It is, nevertheless, very tempting to suppose that *i* is a correct *inductive* argument. We do not want to say that arguments like *i* prove conclusively that hypotheses are true, but there does seem to be good reason for thinking that they support the hypothesis, lend weight to it, or confirm it to some extent. It appears that scientists make frequent use of arguments of the form *i,* and it would be most unreasonable to deny the correctness of the inductive arguments upon which science rests.

Unfortunately, appearances are deceiving. Arguments of form *i* are, as a matter of fact, extremely weak—if not wholly incorrect—even when we regard them as inductive arguments. The trouble is that $i$ is a gross over-simplification of the inductively correct argument used in the confirmation of scientific hypotheses. In particular, $i$ omits two essential aspects of the argument. In view of this fact, it should now be noted that the presentation of examples $a$ and $b$ was incomplete.

The first additional aspect of confirmation that must be considered is the bearing of alternative hypotheses upon the case. The question is: What are the chances that the deduced prediction would be true if the hypothesis we are testing is false and some other hypothesis is true? The same question may be reformulated: Are there other hypotheses that would be strongly confirmed by the same outcome? Consider another example.

$j$]    Small boys are often told that warts can be made to disappear if they are rubbed with onions. Such "cures" often work. The hypothesis is that rubbing with onions cures warts. The initial conditions are that Johnny has warts and he rubs his warts with onions. The observational prediction is that Johnny's warts will disappear. Johnny's warts do, in fact, disappear, and this constitutes a confirmatory instance for the hypothesis.

Has the hypothesis been confirmed by this observation? It is important to realize that there is an alternative explanation of the "cure" which is at least equally supported by the same results. It has been argued that warts are psychosomatic symptoms that can be cured by suggestion. Any method of treatment the patient sincerely believes to be effective will be effective. It is the belief in the treatment, rather than the treatment itself, that brings about the cure. If this alternative hypothesis is correct, then rubbing with grapes would be equally effective, and so would daily recitation of "Mary had a little lamb," provided the patient believes in these treatments. The fact that the observed result is a confirmatory instance of another hypothesis detracts from the confirmation of the hypothesis that onions cure warts. This situation calls for the use of controlled experiments of the sort discussed in section 29.

Example $j$ illustrates what is perhaps the most serious problem in the logic of the confirmation of hypotheses. The concept of a confirmatory instance of a hypothesis is defined by schema $d$; any instance of $d$ in which the conclusion is true provides a confirmatory instance of the hypothesis that stands as its first premise. If we write the schema containing only the statements whose truth has presumably been ascertained, we have the following incomplete deduction, which requires an additional premise to be valid:

$k$]    Statements of initial conditions.
       $\therefore$Observational prediction.

Generally speaking, a variety of statements can be added to an incomplete deduction to make it valid. Any such statement could, therefore, be taken as a hypothesis, and it would have a confirmatory instance in the fact that the observational prediction is true. Moreover, there are other statements of initial conditions, just as true as those actually used, which could have appeared in $k$. When the statements of initial conditions in $k$ are replaced by alternative statements of initial conditions, additional alternative hypotheses become available to allow the valid deduction of the same observational prediction. The fact that the observational prediction is true is, therefore, a confirmatory instance of these alternative hypotheses as well. There are, in fact, an infinite number of hypotheses for which any observed fact constitutes a confirmatory instance. The problem is to select the hypothesis, among all those that could have been used to deduce the observational prediction, that is most likely to be true.

The same situation holds for any finite number of confirmatory instances. Consider Hooke's law once more, and suppose it has been tested a number of times. The results for one elastic object, the steel spring of example $a$, are presented graphically in Fig. 16. The fact that Hooke's law applies to all elastic objects at all times and places, not just to one steel spring reinforces the point. Graphically, Hooke's law says that the plot of deformation against distorting force is a straight line, so the solid line in Fig. 16 represents Hooke's law. The encircled points represent the results

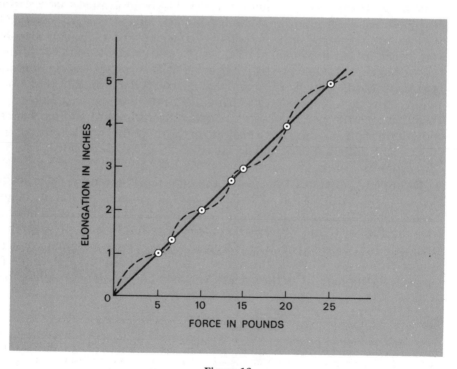

Figure 16

of testing. The broken line represents an alternative hypothesis for which these same results are confirmatory instances. An unlimited number of other curves could have been drawn through the encircled points. Of course, we can always perform additional tests to disconfirm the hypothesis represented by the broken line in the diagram; but for any finite number of additional tests, there will always be an infinite number of additional hypotheses. The problem is: On what grounds can Hooke's law be accepted and the alternative hypotheses be rejected, in view of the fact that the alternatives cannot all be disconfirmed by any finite amount of testing?

This problem leads to the consideration of the second aspect of confirmation that must be added to arguments of form *i*. In order to determine the extent to which a confirmatory instance actually supports a hypothesis, it is necessary to assess the *prior probability* of that hypothesis. The prior probability of a hypothesis is the probability, without regard for its confirmatory instances, that it is true. The prior probability is logically independent of the testing of the hypothesis by way of deduced consequences. In this context, the term "prior" has no temporal connotations. The prior probability may be assessed before or after confirmatory instances are examined; the point is that the examination of confirmatory instances does not affect the assessment of prior probability.

We have now entered the most highly contested area of the controversial territory of this section, for there is serious disagreement among experts concerning the exact nature of prior probabilities.[14] It seems clear, nevertheless, that scientists take them into account when they are considering the confirmation of scientific hypotheses. Scientists often speak of the reasonableness or plausibility of hypotheses; such judgments constitute assessments of prior probabilities. Prior probabilities are not merely measures of someone's subjective reaction to hypotheses, for some hypotheses have objective characteristics that make them antecedently more likely to be true than other hypotheses. Instead of attempting a general analysis of prior probabilities, let us examine a few examples of characteristics that have some bearing upon the prior probabilities of various hypotheses.[15]

*l*]    Simplicity is an important characteristic of Hooke's law, and this characteristic does not depend in any way upon its confirmatory instances. In this respect, Hooke's law is far more plausible than the alternative represented by the broken line in Fig. 16. To be sure, we would not continue to accept Hooke's law if it were disconfirmed by experimental test, but among those possible hypotheses for which the test results are confirmatory instances, Hooke's law

[14]See Salmon, *Foundations of Scientific Inference*, chap. VII, for discussion of a wide variety of views on this subject.

[15]Although these probabilities are often called "a priori probabilities," it should not be supposed that they are a priori in the philosophical sense, i.e., that they can be ascertained without recourse to experience. It is my firm conviction that they reflect our scientific experience in dealing with many types of hypotheses in a wide variety of circumstances.

has the highest prior probability. In the physical sciences, at least, experience has shown that simplicity is a characteristic of successful hypotheses.

m] Medical research scientists know enough in general about onions and warts to regard it as highly unlikely that onions contain any substance that would have any curative power when applied directly to warts. They would know this whether or not they had proceeded to examine confirmatory instances of the hypothesis of example *j*. This hypothesis has a low prior probability.

n] Hypotheses that are incompatible with well-established scientific hypotheses have low prior probabilities. It has sometimes been maintained that mental telepathy occurs in the form of instantaneous thought transfer from one mind to another. This particular telepathic hypothesis has a low prior probability, for it is incompatible with the requirement of relativity theory that no causal process (and, consequently, no process that transmits information) can be propagated with a velocity exceeding that of light.

o] The argument from authority and the argument against the person in their correct forms (sections 24 and 25) may be used to assess prior probabilities. In particular, a scientific hypothesis proposed by a "crank" will usually have a very low prior probability on this and other grounds. The prior probability may be so low that reputable scientists are properly unwilling to spend time subjecting such hypotheses to test.

p] During the thirteenth century A.D., a fairly large region surrounding the "four corners" (where Utah, Colorado, New Mexico, and Arizona meet) was rather densely populated, but in the latter part of the fourteenth century, much of this area was quite suddenly abandoned. Archaeologists are trying to figure out why this abandonment occurred. One possible hypothesis is that the people—who depended to a great extent upon agriculture for their food—left because of a drought. There is, in fact, strong evidence in tree rings that several years of very low rainfall occurred at the end of the fourteenth century. Most archaeologists, however, do not accept the drought as the entire causal explanation. For a variety of reasons, they are convinced that a much more complex explanation is required, and that the drought hypothesis is almost surely an oversimplification. Although the lack of rain played some role, no doubt, many other factors were probably involved. As we noted in the preceding section, causal relations are often quite complicated, and this consideration sometimes allows us to assign low prior probabilities to hypotheses that are too simple.

The assessment of prior probabilities is often a difficult and subtle matter. Fortunately, in many cases a very rough estimate may be sufficient; in fact, in many cases it is enough to know that the prior probability of a hypothesis is not negligibly low—that our hypothesis is not utterly implausible and unreasonable. If the prior probability of a hypothesis is virtually zero, a confirming instance supplies virtually no support for the hypothesis. Otherwise, a confirming instance may supply a significant amount of weight.

As a result of the foregoing discussion, it turns out the schema *i* does not adequately characterize the confirmation of scientific hypotheses. Although schema *i* does represent an indispensable part of the argument, it must be expanded by the addition of other premises. To be inductively correct, the hypothetico-deductive method must assume the following form:

*q*]     The hypothesis has a nonnegligible prior probability.
        If the hypothesis is true, then the observational prediction is true.
        The observational prediction is true.
        No other hypothesis is strongly confirmed by the truth of this observational prediction; that is, other hypotheses for which the same observational prediction is a confirming instance have lower prior probabilities.
        ∴The hypothesis is true.

This is an inductively correct form, and it correctly schematizes many important scientific arguments.

Although any group of experimental data constitutes confirmatory instances for an infinity of possible alternative hypotheses, it does not follow that alternative hypotheses with nonnegligible prior probabilities can always be found. Quite the contrary. Thinking up a plausible hypothesis to cover a particular set of observed facts is the most difficult part of creative scientific work, and it often requires genius. This is a problem of discovery, and logic has no royal roads to solve such problems. The result is that there is seldom a large number of competing hypotheses, for the alternative hypotheses with negligible prior probabilities are not really in the competition. They are the implausible—even preposterous—hypotheses. Thus, when a hypothesis that has an appreciable prior probability is found, it can be highly confirmed by its confirmatory instances. In the rarer cases in which there are several competing hypotheses with appreciable prior probabilities, disconfirmation assumes considerable importance.

Suppose we have a hypothesis *H* for which there are confirmatory instances. There is an unlimited supply of alternative hypotheses for which the same facts are also confirmatory instances. It is, therefore, hopeless to try to disconfirm all possible alternative hypotheses, leaving *H* as the only one that is not disconfirmed. We consider the prior probabilities. Suppose *H* has an appreciable prior probability, and furthermore, we can think of only one alternative hypothesis, *H'*, which also has an appreciable prior probability. If *H* and *H'* are genuinely different, not merely different ways of saying the same thing, there will be some situations in which they will yield different observational predictions. A *crucial test* can be performed by examining such a situation in order to determine which hypothesis, *H* or *H'*, yields the correct observational prediction. Since *H* and *H'* lead to incompatible observational predictions, the observational prediction deduced from at least one of them must be false. Finding that *H'* leads to a false observational prediction disconfirms it. If *H* leads to a true observational prediction, we have good reason to accept *H* as the only hypothesis

that is significantly confirmed by the observational evidence. $H'$ was disconfirmed, and all other alternatives fail to be substantially confirmed by their
confirmatory instances because of their negligible prior probabilities.

$r$]     At the beginning of the nineteenth century an important controversy concerning the nature of light occurred. Some physicists supported the hypothesis that light consists of corpuscles (particles), whereas others maintained
that it consists of waves. The French mathematician S. D. Poisson was able to
demonstrate that, if the wave theory were true, a bright spot should appear in
the center of the shadow of a small disk. As a supporter of the corpuscular
theory, he regarded this as a *reductio ad absurdum* (section 8), but when the
experiment was actually performed the bright spot was observed. This outcome was a dramatic confirmation of the wave theory, since there was no way
for the corpuscular theory to account for this phenomenon. According to the
corpuscular theory the shadow should be uniformly dark.

It should be re-emphasized that the whole procedure of confirmation of
hypotheses is inductive. This means that no scientific hypothesis is ever
completely verified as absolutely true. No matter how carefully and exten-
sively a hypothesis is tested, there is always the possibility that it may later
have to be rejected because of new disconfirming evidence. In inductive
arguments, no matter how much evidence the premises present, it is always
possible for the premises to be true and the conclusion false. There are
various sources of difficulty in the confirmation of scientific hypotheses.
We may make errors in assessing prior probabilities by supposing that a
hypothesis has a negligible prior probability when, in fact, its prior probability is quite high. There may be a hypothesis with higher prior probability
that has not yet occurred to anyone. A hypothesis with a very low prior
probability may turn out to be true; "improbable" does not mean "impossible." Observational and experimental errors are possible. False auxiliary
hypotheses may be accepted and used.

   In the confirmation of scientific hypotheses, as in other kinds of inductive argument, the best insurance against error is to take steps to avoid
accepting conclusions on the basis of insufficient or biased evidence (see
sections 21 and 22). This means that hypotheses must be tested many times
and under a wide variety of conditions if they are to become highly confirmed. Our discussion, so far, has concentrated upon the logical characteristics of the hypothetico-deductive method, schema $q$, much as if we
were dealing with a single application and a single confirmatory instance.
To do justice to scientific method, it is necessary to emphasize the repeated
application of this method to build up a large and heterogeneous body of
confirming evidence or to find disconfirming evidence if there is any. A
familiar classic example will illustrate the point.

$s$]     Newton's theory is a comprehensive hypothesis concerning the gravitational
forces among masses. It has been confirmed by an extremely large number of

observations of the motions of the planets in the solar system and their satellites. It has likewise been confirmed by an extremely large number of observations of falling objects. There are vast numbers of observations of the tides, and these constitute additional confirmatory instances. Torsion balance experiments, which measure the gravitational attraction between two objects in the laboratory, have been performed repeatedly, and these constitute further confirmations. Even with this impressive quantity and variety of confirmatory instances, which does not exhaust the supporting evidence, Newton's theory is not regarded as literally correct. Disconfirming evidence has been found, as illustrated by example *h*. It does serve, however, as an excellent approximation in limited domains of application, and as such, it is extremely highly confirmed.

To a large extent, the importance of Newton's theory lies in its comprehensiveness. It explains a wide variety of apparently diverse phenomena. Before Newton, Kepler had established laws of planetary motion and Galileo had established a law of falling bodies. The laws of Kepler and Galileo had seemed distinct until they were subsumed under Newton's theory, which explained many other facts as well. The unification of restricted hypotheses by means of more comprehensive hypotheses leads to the possibility of hypotheses that can be confirmed by vast amounts and varieties of evidence. Such hypotheses are rich in predictive and explanatory power.

In order to examine the logical characteristics of the confirmation of hypotheses, we have dealt mainly with scientific examples. Similar issues are involved in everyday life as well as in science, for we do make extensive use of hypotheses in the conduct of practical affairs. It does not matter much whether we call them "scientific hypotheses," for there is no sharp dividing line between science and common sense, and we all use a certain amount of scientific knowledge in guiding our decisions and actions. In sections 27 through 29 we discussed causal arguments and their importance in practical situations. Causal statements are hypotheses. Insofar as we accept and use causal hypotheses, to that extent, at least, we have reason to be concerned with the logic of the confirmation of hypotheses. Such hypotheses often play a crucial role in decisions respecting the matters most significant to us: our personal health, our moral attitudes, our relations with other people, the affairs of government, and international relations. Surely there is as much reason to insist upon logical accuracy in matters of practical importance as there is in the abstract pursuit of scientific truth.

# CHAPTER FOUR

# Logic and Language

In order to deal adequately with arguments it is necessary to pay close attention to the nature of language, for arguments, being composed of statements, are linguistic entities. Since language is an extremely complex tool, there are possibilities of error arising out of the use of language itself. This chapter will be devoted to a few important problems of language that have a direct bearing upon the logical correctness or incorrectness of arguments.

## 31. USE AND MENTION

Language operates by means of symbols. If we want to refer to some object—for example, a table—we *use* a word. In so doing, we *mention* the thing to which we are referring. The word is a linguistic entity that somehow has a meaning by virtue of which it stands for some nonlinguistic object. In the next section, we shall discuss the ways in which words are given meanings. There is no particular similarity between the word and the thing to which it refers. The word "table" has five letters but no legs; the table has four legs but it is not composed of letters. A table can be a very useful object for supporting a cup of coffee, but it would not fit conveniently between the covers of a book on interior decorating. The word "table" can easily be placed in a book, but it is no good at all for holding drinks. No one would ever be tempted to confuse the word "table" with the piece of furniture to which it refers, though in other contexts the confusion of the name with the object named can easily occur.

Sometimes we want to talk about language itself, as we have been doing constantly throughout this book. In that case, we follow the same procedure as with the table. In order to mention an entity—even if that entity is itself a linguistic object such as a word—we must make a name by means of which to refer to it. The standard practice is to enclose it in quotation marks; the word along with the surrounding quotation marks constitute a name for the word. We mentioned the word "table" three times in the preceding paragraph by using just such a symbol. The following two statements are both correct:

*a*]   The table has four legs.

*b*]   "Table" has five letters.

The following sentence is nonsense:

*c*]   Table has five letters.

It is ungrammatical, for it confuses use and mention of a word; it violates the general principle that to *mention* an object we must *use* a name that is distinct from the object being mentioned. The fact that we are talking about a word is no license to confuse the object being discussed with the words used in the discussion.

The danger of confusing use and mention can be illustrated with a mathematical example.

*d*]   $\frac{9}{12}$ has a nine in its numerator.
  $\frac{3}{4} = \frac{9}{12}$.
  $\therefore \frac{3}{4}$ has a nine in its numerator.

This argument might appear valid, for the conclusion results from the first premise by substituting equals for equals. Yet the premises seem to be true and the conclusion false.

In order to clarify this example, let us begin by noting that numbers are abstract objects of some sort, and numerals are the names we give to them. Twelve, for example, is the *number* of apostles; this number is designated by a variety of *numerals*—for example, "12," "XII," "a dozen," "$\frac{36}{3}$," etc. The first statement in argument *d* can only be construed as a statement about a numeral; as such, it is not correctly written. There is a certain rational number that is denoted by various numerals—for example, "$\frac{3}{4}$," "$\frac{6}{8}$," "$\frac{9}{12}$," "0.75." The last of these numerals is not written in fractional form, so it does not even have a numerator, and those that do have numerators have different ones. The conclusion is likewise a statement about a numeral. If we want to talk about numerals, we must make names for them, and we can do so by the method just described. When we rewrite the argument properly,

*e]*    "$9/12$" has a nine in its numerator.
       $3/4 = 9/12$.
       ∴"$3/4$" has a nine in its numerator.

we see that it loses any appearance of validity. Of course, we could make it into a valid argument by replacing the second premise,

*f]*    "$9/12$" has a nine in its numerator.
       "$3/4$" = "$9/12$."
       ∴"$3/4$" has a nine in its numerator.

but the second premise is now patently false, for it says that two numerals that are not at all alike are identical.[1]

The confusion of numbers with numerals seems nowhere so common as in talk of *numbers* to the base ten or binary *numbers*. Actually, there are no such things as binary numbers, any more than there are Roman numbers and Arabic numbers. Roman *numerals* and Arabic *numerals* are simply different ways of naming the very same numbers; decimal notation and binary notation are, likewise, two different systems of numerals for referring to the same numbers. Thus, for example, the statement

*g]*    The number 100 is a perfect square in the system of binary numbers as well as in the system of numbers to the base 10, for $100_2 = 4 = 2^2$ and $100_{10} = 10^2$

involves a horrible confusion. The correct statement is

*h]*    The symbol "100" is a numeral in both the base 2 notation and also the base 10 notation; in these two different systems of notation this numeral refers to two different numbers, but both of these numbers are perfect squares.

If the "new math," with its emphasis upon understanding mathematical concepts, should do anything, it ought to help us distinguish clearly be-

---

[1]The word "nine" in English is ambiguous; sometimes it stands for a number and sometimes for a numeral. This fact, no doubt, tends to facilitate the confusion of use and mention in arithmetical contexts. In arguments *d* to *f* we are obviously using "nine" as a name of an Arabic numeral.

The perceptive reader might ask why we reject argument *e*, since its conclusion seems to result from substitution of equals for equals inside the quotation marks in the first premise. What is wrong with that? The answer is that the name of the numeral used in the first premise must be taken as a single word, and that substitutions are not permitted for parts within words. Thus, even though ten equals five plus five, we will not tolerate a translation of "Ladies and gentlemen, your attention please!" into "Ladies and gentlemen, your atfive-plus-fivetion please!"

tween numbers and their names, but I fear that it has, with its extensive reference to different systems of numerals, actually engendered confusions like *g*.

Proper differentiation between the use and mention of symbols leads to the recognition of a hierarchy of languages. When we want to talk about one language—for example, French—we often do so in a different language—for example, English. The language being mentioned is the *object language* (it is the object of discussion), whereas the language being used to talk about it is the *metalanguage*. In a beginning French textbook written for English-speaking students, for instance, French would be the object language and English would be the metalanguage. If, however, the textbook is an English grammar written for English-speaking students, English constitutes both the object language and the metalanguage. In this case it is especially important to distinguish the instances in which English is the object language from those in which it is the metalanguage. The use of quotation marks to make names of linguistic expressions is extremely helpful in this regard. Consider, for example, statements *a* and *b; a* is in the object language, whereas *b* is in the metalanguage, for it contains an expression in quotes that is the name of a word in the object language. Likewise, the statement

*i*]     Man's mortality fills me with despair

is in the object language, and

*j*]     "All men are mortal" is a trite example of an *A* statement

is in the metalanguage.[2]

To emphasize the importance of observing the distinction between object language and metalanguage, consider an example famous from antiquity:

*k*]     Epimenides, the Cretan, says that all Cretans are liars.

Is his statement true or false? Neither answer seems acceptable. This is the *liar paradox;* it can be put in more modern dress and expressed more precisely in terms of the statement

*l*]     This statement is false.

---

[2]Displaying a statement or other expression on a separate line is also a way of mentioning it; such display is a satisfactory substitute for quotation marks. Using quotation marks for the same purpose, we could say, "The statement, 'All men are mortal,' is a trite example of an *A* statement" is a statement in the metalanguage. Here, we have alternated single quotes with double quotes for clarity, and we have *used* a sentence in the metametalanguage in order to *mention* a statement in the metalanguage. Evidently, we can construct as many levels as we wish in our hierarchy of languages.

Is statement *l* true? If so, it is false. Is statement *l* false? If so, it is true. We seem to have a statement that is false if and only if it is true. Such a statement is a plain contradiction. The source of the difficulty is that statement *l* violates the distinction between object language and metalanguage—that is to say, the distinction between use and mention—for it is being used to mention itself. We must rule it out as a nonsensical sentence that can be neither true nor false. We now realize that failure to respect these distinctions may lead to outright logical inconsistency.

## 32. DEFINITIONS

A word is a large class of physical things or events such as ink marks, graphite marks, or sound waves. A particular word is used many times; it has many occurrences. The word "language," for example, occurs frequently in the preceding section. It is the same word in each of these occurrences, and each occurrence is a physical thing. The word is the class of all such occurrences—oral or written—past, present, or future. Words are not, however, merely collections of physical things or events, for words have meaning. Words are symbols.

The meaning of a word is not a natural attribute that people discover; meaning is given to a word by people who agree to let it have that meaning. For example, there is no intrinsic characteristic of the word "cat" that makes it refer to feline animals; it does so because English-speaking people have adopted a convention to that effect. This is not intended to suggest that people once sat down at a conference table and formally decided the meaning of words. For the most part, these conventions, like many other conventions, have grown gradually and informally over a long period of time. As language continues to grow and develop, these conventions are still subject to change. The important fact is that other conventions could have been adopted without being false or incorrect. Indeed, there are many different languages—English, German, Russian, etc.—all with different conventions. None of these languages is false and none is "the true language."

A word has meaning if there is a convention establishing its meaning. Definitions express these conventions in the metalanguage. The convention may have been laid down formally by means of a definition, or it may have grown up informally by way of customary usage. In either case, the definition, as a formulation of a convention, is neither true nor false.

Offering a definition is like making a proposal. One may accept it or reject it, but the proposal, itself, is not true or false. If a young man's proposal, "Let's get married," met the response, "That's false," it would be a nonsensical reply. Likewise, there may be good reasons for rejecting a proposal to use a certain word in a certain way, but falsity is not one of them. Nor is truth a reason for accepting such a proposal.

Moreover, when the convention governing the meaning of a word has developed informally, a definition may be offered as an explicit formulation of that convention. Again, the definition is neither true nor false; it is more like a rule than like a statement of fact. Rules, like proposals, can be accepted or rejected, complied with or violated. For example, certain conventions of etiquette have developed informally in our culture. These conventions are formulated in rules such as, "Do not eat peas with your knife." This rule is neither true nor false, but statements that are true or false can be made about the rule. For instance, it is true to say that the foregoing rule expresses a currently accepted convention of etiquette. Similarly, although a particular definition is neither true nor false, the statement that this definition expresses an accepted convention is either true or false. It is important to realize that the statement about the definition is different from the definition itself.

In most cases, the meaning of a word has two aspects. Consider the word "logician." In the first place, this word refers to various people such as Aristotle, George Boole, Gottlob Frege, Bertrand Russell, Kurt Gödel, W. V. Quine, and many others. These people—that is, all people who are logicians—constitute the *extension* of the word "logician." The extension of a word consists of the class of all objects to which that word correctly applies. Extension is one aspect of the meaning of the word. In the second place, there are certain properties that distinguish logicians from all other people and things. A logician is a person who is skilled in logic. In order to qualify as a logician, an object must have the properties of being human and being skillful in logic. The *intension* of the word "logician" consists of these two properties. The intension of a word consists of the properties a thing must have in order to be in the extension of that word. The extension of a word is the class of *things* to which the word applies; the intension of a word is the collection of *properties* that determine the things to which the word applies.

There are many ways of specifying the meanings of words; consequently, there are many different types of definitions. To begin with, we may specify the meaning of a word through its extension, or we may specify its meaning through its intension. There is thus a basic distinction between *extensional definitions* and *intensional definitions*.

There are two fundamentally different ways of indicating the extensions of words. First, we may simply point to objects in the extension of the word. To give the meaning of the word "dog," we can point to a variety of dogs. This method of indicating the extension of the word is called *ostensive definition*. Another method of indicating the extension of a word is to name some of the objects in its extension (if the objects in the extension have proper names). Thus, one can mention examples of the extension of the word "dog" by naming various dogs: Fido, Rover, Spot, Rex, Beauregard, etc. An ostensive definition is a *nonverbal* extensional definition, for the meaning of the word is given, not by using other words to explain its meaning, but by pointing to the actual objects. Naming members of the extension, on the other hand, is *verbal* extensional definition, for the meaning of the word is explained by the use of other words, the names of the members of the extension.

Whether one gives the extension of a word verbally or nonverbally, it is usually impractical or impossible to indicate every member of the extension. It would be impossible to point out each member of the extension of the word "dog," because this word applies to dogs as yet unborn. Furthermore, it would be impractical to point out every living dog to show the meaning of the word, because there are so many dogs and they are so widely scattered. Very often, then extensional definitions consist of indicating, either verbally or nonverbally, some members of the extension, assuming that other members of the extension can be recognized on the basis of their similarity to the examples. This process of definition suffers some imprecision, yet the meanings of many words are effectively conveyed by extensional definitions.

A moment's reflection should be sufficient to realize that some words must be defined nonverbally. If the meaning of a word could be given only by using other words, it would be impossible to convey the meaning of any word. Unless some words had their meanings given nonverbally, there would be no words with meanings that could be used to explain the meanings of other words. Imagine finding a Sanskrit dictionary in which every Sanskrit word is defined in terms of other Sanskrit words. You could memorize every definition in that dictionary, but you would not know what any of the words mean, for you would not know to what things these words refer. Something like ostensive definition is necessary to relate some of the words to things; it is not sufficient merely to relate all of the words to each other.

Intensional definitions are verbal. One important type of intensional definition is the *explicit definition*. An explicit definition consists of giving a word or phrase that means the same as the word being defined. For example,

a]   "Mendacious" means "deceitful."
    "Pentagon" means "five-sided plane figure."
    "Bachelor" means "unmarried adult male."

In each case, the word being defined appears on the left; it is called the *definiendum*. The word or phrase on the right does the defining; it is called the *definiens*. The definition itself occurs in the metalanguage as a proposal or rule about the use of words in the object language.

A definition is circular if the *definiendum* occurs in the *definiens*. For instance,

*b]*    "Pentagon" means "plane figure having the shape of a pentagon"

is circular because the word to be defined is used in giving the definition. Such definitions are useless. Definitions can also be circular in a less direct manner. For example, the following three definitions taken together are circular:

*c]*    "Mendacity" means "lack of veracity."
        "Veracity" means "absence of prevarication."
        "Prevarication" means "mendacity."

Three words are defined, but each is defined in terms of the other two. Unless a meaning is independently given for one of the three, none of them achieve meaning from this series of definitions.

Definitions of another type are often used to introduce new terms, or new meanings for old terms, in scientific contexts. The sciences—physical, biological, and social—endeavor to provide *precise* statements that contain *objective* information about the world. If this aim is to be achieved, scientific terms must have exact meanings in reference to objects and events found in the world. *Operational definitions* are often used by scientists to provide a suitable scientific vocabulary.[3]

The basic idea behind an operational definition is that a term is defined by specifying some *physical operation* that provides a criterion to determine whether the term applies to an object. Suppose, for instance, that we want to use the concept of temperature. We will need an appropriate way to measure temperature.

*d]*    To say, for example, that John Jones is running fever of 102 degrees *means:* If a suitably calibrated thermometer is placed in his mouth and held under his tongue long enough to come into thermal equilibrium with his body, the end of the mercury column will coincide with the mark labeled "102."

The concept of hardness of minerals can also be operationally defined.

*e]*    To say that diamonds are harder than glass *means:* If a sharp corner of a diamond is drawn firmly across a glass surface it will leave a scratch; if a sharp

---

[3]The term "operational definition," was invented by the physicist Percy W. Bridgman, who also advocated a philosophical view called *operationism* or *operationalism.* According to this doctrine, *every* legitimate scientific term must be operationally defined. In discussing operational definitions, I do *not* intend to advocate the operationist philosophy of science. We can readily admit that operational definitions are often useful without insisting that every scientific term must have an operational definition. I seriously doubt that the term "electron" can be defined operationally.

corner of a piece of glass is drawn firmly across the surface of a diamond it will not leave a scratch.

The concept of human intelligence has also been approached operationally. Psychologists have devised a number of intelligence tests and have defined the "intelligence quotient" or IQ. Some psychologists have used such intelligence tests as operational definitions of "intelligence."

*f]* To say that Mary Smith is more intelligent than John Brown *means* that Mary Smith achieved a higher IQ rating than did John Brown, based upon their scores on some particular intelligence test (e.g., the Stanford-Binet).

It should be explicitly recognized that the passing out of test papers, the marking of such papers by individuals taking the test, and the scoring of the answer sheet by an optical scanning device constitute a series of *physical* operations even though the term being defined refers to a psychological characteristic of human beings.

In each of the foregoing three examples it should be noted that we begin with an imprecise commonsense concept—temperature, hardness, intelligence. Everyone has a vague intuitive notion of what is meant by saying that today is a hot day or that someone is running a fever. We all have the same kind of intuitive idea of the meaning of the statement that granite is hard but chalk is not very hard. All of us have a similar sort of understanding of the claim that Einstein's intelligence was far above average. The aim of an operational definition is to render a term of that sort precise by specifying a definite operational procedure—placing a thermometer in the patient's mouth, drawing a sharp corner on one mineral across the surface of another, administering an IQ test. The operational definition *may* involve logical or mathematical manipulations, such as calculating an IQ from a raw test score, but it *must* involve some physical operation of the previously mentioned sort. Operational definitions share a fundamental property with ostensive definitions: Each provides some direct connection between the words in our language and the nonlinguistic physical facts that we want to be able to talk about. Operational definitions are extremely important, but they involve certain dangers and limitations, which will be discussed later.

Many words, like "dog," "run," and "red," refer to objects, events, or properties. Such words have extensions and intensions. Other words have meaning only as they function in a linguistic context. Words like "if," "unless," "the," "only," "is," "not," and "or" do not refer to anything. For instance, there is no such thing as an *unless,* there is no such event as *unlessing,* and there is no such property as *being unless.* Words of this sort have neither intension nor extension; in fact, they have no meaning in isolation. They have purely grammatical functions, and their meanings come from their function in providing structure for the statements in which they occur. We give the meanings of these words by showing how they function in a context. This method of specifying meanings is called *contextual definition.*

Since logic is primarily concerned with form or structure, many of the most important logical words are defined contextually. We have already encountered many such definitions. For example, in discussing categorical statements we had occasion to note that statements of type *A*, "All *F* are *G*," were equivalent in meaning to statements of the form "Only *G* are *F*." This is a contextual definition of the word "only." There is no single word or phrase that is equated in meaning to the word "only"; instead, the context in which the word "only" occurs has the same meaning as a statement that does not contain the word "only." The truth tables, for another example, provide contextual definitions of the truth-functional connectives.

Contextual definitions may be contrasted with explicit definitions on the following grounds. If a word that is explicitly defined occurs in a statement, we may replace the defined word by its *definiens* without changing the meaning of the statement.

*g*]    In the statement "Fred Smith is a bachelor," we may replace the word "bachelor" by the phrase "unmarried adult male," with the result that the statement "Fred Smith is an unmarried adult male" means the same as the original statement.

By contrast,

*h*]    In the statement "Only mammals are whales," our contextual definition does not provide any word or phrase with which to replace the word "only." Our definition does permit us to replace the whole statement in which the word "only" occurs with another statement, "All whales are mammals," which has the same meaning as the original statement. The meaning of the word "only" is specified by the definition, because the definition enables us to express, without using the word "only," what was originally expressed with the help of the word "only."

We have described some of the different types of definitions; now we must discuss some of the purposes definitions are designed to fulfill. Although definitions are not true or false, their adequacy can be judged in terms of their ability to fulfill certain functions.

1. Some definitions are designed to characterize the customary usage of a word. These definitions attempt to make explicit the conventions followed by people who speak the language, or perhaps those who speak it correctly. Definitions given in dictionaries have this function.

When we look up a word in the dictionary to find out what it means, it might be tempting to say that we find the true definition. A dictionary gives a large number of definitions, and these definitions purport to be conventions to which speakers of the language conform. A previous point applies here. For purposes of logical clarity, it is essential to distinguish carefully between definitions and statements about definitions. A definition itself has the force of a proposal to use a certain word with a certain meaning; as such, it is neither true nor false. The statement that a particular definition is the accepted one is a statement about the definition, not the definition itself. This statement is either true or false.

2. Sometimes we define a new word because there is no established way of briefly expressing an important meaning. For example, we might wish to make repeated reference to those months of the year that have fewer than thirty-one days. As a convenient abbreviation, we might coin the word "monette" and define it as "month having fewer than thirty-one days."

3. A word is *vague* if there are objects that are neither definitely included in nor definitely excluded from its extension. Definitions often have the purpose of making vague words more precise. For example, the word "rich" is vague. Some people have very little money; they are definitely not rich. Others have millions; they are definitely rich. Some people have quite a lot of money, but they are not fabulously wealthy. Even if we know how much money such people have, we cannot say whether they are rich or not because of the vagueness of the word "rich." We might wish to make this word more precise by a definition such as the following: "Rich" means "has a fortune of at least one million dollars."

4. Sometimes we seek an intensional definition for a term whose extension is quite well known. For instance, most of the time we have very little trouble in applying the term "human being"; when we encounter an object we can almost always say definitely whether or not it is a human being. Still, we might have considerable difficulty in saying what properties distinguish human beings from nonhumans. The problem is to find an intensional definition that will provide the extension we already accept for the term.

Although we use the term "human being" quite adequately in most contexts, its extension is not precisely determined. The case is typical. There are many objects that definitely belong to the extension of the term; there are many other objects that definitely fall outside its extension; and there are some objects that are borderline cases—neither definitely within the extension nor definitely outside the extension. To find an adequate intensional definition of "human being" requires that we find a set of properties shared by all the objects definitely within the extension of the term but not shared by any of the objects definitely outside its extension. The borderline cases can be dealt with as we see fit.

If an intensional definition is proposed, it must not be too broad or too narrow. The definition will be *too broad* if it admits into the extension some objects that are definitely outside the extension. The defnition will be *too narrow* if it excludes from the extension objects that are definitely within the extension. Notice that a definition could be both too broad and too narrow. For example, the definition " 'human being' means 'rational animal' " has been proposed. There is reason to suppose that this definition is too broad in some respects and too narrow in others. We would normally regard tiny infants, severely retarded individuals, and insane persons as human beings. However, it is doubtful that such beings are rational, so the proposed definition would seem to exclude them from the extension of "human being." Thus, the definition is too narrow. At the same time, certain apes seem to be quite intelligent and capable of elementary reasoning. Such creatures, which are clearly excluded from the extension of "human being" as we understand the term, would be included under the proposed definition. In this respect the intensional definition is too broad.

When we have succeeded in framing an intensional definition that is neither too broad nor too narrow, we must still consider how it disposes of the borderline cases. To pursue our previous example, we shall find borderline cases if we ask when an organism becomes a human being. Does a person first qualify as a human being at the moment of birth? Is an unborn baby a human being? Does a fetus become a human being when the mother first "feels life"? Is the fertilized egg a human being from the moment of fertilization? These are not purely academic questions; legislation stipulating that human life begins at conception has been seriously proposed. The issue is hotly debated. Questions of the following sorts are involved. Does an unborn child have any legal rights? Can an unborn child inherit money or be the beneficiary of a life insurance policy? Is abortion murder? (By definition, it is impossible to murder anything that is not a human being.)

Even if we have succeeded in framing an intensional definition that deals satisfactorily with the borderline cases we have already encountered, we may still wish to consider certain additional borderline cases we have not yet encountered, and may never encounter. For example, suppose a space ship landed on earth carrying beings from another planet who were obviously intelligent and similar to earth people in many other respects. Suppose further that someone killed one of these beings without any provocation. Would this be murder? It would depend upon our definition of "human being."

Until the term "human being" is clearly defined, it does not make sense to ask whether such visitors from space are *really* human beings, for the answer depends upon the definition of "human being." Whether a given definition is reasonable and useful is, nevertheless, a very important question. There are numerous legal, ethical, biological, sociological, anthropological, and psychological considerations relevant to this question. They do not tell us whether a given definition is true, but they do help us to appraise the adequacy of definitions.

5. Some definitions are designed to introduce a word that will have theoretical importance and utility. Such definitions are common in science. Words like "work" and "energy" are given precise definitions in physics, not so much to remove the vagueness of their everyday meanings, but to

provide words that can be used to state important physical generalizations. Indeed, the ordinary meanings are deliberately changed to provide useful physical concepts.

Operational definitions, as we noted, are often used to introduce precise scientific terminology. It is important to say something about their limitations. Take the concept of temperature. If we are considering a particular operational definition, we must insist that it not depart too radically from our subjective judgments. The temperature of a steaming cup of coffee must turn out to be higher than that of a glass of icewater; the temperature on a typical summer day in the Sahara Desert must turn out to be higher than that of a typical winter day at the North Pole. A definition in terms of the readings on mercury thermometers does yield such results. Some of our subjective temperature judgments will, however, be rejected. Our sense of coldness will be different on a windy winter day than on a calm day when the thermometer gives the same reading. We realize, however, that our subjective judgments are sometimes unreliable, and we are willing to accept the thermometer as an objective standard.

A satisfactory operational definition of temperature will also have to fit reasonably well with more sophisticated scientific theories. One important factor is that our operational definition applies only over a limited range; we cannot use a mercury thermometer to measure the temperature of the surface of the sun or the temperature of liquid helium. However, we must require our operational definition to fit consistently with operational definitions that apply to temperatures above and below the range of the mercury thermometer. Another crucial consideration arises from the fact that the temperature of a gas is also defined theoretically in terms of the average kinetic energy of its molecules. Since molecules, their masses, and their velocities cannot be individually and directly manipulated in the laboratory, this definition is not operational. Nevertheless, the operational definition in terms of the mercury thermometer fits reasonably well with this theoretical definition. The operational definition actually helps to bridge the gap between our direct sensations of temperature and the concept of temperature that appears in more advanced physical theories.

Not all operational definitions are as satisfactory as the foregoing definition of temperature. Let us return to the concept of intelligence. Many intelligence tests, it has been charged, have a bias in favor of white middle- to upper-class Americans. If native American Indians, or members of some other ethnic minority, get lower scores on these tests on the average, it may not mean that they are less intelligent than white middle-to upper-class Americans. For instance, one test included the question "Who discovered America?" The answer "Columbus" was good for two points; the answer "Leif Ericcson" was awarded one point. An American Indian child who answered "We did" received no points. Because the question of the relative intelligence of different races has enormous social significance, it is important to be sure that our tests measure intelligence rather than socio-economic status. To say that intelligence is, by definition, what is measured by intelligence tests surely begs the basic issue. A fundamental question concerning operational definitions is whether the operation stipulated actually measures the property we intend. Inappropriate operational definitions are likely to yield concepts that lack theoretical significance.

In philosophy, too, we seek definitions that will provide theoretically useful concepts. For example, philosophers have tried to define the word "free" (as it occurs in the phrase "free will") so that it will mark a *significant* distinction between free and unfree acts. The resulting concept should enable us to state the connection between freedom and responsibility. It should help us to explain what it means to say that a person could have acted differently, and it should help us to clarify the relation, if any, between freedom and causal determination.

6. In addition to intensions, extensions, and grammatical functions, words have emotive force. A book that goes into great detail might be described by one person as thorough and scholarly but by another person as tiresome and pedantic. It is not so much that the two people are making different statements of fact about the book as that they are expressing different attitudes toward it. For many people "thorough" and "scholarly" are terms of praise; for almost everyone "tiresome" and "pedantic" carry strong negative connotations.

Definitions are often designed to transfer emotive force. This can be done in either of two ways. First, we may take a word that has a great deal of emotive force and define it so that it will apply to something we wish to applaud or condemn. For instance, one might define "socialistic" as "tending to equalize wealth by government action." Since the graduated income tax has the effect of equalizing wealth, the word "socialistic" applies to it. Among people for whom the word "socialistic" has negative connotations, this tends to transfer the negative attitudes to the graduated income tax itself. Among people for whom the word "socialistic" has positive connotations, the effect would be just opposite. Definitions of this kind transfer emotive force from the *definiendum* to the *definiens*. The *definiens* clearly applies to the graduated income tax, so the emotive force of the *definiendum*—"socialistic"—is transferred to the graduated income tax via the *definiens*.

Second, the process may be reversed. Suppose a certain drama is admittedly naturalistic. Someone might define "naturalistic" as "glorifying the meanness of human nature and the sordidness of human existence." This definition transfers negative emotive force from the *definiens* to the word "naturalistic"—the *definiendum*—and thence to the play itself. Definitions whose main function is the transfer of emotive force are called *persuasive definitions*.

The foregoing examples could easily give the impression that all persuasive definitions are illegitimate. This is not true. We need words with emotive force to express our feelings, emotions, and attitudes; persuasive definitions help to provide the necessary vocabulary. However, persuasive definitions can lead to difficulty if, in the process of transferring emotive force, we also modify the established descriptive meanings of our words. If the modification of descriptive meaning goes unnoticed, confusion can result.[4]

The preceding list of purposes of definitions is not intended to be exhaustive, nor are these purposes mutually exclusive. In discussing the definition of "human being," we were concerned with characterizing customary usage to some extent (purpose 1), making a somewhat vague term more precise (purpose 3), providing an intensional definition for a term whose extension is fairly clear (purpose 4), and providing a term with theoretical importance and utility (purpose 5).

Some of the most important philosophical problems are basically problems of definition. Philosophers ask: What is justice? What is art? What is religion? What is knowledge? What is truth? In each of these cases, the question could be rephrased: How should we define the word "justice"? How should we define the word "art"? etc. Notice that this transformation takes what appears to be a question in the object language and reformulates it as a question in the metalanguage. It will not do to answer that definitions are conventions, so one definition is as good as another. Definitions *are* conventions, but some conventions achieve their purposes better than others. Finding an adequate definition is often a delicate matter.

## 33. ANALYTIC, SYNTHETIC, AND CONTRADICTORY STATEMENTS

In section 12 we saw that there are certain statements, known as tautologies, whose truth value is T under all circumstances; we observed that these statements constitute a small portion of all statements whose truth can be certified by logical means alone. Now that we have discussed definitions, it is time to consider the broader class. Let us begin with the tautological form

a]    $p \supset p$

which has an instance,

b]    If $x$ is a bachelor, then $x$ is a bachelor.

---

[4]The term "persuasive definition" was originated by Charles L. Stevenson; see his *Facts and Values* (New Haven, Conn.: Yale University Press, 1963), Essay III. Stevenson provides many excellent examples that illustrate both the utility and the dangers of persuasive definitions.

This obvious truism holds generally; hence,

*c*]    All bachelors are bachelors.

is a logical truth. If we now invoke the definition

*d*]    "Bachelor" means "unmarried adult male,"

we can substitute in *c* and assert

*e*]    All bachelors are unmarried adult males.

from which it follows that

*f*]    All bachelors are unmarried.

Logical truths like *c* are statements whose truth follows from their logical form—that is, the meanings of the logical terms—alone. The class of analytic statements contains all such logical truths, as well as all statements like *e* and *f* whose truth follows from logical truths by virtue of definitions. Statement *f* is not, itself, a definition, but no information other than a knowledge of the meanings of its logical and nonlogical terms is needed to establish its truth. It is not necessary to observe a large number of bachelors to ascertain the truth of *f*. Since a bachelor is, by definition, an unmarried adult male, the word "bachelor" cannot correctly be applied to any person who is not unmarried. Statements of this type, whose truth follows from the definitions of the words (logical and nonlogical) that occur in them, are known as *analytic statements*.[5]
   The statement

*g*]    Some bachelors are married.

is like statement *f*, except that the meanings of the words occurring in *g* make it false rather than true. Statements of this type are *contradictory statements* (or self-contradictions, or merely, contradictions). A contradictory statement is one whose falsity follows from the meanings of the words that occur in it. In a broad sense, then, analytic statements and contradicto-

---

[5]W. V. Quine has vigorously attacked the analytic-synthetic distinction; see the essay "Two Dogmas of Empiricism" in his book *From a Logical Point of View*, 2nd ed. (New York: Harper Torchbooks, 1963). Quine's misgivings, which are based upon subtle difficulties about the identification of definitions in rich complex languages such as English, are not shared by all philosophers. Since we are assuming—for purposes of the present elementary discussion— that many definitions are available, we shall not abandon what seems to me an extremely useful distinction. Moreover, even if Quine's view is correct, the import of his arguments cannot be appreciated without an understanding of the distinction presented here.

ry statements may be considered *logical truths* and *logical falsehoods,* respectively.

By contrast,

*h*]     Some bachelors do not own cars.

*i*]     All bachelors are blind.

are statements whose truth or falsity is not determined solely by the meanings of the words they contain. They are called *synthetic statements.* To be sure, you have to know the meanings of the words that occur in them before you can find out whether they are true or false, but it would be possible to understand the meanings of the words perfectly without knowing whether either one is true or false. Statement *h* is obviously true, but there is nothing in the definition of the word "bachelor" that implies that some bachelors do not own cars. It is a matter of fact, over and above the meaning of the word, that some bachelors do not own cars. Similarly, statement *i* is obviously a false sentence, but again this is not a consequence of the definitions of the words. The only way to find out that *h* is true and *i* is false is to investigate bachelors. It is not sufficient merely to investigate the word "bachelor" (and the other words in these statements). Synthetic statements are not logical truths or falsehoods; they are *factual statements.*

There are important consequences of these distinctions. The reason that the truth of an analytic statement can be ascertained without recourse to anything beyond the meanings of words is that analytic statements contain no information about matters of fact outside of language. Whatever information is conveyed by an analytic statement is information about language itself and not about the facts that language refers to. It is not that analytic statements refer explicitly to language; rather, they express relationships among definitions. Definitions are, as we have said, conventions. These conventions are neither true nor false. The conventions do, however, have consequences, and analytic statements are among the consequences of our definitions.

We may explain in the following way why analytic statements have no factual content. Suppose there is a room whose contents we know nothing about. We can imagine all sorts of possibilities concerning what is in that room, but we have no way of knowing which of these imaginable possibilities is actually true. Now, suppose we learn that the synthetic statement "There is a book in the room" is true. We can immediately exclude as *not actual* any of the imaginable possibilities about the contents of the room that did not include at least one book among the contents. For example, we now know that the room is not completely bare; we know that it is not completely filled with corn flakes to the exclusion of everything else; we know that it does not have just a bed, chair, table, lamp, and rug, and so on. Now we have some information about the contents of the room, but not very much. Next, suppose we learn that the statement "There is exactly one book in the room, and this book is green, has hard covers, has 348 pages, is a mystery novel, and rests upon a desk" is true. Now we have much more information about the contents of the room, for the truth of this latter statement is incompatible with many more imaginable possibilities than the truth of the former is. For example, we now know that the room does not have more than one book in it; we know that it is not without a desk; we know that it does not contain a desk with a paperback philosophy book; and so on. All of these possibilities that have been excluded were compatible with the truth of the former statement. In general, the amount of factual information in a statement is a function of the number of possibilities its truth excludes. The more information a statement contains, the fewer possibilities it leaves open.

Let us consider analytic statements from this standpoint. How many possibilities does the truth of an analytic statement exclude? The answer is *none*. Since an analytic statement is necessarily true, it will be true regardless of what circumstances hold. Its truth does not exclude any imaginable possibilities, and knowing it to be true does not enable us to draw any specific conclusion about what possibilities are actualized. Suppose, referring back to the previous example, we were to learn that the statement "All green books in the room are green" is true. This statement is analytic and it is completely uninformative. It does not tell us whether there is a book in the room (see section 13), and it does not tell us anything about the color of any book that might be in the room. It is true regardless of the actual contents of the room. It is a statement that cannot be false, and for this reason it does not convey information.

One important feature of analytic statements is that observational evidence is not relevant to their truth. Consequently, it would be pointless to try to refute them by reference to observational data. Such attempted refutation would be irrelevant. For example, many (if not all) truths of mathematics are analytic. Consider the statement "Two plus two equals four." We would establish the truth of such a statement by reference to the definitions of "two," "four," "plus," and "equals." Small children sometimes learn their sums by counting fingers, blocks, or apples, but the truths of arithmetic do not rest upon observational evidence of that sort. If they did, we would have to consider negative observational evidence, as well. For instance, it is a fact that two quarts of alcohol mixed with two quarts of water yield less than four quarts of solution. If observational evidence were relevant, we would have to conclude that two plus two sometimes equals four but sometimes does not. We do not draw any such conclusion, however, because the experimental facts cited are not relevant. We say instead that if we put two quarts of alcohol into a container and two quarts of water into the same container, then we put four quarts of liquid into the container. The fact that the resulting solution occupies less than four quarts volume is an interesting physical fact that has no bearing upon any truth of arithmetic.

Analytic statements, then, are necessarily true, and they have no factual content. It is easy to see that no synthetic conclusions can be validly deduced from analytic premises alone. As we have seen, in a valid deductive argument there can be no information in the conclusion that is not in the premises. If all of the premises are analytic, they have no factual content. Therefore, the conclusion cannot have factual content either. Arguments are often given, however, in which the premises are analytic and the conclusion has content. Such arguments must be invalid. For example,

j]    People have sometimes argued for fatalism on the basis of the premise "Whatever will be, will be." Certainly the premise, taken literally, is analytic; it says only that the future is the future. One could hardly deny the premise by maintaining that some things that will be, won't be. The conclusion frequently drawn from the premise is that the future is completely predetermined and that human action and human choices cannot have any effect upon the future. Such an argument is invalid, and it can be seen to be invalid precisely because it proceeds from an analytic premise to a synthetic conclusion.

k]    In the past, many a businessperson has tried to justify unscrupulous practices by appealing to the statement "Business is business." Superficially, this statement looks analytic; but if it were analytic, it could not support the far-from-analytic conclusion that dishonesty and irresponsibility are legitimate tactics in business. If the premise is to support the conclusion, it must mean something like "Business is not, and cannot be, conducted ethically." Putting the premise in a form that looks analytic gives it an appearance of indubitability; stating the synthetic premise literally is rhetorically less effective, for it no longer seems so unquestionable. Much of the same sort of remark applies to the slightly more complicated contemporary formula, "The business of business is business." It certainly cannot constitute a logical justification for the conclusion that the business of business is to make money by any means, no matter how unethical.

l]    People have gloomily concluded that decency, altruism, and consideration of others are completely absent in mankind. The premise from which this conclusion is deduced is "People never act unselfishly." This premise is not obviously analytic; but when it is challenged, we find that no conceivable factual evidence could possibly refute it. When we point out that saints and heroes have sacrificed everything for others, we are told that they did so because they wanted to, so they were really acting selfishly. It appears that no act would be unselfish unless it were motivated by a motive that the agent did not have. But to be motivated by a motive that one does not have is logically impossible. Hence, the premise turns out, after all, to be analytic, and the argument must therefore be invalid.

## 34. CONTRARIES AND CONTRADICTORIES

Two statements may be related in such a way that if one of them is true, the other must be false; and if one of them is false, the other must be true. We may not know which is the true one and which is the false one, but we can be certain that one of them is true and the other is false. Such statements are called *contradictories* of each other; the relation between them is called *contradiction*. The following pairs of statements are contradictories; you should satisfy yourself that in each pair it is impossible for both to be true, and it is impossible for both to be false.[6]

*a*]      All horses are mammals. Some horses are not mammals.

*b*]      No logicians are philosophers. Some logicians are philosophers.

*c*]      It is raining here. It is not raining here.

In general, for any statement *p*, *p* and *not-p* are contradictories. Furthermore, any statement of the form "*p* or not-*p*" is analytic and, consequently, necessarily true; this is called the *law of excluded middle* or *tertium non datur*. Also, any statement of the form "Not both *p* and not-*p*" is analytic; this is called the *law of contradiction*. These logical laws express the fact that every statement is either true or false and no statement is both true and false.[7]

Two statements can be related to each other in such a way that it is impossible for both of them to be true, but it is possible for both to be false. In such cases the statements are called *contraries* and the relation between them is called *contrariety*. For example, the following are contraries:

*d*]      It is cold here. It is hot here.

For any given time and place, it is impossible that it should be both cold and hot, but it is possible for the temperature to be moderate. Thus, both statements can be false, but they cannot be true.

Failure to understand the difference between contraries and contradictories has led to much confusion.

*e*]      In example *f*, section 9, we referred to the dilemma of free will. This dilemma concludes that freedom of the will does not exist because it is incompatible with both determinism and indeterminism. Some people have rejected this dilemma on the grounds that there may be some third alternative besides

---

[6]In section 13 we noted the relation of contradiction between *A* and *O* statements and between *E* and *I* statements.

[7]In section 12 we showed that the law of excluded middle is a tautology; it is a simple matter to make a truth table that will do the same for the law of contradiction.

determinism and indeterminism. To deal with this objection we must be clear about the meanings of the words "determinism" and "indeterminism." Determinism is the doctrine that everything is causally determined. Indeterminism is the doctrine that something is not causally determined. A third doctrine, which we shall call "chaoticism," is the doctrine that nothing is causally determined. It is easy to see that determinism and indeterminism are contradictory doctrines; one of them must be true. Determinism and chaoticism, on the other hand, are contrary doctrines; both would be false if some things were causally determined and some were not. If the free-will dilemma used as a premise the statement "Either determinism or chaoticism holds," it would be open to the objection that there is a third alternative. Actually, the premise is "Either determinism or indeterminism holds." This premise is analytic; it is an instance of the law of excluded middle.

*f]*   There is an unfortunate tendency on the part of many people to "think in extremes"[8]—for instance, to regard everything as wholly good or wholly bad. We are all too familiar with our compatriots who believe that our nation can do no wrong, whereas other nations can do no right, except when they cooperate with our goals. Likewise, we are all too familiar with people who believe that their political party is on the right side in every political dispute, whereas the opposition party is always in the wrong. Thinking in extremes is a confusion of contraries with contradictories; it is the error of treating contrary statements as if they were contradictories. "X is wholly good" is contrary to "X is wholly bad"; thinking in extremes proceeds as if they cannot both be false.

*g]*   Some people have suggested that logic is dangerous because it leads to thinking in extremes. This results from the principle that every statement is either true or false. It would be better, so the allegation goes, to regard statements as true to some extent and false to some extent, in order to avoid this species of thinking in extremes. Strangely enough, this criticism of logic rests upon the same error as that committed in thinking in extremes, the confusion of contraries and contradictories; "$p$ is true" and "$p$ is false" are not contraries and should not be treated as such. There is nothing in logic that proposes the confusion of contrariety and contradiction; rather, the study of logic should end the confusion.

## 35. AMBIGUITY AND EQUIVOCATION

It is a well-known fact that a single word may have a variety of meanings. There is usually no harm in this phenomenon, for the context generally determines which of the several meanings is intended. For instance, the word "table" has one meaning in which it refers to furniture and another in which it refers to lists (as in "table of contents" or "table of logarithms"), but this multiplicity of meanings could hardly ever lead to confusion. There are cases, however, in which a word is used in such a way that we cannot tell

---

[8]Thinking in extremes has often been called *black-white thinking*. This would be a good name for the error except for its unfortunate tendency to reinforce the identification of white with good and black with bad.

which of its several meanings is intended. In such cases, we say that the word is being used *ambiguously*, for the statement in which it occurs is open to at least two distinct interpretations. In the absence of additional context, the statement "Roxanne is dusting her plants" may mean that she is cleaning the plants by removing dust from them or that she is protecting them by applying an insecticidal dust.

Multiplicity of meaning leads to logical difficulty if the same word is used in two different senses in the same argument and if the validity of the argument depends upon that word maintaining a constant meaning throughout. Such arguments commit the *fallacy of equivocation*. Consider a trivial example:

a]    Only man is rational.
       No woman is a man.
     ∴All women are irrational.

This argument would be valid if the term "man" had the same meaning each time it occurred. However, for the first premise to be true, "man" must mean "human being," whereas, for the second premise to be true, "man" must mean "human male." Thus, if the premises are to have any plausibility whatever, the term "man" must shift its meaning. We would surely be misconstruing the premises if we understood the term "man" to mean the same in both. The result is an equivocation, which destroys the validity of the argument.

Let us consider some less trivial examples:

b]    The normal male college freshman has a lively interest in athletics and liquor and a consuming preoccupation with sex. These things engulf his attention. Poetry, for instance, leaves him cold. Once in a while, however, you run across a freshman who is entirely different. He spends much of his free time reading, and perhaps even writing, poetry. He does so because he likes to. He is an abnormal case. Often he has an abnormally high IQ. He is not interested in the things that interest normal boys of his age. He is a boy set apart from other boys. When we encounter boys of this kind we ask ourselves, "What can be done for them?" Surely there must be some way to help them achieve a normal adjustment to life!

The word "normal" in this passage shifts from one meaning to another. Toward the beginning, the word "normal" means simply "average"; at the end, it means "healthy." "Average" is purely statistical term which has no valuational content; "healthy" is, among other things, an evaluative term. There is, in this passage, an implicit argument of the following sort:

c]    A college freshman who likes poetry is an abnormal boy.
       An abnormal boy is an unfortunate case.
     ∴A college freshman who likes poetry is an unfortunate case.

This argument contains an equivocation on the word "normal." Arguments of this sort have been seriously proposed as arguments for mediocrity and conformity.

d]     If you think that a brick wall is solid, you are quite wrong. Modern science has shown that things like brick walls are made up of atoms. An atom is something like the solar system; electrons revolve around the nucleus much as the planets revolve around the sun. Like the solar system, an atom is mostly empty space. What common sense regards as solid, science has shown to be anything but solid.

The equivocation that may well be present in this passage involves the word "solid." On the one hand, common sense may be right in regarding a brick wall as solid—meaning that it is strongly resistant to penetration. On the other hand, science may also be right in regarding the same brick wall as lacking solidity—meaning that it is not composed of tightly packed material particles.

e]     Example l of section 33 affords a good example of equivocation. To defend the premise "People never act unselfishly,"the author of the argument takes the word "selfish" to apply to any act whose motivation comes from the person who performs it. When the word "selfish" is construed in this manner, the premise becomes analytic, and hence, irrefutable. When, however, attention is turned from the defense of the premise to the deduction of a conclusion from it, the author of the argument changes the meaning of the word "selfish." Now the word "selfish" applies to acts in which the agent ignores the interests of other people. With this latter meaning of the word "selfish" the premise is no longer analytic. It is not true by definition (or even true at all) that people are never motivated to take account of the interests of other people. Saints, heroes, and ordinary people act from their own motives. Still they are sometimes decent, considerate, and altruistic, for these very motives include a concern for the welfare of others.

# 36. CONCLUSION

Now that we have dealt with a fairly wide variety of topics in logic, it is time to reconsider the goals we have been attempting to achieve. In the very first section of the book, it will be recalled, we emphasized a basic distinction between statements that are supported by evidence and those that are not. The book has been devoted almost entirely to an elaboration of that distinction and a discussion of the ways in which statements can be supported by evidence. This has been the chief focus of our excursion into the field of logic.

We noted at the outset that statements supported by evidence are the conclusions of arguments. The evidence that is taken to support the conclusion is formulated in the premises. As we have seen, there are two kinds of support, deductive and inductive. If we are to be justified in accepting the conclusion of an argument on the basis of the evidence certain conditions must be fulfilled:

First, we must have good reasons for accepting the premises as true.
Second, the argument must possess a logically correct form.
Third, in the case of inductive arguments, we must satisfy the requirement of total evidence.

We have examined a number of basic correct forms of each type. In order to facilitate detection and avoidance of common logical mistakes, we have also discussed a number of fallacies of various sorts.

We have, for the most part, directed our attention to the logical relationship between the premises and conclusions of arguments, leaving aside the question of truth or falsity of premises. Moreover, although we have often remarked on the requirement of total evidence in connection with induction, we have not given a great deal of consideration to the question of whether it is, in fact, satisfied in particular example. This has enabled us to deal with the logical properties of arguments in abstraction from such factual questions as the truth values of the premises and whether they encompass all of the available relevant evidence. The main object of our interest throughout the book has been the nature of the relation of *evidential support*.

What should be the result of these studies? We should, in the first place, be able to distinguish between unsubstantiated assertions and those for which supporting evidence is offered. We should be able to distinguish between the appeal to supporting evidence and mere emotional appeals. It is an interesting—and perhaps disillusioning—experience to examine ordinary newspapers, magazines, radio programs, television shows, etc., in a serious attempt to find arguments. They are few and far between. For the most part, one finds unsubstantiated assertions mixed with emotional appeals. This is not to deny that appeals to our emotions have important uses; they are, I should think, quite appropriate in such contexts as fund drives for worthy charities, efforts to persuade people to engage in worthwhile activities, or attempts to influence their feelings in ways we consider desirable. The point is simply that appeals of these sorts should not be mistaken for logical arguments.

In cases in which evidence is offered, we should be able, in addition, to assess critically the quality of the arguments employed. When the evidence is inadequate we should be able to see what kind of additional evidence would be needed to make the argument compelling. As a result, we should be able to function more intelligently in our public and private roles as consumers, citizens, and individuals seeking personal satisfaction.

Third, we should also be able to apply these critical techniques to our own thinking, thereby improving our ability to evaluate the results of our own intellectual efforts. This should enable us to function more rationally in deliberating, formulating plans, making choices, and deciding what to do. Even more importantly, the study of logic may contribute in some small way to our achievement of more reliable knowledge and deeper understanding of the world in which we live. Logical skill is no substitute for factual knowledge, but it is a tool for critical evaluation of knowledge claims.

It should be re-emphasized, in conclusion, that our survey of logic has been conducted at an extremely elementary level. We have barely scratched the surface. Both deductive and inductive logic are highly developed fields of study in which profound and far-reaching results have been achieved. If would be gratifying indeed if readers of this book were motivated to learn more about the areas with which we have been concerned. Some bibliographical suggestions follow.

# For Further Reading

This book gives, at best, a glimpse into the nature of logic. In its brevity it excludes much important material. If your curiosity about logic has been aroused, further reading will be helpful in two ways. First, you may want lengthier and more detailed discussions of topics we have treated only briefly. Second, you may want to expand your view of the field by learning something about subjects we have had to omit entirely. There are many excellent books on logic that will serve either or both of these purposes. The following are easily available and are among the best.

## GENERAL INTRODUCTIONS TO LOGIC

BEARDSLEY, MONROE C. *Thinking Straight,* 3rd ed. Englewood Cliffs, N.J.: Prentice-Hall, Inc., 1966.

BRODY, BARUCH. *Logic: Theoretical and Applied.* Englewood Cliffs, N.J.: Prentice-Hall, Inc., 1973.

COHEN, MORRIS R., AND ERNEST NAGEL. *An Introduction to Logic and Scientific Method.* New York: Harcourt Brace Jovanovich, Inc., 1934.

COPI, IRVING M. *Introduction to Logic,* 6th ed. New York: Macmillan, Inc., 1982.

EATON, RALPH M. *General Logic.* New York: Charles Scribner's Sons, 1931.

FOGELIN, ROBERT J. *Understanding Arguments.* New York: Harcourt Brace Jovanovich, Inc., 1978.

KAHANE, HOWARD. *Logic and Contemporary Rhetoric,* 3rd ed. Belmont, Calif.: Wadsworth Publishing Co., Inc., 1980.

MICHALOS, ALEX C. *Principles of Logic*. Englewood Cliffs, N.J.: Prentice-Hall, Inc. 1969.

## INTRODUCTIONS TO SYMBOLIC LOGIC

If you would like to learn more about deductive logic as a modern formal science, the following books will be helpful. They presuppose no previous acquaintance with logic, but they go far beyond our brief survey of symbolic techniques.

HUNTER, GEOFFREY. *Metalogic*. Berkeley and Los Angeles: University of California Press, 1973.

KALISH, DONALD, AND RICHARD MONTAGUE. *Logic: Techniques of Formal Reasoning*, 2nd ed. New York: Harcourt Brace Jovanovich, Inc., 1980.

MASSEY, GERALD J. *Understanding Symbolic Logic*. New York: Harper and Row, Publishers, Inc., 1970.

MATES, BENSON. *Elementary Logic*, 2nd ed. New York: Oxford University Press, 1972.

MENDELSON, ELLIOTT. *Introduction to Mathematical Logic*. New York: D. Van Nostrand Company, 1964.

## INDUCTIVE LOGIC

Unlike deductive logic, inductive logic is not a well-developed discipline with standard systems one can learn. The following books will help you to see the present state of understanding of the problems in the field.

GIERE, RONALD N. *Understanding Scientific Reasoning*. New York: Holt, Rinehart & Winston, 1979.

HEMPEL, CARL G. *Philosophy of Natural Science*, Chaps. 1–4. Englewood Cliffs, N.J.: Prentice-Hall, Inc. [*The Foundations of Philosophy Series*], 1966.

SALMON, WESLEY C. *The Foundations of Scientific Inference*. Pittsburgh, Pa.: University of Pittsburgh Press, 1967.

SKYRMS, BRIAN. *Choice and Chance*, 2nd ed. Belmont, Calif.: Dickenson Publishing Co., Inc., 1975.

## LOGIC AND LANGUAGE

Although all the books previously listed as general introductions to logic contain discussions of material contained in our Chapter 4, the following books are excellent supplementary sources.

ALSTON, WILLIAM P. *Philosophy of Language.* Englewood Cliffs, N.J.: Prentice-Hall, Inc. [*Foundations of Philosophy Series*], 1964.

HOSPERS, JOHN. *An Introduction to Philosophical Analysis,* 2nd ed. Englewood Cliffs, N.J.: Prentice-Hall, Inc., 1967.

## PHILOSOPHY OF LOGIC

If you would like to penetrate more deeply into the philosophical problems at the basis of deductive logic, the following book by Quine is unsurpassed. The book edited by Copi and Gould is an anthology of classic readings in the philosophy of deductive and inductive logic.

COPI, IRVING M., AND JAMES A. GOULD, EDS. *Readings on Logic,* 2nd ed. New York: Macmillan, Inc., 1972.

QUINE, WILLARD VAN ORMAN. *Philosophy of Logic.* Englewood Cliffs, N.J.: Prentice-Hall, Inc. [*Foundations of Philosophy Series*], 1970.

# Argument Forms (Correct and Fallacious)

Page numbers indicate the place at which the argument forms are introduced and explained.

# Index

Coffee:
  beans, 89–95 *passim*
  evening consumption of, 113–17 *passim*
Cohen, Morris R., 165
Coincidence, confused with causation,
  119–20, 123
Cold, common, remedies for, 119, 121–22
Collective statement, 55–56
Color matching, perceptual, 79
Columbus, Christopher, 152
Comet, 123
Common cause, 123–25
Communists, 103, 104
Composition, fallacy of, 56
Compound statements, 38
Comprehensiveness of hypotheses, 139
Conclusions:
  content of, 15–18, 87, 158
  discovery of, 12
  about future, 18
  identification of, 6–8
  incompatible, 96
  indicator words, 6–7
  of inference, 9
  justification of, 1, 4, 9–14, 162
  necessitated by premises, 6, 15–21, 27,
    95–96
  of scientific argument, 16, 127–28
  as supported statement, 1–5, 9, 162
  synthetic, 158
  truth independent of validity, 20–21
  about unobserved facts, 108
  unwanted, 35
  used as premise, 94
  (*see also* Consequences; Justification)
Concomitant variation, method of,
  117–18, 126–27
Conditional arguments, 25–31 (*see also* Affirming the antecedent; Affirming the
  consequent, fallacy of; Denying the antecedent, fallacy of; Denying the
  consequent)
Conditional statements, 23–27, 37–38,
  41–50 *passim*, 63, 85–86
  logical core of, 41, 86
  material, 38, 40–41, 51, 110, 114–15
  tautological, 50
  (*see also* Universal conditional
    statements)
Conditions:
  necessary, 47, 114–15
  necessary and sufficient, 48
  sufficient, 47, 114–15
Confirmation, 87, 128–39 *passim*
Confirmatory instances, 128, 133–39
  *passim*
Confusion:
  of cause with effect, fallacy of, 123–25
  of contraries with contradictories,
    159–60
  of use and mention, 141
Conjunction, 38–40, 42, 85
Connective:
  binary, 39
  non-truth-functional, 39
  ordinary vs. truth-functional, 39

singular, 39
  truth-functional, 38–41
Connotation, negative/positive, 153
Consensus:
  argument from, 100–101, 104
  negative argument from, 104
Consequences:
  consideration of, 5, 10
  of definitions, 156
  of hypotheses, 128–29
  unacceptable, 33
Consequent, 23–29 *passim*, 37, 40–45 *passim*, 59–60, 86 (*see also* Affirming the
  consequent, fallacy of; Denying the
  consequent)
"Consequently," 6
Contamination of hands, 110, 120
Content:
  of analytic statements, 156–58
  of categorical statements, 50
  of conditional statements, 24
  vs. form, 19–21, 24
  implicit, 16
  of premises and conclusions, 15–17, 87,
    158
  validity independent of, 20–21
  (*see also* Knowledge)
Context:
  of discovery (*see* Discovery)
  of justification (*see* Justification)
Contextual definition, 149
Contraceptives, oral, 120
Contradiction:
  hidden, 35
  in inductive conclusions, 96
  law of, 159
  necessarily false statement, 155–56
  in *reductio ad absurdum*, 32–33
  relation between statements, 52, 81,
    159–60
  self-, 32, 35, 52n, 96, 155
  (*see also* Incompatability)
Contradictory statements (*see*
  Contradiction)
Contraposition, 24, 44–45, 49, 115
Contrariety, 159–60
Control, of future, 108–9
Control group, 121–22, 124
Controlled experiment, 118–27, 133
Controversy:
  re causal relations, 125
  re confirmation, 135
  re free will, 28, 36–37
  re induction, 89, 128
  re philosophy of language, 3n
  re prior probability, 135
  theological, 36
  use of dilemma in, 35
  (*see also* Disagreement; Disputation)
Convention, 144–45, 149, 154, 156
Converse, 74, 78
Copi, Irving M., 52n, 165, 167
Correctness, logical (*see* Logical
  correctness)
Counterexample, method of, 21–23,
  29–30